Uncoding the Digital

Also by David Savat

DELEUZE AND NEW TECHNOLOGY (*co-edited with Mark Poster*)

Uncoding the Digital

Technology, Subjectivity and Action in the Control Society

David Savat

The University of Western Australia, Australia

palgrave
macmillan

First published 2013 by
PALGRAVE MACMILLAN

Palgrave Macmillan in the UK is an imprint of Macmillan Publishers Limited, registered in England, company number 785998, of Houndmills, Basingstoke, Hampshire RG21 6XS.

Palgrave Macmillan in the US is a division of St Martin's Press LLC, 175 Fifth Avenue, New York, NY 10010.

Palgrave Macmillan is the global academic imprint of the above companies and has companies and representatives throughout the world.

Palgrave® and Macmillan® are registered trademarks in the United States, the United Kingdom, Europe and other countries.

ISBN 978–0–230–27815–8

This book is printed on paper suitable for recycling and made from fully managed and sustained forest sources. Logging, pulping and manufacturing processes are expected to conform to the environmental regulations of the country of origin.

A catalogue record for this book is available from the British Library.

Library of Congress Cataloging-in-Publication Data
Savat, David.
   The uncoding the digital : technology, subjectivity and action in the control society / David Savat.
      p.   cm.
   Summary: "Examining the impact of digital media on surveillance, power and people's capacity for action, this book explores how people act, and are acted upon, in an increasingly connected world"—Provided by publisher.
   ISBN 978–0–230-27815–8 (hardback)
   1. Technology—Social aspects.   2. Human behavior.
   3. Social control.   I. Title.
   T14.5.S28 2012
   303.48′3—dc23   2012022280

10 9 8 7 6 5 4 3 2 1
22 21 20 19 18 17 16 15 14 13

Printed and bound in the United States of America.

To Katinka, for all the joy

Contents

Tables and Figures

Table

Figures

Acknowledgements

This book has been a long time coming. There are numerous people whom I would like to thank in that process. In the first instance those whose conversations and questions enabled me to think differently about a problem deserve the most thanks. Conversations with students and colleagues over the past couple of years have been especially helpful in that respect, as have conversations with many friends.

The person who features high on the list is Ian Cook, whose questioning and challenging was always productive as was that of Horst Ruthrof in the earlier stages of the research. Conversations with Tauel Harper were also useful at key moments in the research. Friends and family members, including those who provided fruitful distraction, as well as Stewart Woods, Helen Merrick, and all those who continue to enable me to recognize the value of play, need to be thanked. In addition many friends and colleagues are thanked for their patience and support over the years, most notably staff in Communication and Media Studies at the University of Western Australia, Australia, including Ian Saunders, Larissa-Sexton-Finck, Linda Cresswell, Ines Bortolini, and Hui Chuin Poa, as well as my parents Marga and Jaak.

A special thank-you for patience and understanding should go to Felicity Plester and Catherine Mitchell at Palgrave Macmillan – I suspect my repeated delays could only be read as recalcitrant in nature.

Elements of Chapter 4 appeared in 'Introduction: Deleuze and New Technology', in *Deleuze and New Technology* (2009, ed. Mark Poster and David Savat, Edinburgh: Edinburgh University Press). Aspects of the argument presented in Part I appeared in 'Deleuze's Objectile: From Discipline to Modulation', in *Deleuze and New Technology* (2009, ed. Mark Poster and David Savat, Edinburgh: Edinburgh University Press). Aspects of the argument presented in Part II appeared in '(Dis)Connected: Deleuze's Superject and the Internet', in *The International Handbook of Internet Research* (2010, ed. Jeremy Hunsinger, Lisbeth Klastrup, and Matthew Allen, used with kind permission from Springer Science + Business Media B.V.).

The image *Colored Liquids*, used for the front cover, was created by Paul Taylor and was sourced from Getty Images.

Finally, my greatest thanks go to Katinka, for encouragement and unending patience, and for continuously demonstrating that, as Yoda states, 'there is no try'.

Introduction

In the game *Rift*, released in 2011, the player's character exists in a world that is under constant threat. At any moment rifts can appear through which creatures from another plane enter the player's world to interrupt their normal day-to-day quests. When such rifts erupt, players team together to eliminate the rifts and the creatures that come through them. Such a game world, a world of contingency and anxiety about what might happen next, is one that some suggest we live in today. It is a world of so-called known and unknown unknowns; a world where through our screen reality we are frequently reminded that if we are not with a team, we must be against that team. *Rift* similarly has two factions, and while at times members of each might help close a rift together, they – so the players are informed – remain fundamentally opposed to each other and effectively in a state of conflict with one another.

In *Rift*, that conflict is based on the different approach to technology that each faction has taken. The Guardians are the faction that is opposed to harnessing the power of technology. They are firmly of the view that the desire to harness the power of technology, the possibilities and worlds it opens up are precisely what caused the instability in the world, ultimately enslaving people to a state of insecurity and anxiety because they ceased their respect for their gods. Only through following the gods of their world can their world be saved. The Defiant, on the other hand, are firmly of the view that only through the use of technology can the world be saved. Respecting the gods in that respect is tantamount to doing nothing.

Even within each faction, players compete against each other – a competition of who has the best gear, who can get into the best raid groups and who has the most achievements. This too shouldn't be unfamiliar.

As Wark has pointed out, 'gamespace wants us to believe we are all nothing but gamers now, competing not against enemies of class or faith or nation but only against other gamers' (2007, paragraph 024). Indeed, the binary distinction upon which the conflict of the factions in *Rift* is said to be founded is one that is much repeated in much theorizing about technology. While this takes many guises, it generally falls into a distinction of technology in some way enslaving people, or technology extending what it means to be human (Arthur 2010).

This book initially started through an interest in theorizing the relation between politics and technology. There was always a perception on my part that technology was not a primary concern in much thinking about politics. As Stiegler similarly commenced his three-volume *Technics and Time* (1998; 2009a; 2010b), the question of technology 'seemed only secondary' not such a long time ago (1998, iv). Indeed, when technology was taken up as an issue within political thought, it was often treated as some autonomous force (Feenberg 1999; Poster 2001b; Winner 1977) – autonomous because technology is generally treated as something that is outside of being human. It is invariably constructed as a force that has an impact on human being. This impact is usually classified as determinist or indeterminist, or neutral or not neutral. In short, it is treated either as a neutral tool whose effects depend on its use, or it is treated as non-neutral; that is, as always having a political effect, regardless of the use to which it is put.

Such a construct of technology as an autonomous force has taken a number of different forms in thinking about technology and its relationship to politics. Some feminist theorists, for example, have examined the relationship between technology and gender, arguing that technology is 'imprinted with patriarchal designs' (Wajcman 1991, 163). Political economists, on the other hand, have looked at technology more in terms of its function as a productive force within capitalism (Clark 1985). Others again have argued that technology, as 'technique', has taken over the modern world (Ellul 1964) – indeed, that technology, as a specific form of rationality, is an ideology that has become hegemonic (Marcuse 1964). This is a view based upon the work of Adorno and Horkheimer and other members of the Frankfurt School (Horkheimer and Adorno 1982). Of course, there have been other approaches that have taken a more positive view of the political impact of technology, of which McLuhan's (1964) is a good example. A positive view is also found in the work of Benjamin (1969), also of the Frankfurt School.

What these different approaches to thinking about politics and technology are reflective of are different uses of the word 'technology'.

In short, care needs to be taken when discussing these various approaches to theorizing the relationship between politics and technology. The main reason for this is that when authors use the word 'technology' they are not all discussing the same thing. One of my main concerns, therefore, is with the initial construction of the distinction between politics and technology. More specifically, the issue is with the initial act of constructing a category 'technology', thereby separating 'technology' from politics and human being. The very construct 'technology' seems to imply that it is something that stands separate and is therefore autonomous from human being. In other words, the act of distinguishing between politics and technology, between human being and technology, establishes by default a relation between these categories, thereby forming the basis of discussing such a relation in terms of cause and effect. Whether that is somehow escapable, or is even worth escaping from, is highly questionable, but certainly in the context of digital technologies such a clear distinction, I argue, is extremely problematic. It is a concern that underlies this whole book and something I will return to in Part II, which deals with the interface.

My concern with this problem regarding the distinction between technology and politics was first triggered by the essay Habermas wrote in response to Marcuse's *One-Dimensional Man* (Habermas 1971; Marcuse 1964). Marcuse had argued that technology, as a rationality, had become hegemonic. According to him, the solution to that predicament was that people in modern societies had to do away with their technology and invent a new one. Habermas, while appreciative of Marcuse's work, responded by arguing that technology is not an ideology but is something that is part of what it means to be human (Habermas 1971). The key to his argument was that technology may be a rationality, but it is a very specific one and not the only form of rationality available. Technology is a form of rationality that, he argued, corresponds to work. In short, technology is a central characteristic of what it means to be human, and therefore is not something that can be replaced or done away with.

This point, that technology has a constitutive role in what it means to be human, was also previously made by Heidegger (1993a). However, according to him, technology is more than that: technology is neither simply a means to an end nor just a practice (Stiegler 1998). It is, in fact, both these things at once. Indeed, according to Heidegger, technology is what he calls a 'revealing', a 'coming to presence of man [*sic*]' (1993a). Technology is therefore not neutral because it is an expression of human being. It is how we bring ourselves forth in the world and how we bring the world forth to us. According to Heidegger, modern technology is a specific form of revealing – a form that takes the character of an enframing, which in effect is turning the world into a resource, including ourselves. It is this latter distinction, of modern technology as somehow different from non-modern technology, that I find problematic with Heidegger. The main reason for this is that modern technology, and, according to some, digital technology in particular, is constructed as both unitary and entirely negative. In my view, and taking my initial cue from Guattari (1992), this is far too pessimistic and negative a view of modern technology. As Hayles (2009) points out, following Heidegger's approach, which Stiegler urges us to do (Stiegler 1998; 2009a; 2010b), might not offer the best way forward, especially when considering digital technology. Instead, as a number of people have in recent years suggested (Clough et al. 2007; Hayles 2009; Reid 2009), Deleuze's approach might be a more fruitful starting point.

Technology is not something that is outside of us. As Arthur states, 'to have no technology is to be not-human' (2010, 216). This is not necessarily an easy point to maintain. As Clough (2008, 8) points out, even Hansen in his *New Philosophy for New Media* (2004), and whose work on affectivity and digital media is important (2006; 2009), makes the error of wanting to differentiate 'properly human perceptual capacities from the functional processing of information in hybrid human-machine assemblages' (2004, 101). Technology, as I will argue in more detail in Part II, is the link between our being and our doing or, rather, it is the expression of our being as doing. To construct it, therefore, as negative is extremely problematic. That's because, if indeed it is of such a negative character, it brings bad tidings concerning our being.

It is at this point that the work of Mumford, Foucault, Deleuze, and Guattari came to be very useful in my coming to terms with an appropriate conceptualization of technology and its relation to politics. Foucault's conceptualization of both power and discourse (1970; 1979), for instance, is very useful in understanding technology as having productive functions. Just as discourse has a productive function in terms of its constitution of ourselves – that is, in terms of how it enables us to say some things but not other things (Foucault 1970) – so too is technology productive. In other words, technologies, which I explain in more detail in Part II, function as a discourse. Different technologies enable us to do different things, including think different things. Of course, at the same time they close off other possibilities.

In that respect, different technologies are different forms or ways of becoming (Deleuze 1995; Guattari 1992; 1995). When we talk about technology, then – and this point is made strongly by Mumford (1947) – we are always talking about a human-machine assemblage. This means that the questions of what a human being is, of how human beings exist, and of how they exist in relation to one another are at least in part answered by looking at their technologies. This, of course, is not to deny that different human-machine assemblages produce and express very negative ways of existing, of doing and of being. Marx, the first major theorist of technology (Mumford 1947, 464), was well aware of technology's productive functions in both its negative and its positive aspects, as his analysis of the division of labor and the effects of industrialization shows (Marx 1990).

Technology is, as Deleuze stated (1992), an expression of how we live. Technology expresses how we live our day-to-day existence and how we organize ourselves, in terms of both our relations to one another and the sorts of subjects we constitute ourselves as. From this perspective, technologies are not determining (Deleuze 1992). Indeed, in my view, to suggest this is akin to suggesting that language is determining. From my perspective, then – and this is the perspective I rely on and try to develop further throughout this book – all human being is technological being. Different technologies express different forms of human being, both on a macro scale (in terms of specific social forms producing specific types of technology) and on a micro scale (in terms of specific technologies enabling specific forms of being). From Deleuze's perspective, technology and politics are therefore deeply implicated with one another. As Bergen explains, for Deleuze 'politics [is] the orientation of every assemblage' (2010, 34). This makes any separation of technology and politics problematic, though I do not think that this is avoidable. More importantly, I do not think it should be avoided, even if it could be, because it is precisely this problem that alerts us to the political dimension of technology as human being.

This brings me to a second concern of the book. If different technologies, or if different types of machine, express different social forms, then what sort of a social form and, more importantly, what sort of a politics is expressed by those machines we categorize as digital technology, if, indeed, they constitute such a different type of machine in the first place? This is the central question of Deleuze's 'Postscript on the Societies of Control' (1992), and in this he offered a number of different directions to take.

One of his main suggestions is that digital technologies express entirely new forms of control that do not belong to disciplinary power, but instead form part of a new mode of power he referred to as control or modulation. It is this suggestion that I want to pursue further in Part I, especially since a number of authors have also been arguing that discipline and other forms of surveillance and control have intensified through the use of digital media, rather than been surpassed (Chun 2006; Gandy 1993; Lyon 2001; 2006; 2009; Poster 1995). More importantly, I am interested in what this means in terms of how subjects are acted upon and constructed in the context of digital technologies, especially in terms of how these different forms of control reflect a different politics.

At the same time, in some of his work, Guattari (1992; 1995) argued that digital technologies were constructing human-machine assemblages that would enable entirely new and different forms of subjectivity to emerge. New forms of subjectivity could emerge, he argued, that would not be subject to the massive apparatuses of control associated with digital technologies, which was a position that differed from Deleuze's. This argument – that digital technologies enable entirely new forms of subjectivity – is explored by a number of people (Crandall 2010; Hayles 2009). However, not many, beyond pointing out that our politics will be different, fully explore how this might affect our understanding of politics. Certainly the work of, for example, Galloway (2004), Thacker (2005; 2008), and Cooper (2008; 2010), as well as, for example, Dillon and Lobo-Guerrero (2008), is important here, but it is the possibility of new forms of subjectivity emerging in the context of digital technologies, and what this implies for our understanding of politics, that interests me more specifically in Part II.

These two concerns – the conceptualization of the relation between politics and technology, and the question of what sort of politics is expressed by digital technologies – I explore by way of three different themes, which are reflected in the three parts of this book. In the first part I examine how people are acted upon by examining the operation of power through the assemblage of the database. Here I argue that discipline has not reached its end, as Deleuze, for example, suggested (1992). Instead, taking my initial cue from Poster (1995), I argue that databases constitute a significant amplification of the disciplinary mode power as Foucault developed it in *Discipline and Punish* (1979). However, in addition to this I present the case that this amplification of discipline, through the digitization of discipline's writing apparatus, produces a range of effects that are not of the disciplinary mode of power. These effects are instead reflective of the operation of mechanisms that belong to a very different mode of power, which Deleuze identified as modulation, and they have received a lot of attention more recently.

Much like, for example, Massumi (2009), I argue that this modulatory mode of power operates through pre-emption. However, I also want to try to identify the specific mechanisms and instruments of this new machine, in the process arguing that it produces not the individual but a very different type of object. Deleuze and others refer to that object as the dividual, differentiating it from discipline's product that is the individual. However, I'm of the view that dividuality is the product of the simultaneous production of discipline and modulation. Indeed, more significant I think is that modulation's specific product is a type of object that Deleuze in *The Fold* (1993) refers to as an objectile. This objectile has no form and is continually changing. In short, it is a process rather than an object. It is in a very significant sense a flow of information or code. It continues to be important to stress in that regard that modulation should not be seen as replacing discipline, as some are inclined to. In the context of databases, we need to recognize that different modes of power operate in one and the same moment yet can produce very different, and at times antagonistic, effects. One of those effects is the construction of the dividual.

The second assemblage I examine forms the focus of Part II. This is the assemblage of the interface. Here I explore the constitution of subjectivity in the context of digital technologies. I develop a more detailed explanation of the view that human being is technological being. Through the use of the work of Mumford (1947), Deleuze and Guattari (1987), and Arthur (2010), I further develop the position that different types of technology are expressive of what I call larger technological ensembles. It is through this concept of the technological ensemble that I distinguish between what one might call the industrialized or motorized mechanical ensemble and the digital ensemble. Each of these ensembles expresses, and requires, a specific form of being or existence. In short, they express different forms of subjectivity, central to each of which are differing constructs of the political. The form of subjectivity we know as the individual is central to the construct of the political in the industrialized mechanical ensemble. With the digital ensemble, however, a form of subjectivity is expressed that many have characterized as fluid. I argue that its construction of the political is very different from that of the individual so central to modern political thought. Indeed, I argue that it is in the interface, at the point of human-machine assemblage, that a very different sense of the political emerges – one in which flow is critical.

Of course, if we run with the argument that subjectivity in the context of digital technologies is fluid or formless in character, as much of the literature does, then this raises significant questions about not only our construct of the political but also, perhaps more signficantly, how these formless beings can be said to act. Traditionally, politics – certainly in our day-to-day language – continuously makes use of a conceptualization and terminology of political action as performed by solid entities. Given that we are embodied beings, that is perhaps unavoidable. Although, as Cohen (2009) points out, that doesn't mean we can't think differently about embodiment. However, while such a conceptualization of political action might be useful in describing the political actions of the political entities so central to modern political thought, such a conceptualization makes little sense in the context of the assemblage that is the network. In short, in Part III I explore the idea that if we construe the actor as being a fluid entity, whether gaseous or liquid, then its actions must also be conceptualized as fluid. In that respect I attempt to develop a conceptualization of action that may be of use in describing action as it occurs in the context of the network. It is for this reason that I argue that politics in the context of digital technologies may very well be understood as a politics of fluids – not only in terms of, for example, Castells' space of flows (2005), where flows are treated as a river that flows, but more in terms of the characteristics that are specific to fluids. Fluids, for one thing, don't move. Instead they have rates of flow. They have speed. And it is such aspects of flow that, for example, foreign exchange traders experience as their screen reality (Knorr-Cetina 2007) that I want to consider in more detail.

I by no means hereby suggest that using a concept of the fluid is the only way to think about politics in the digital. This might result in the same accusations that are leveled at the work of Bauman (2000; 2003; 2005), who is sometimes accused of reducing everything to the fluid (Jay 2010; Pollock 2007). Indeed, it is for this reason that I explore the idea of the boundary layer in Chapter 8. This layer is precisely the surface where a fluid encounters a solid. My point is that if we argue that power operates, through our digital machines, to produce an increasingly formless or turbulent world (Cooper 2010; Massumi 2009; Terranova 2007), and if we argue that we constitute ourselves as a formless – not patternless – flow of information through our digital machines, then we need to remind ourselves that the network is not a space through which fluids flow. The network's infrastructure might have such an aspect of movement, but the actual 'world' that this infrastructure produces, and is used to produce, is not spatial. It is in that respect that I think a focus on the more specific attributes of flow, rather than temporality as such

(Hansen 2009; Stiegler 1998; 2009a; 2010b), which clearly are related, could be worthwhile.

Finally, I think it is important to be guarded against developing some general theory of the politics of the digital. What one can do, however – indeed, what I think must be done – is to try to come to terms with a language of the politics of the digital. Mumford, in *Technics and Civilization*, predicted

> [a] world that is united physically by the airplane, the radio, the cable, must eventually, if cooperation is to increase, devise a common language to take care of all its practical matters...Precisely as the boundaries of mechanical intercourse widen and become world-wide, a universal language must supplant the tongue of even the most influential national aggregation.
>
> (Mumford 1947, 293)

In many ways the language of binary code in combination with Boolean logic is that universal language. As Lyotard (1984) warned over three decades ago, such a new language is a language that must be developed and learned if one is to cope effectively within that world; especially if one is to be able to avoid, or at least be aware of, the various forces and pressures exerted upon and through oneself as a machinic assemblage. Such an effort, as Hayles (2009), Massumi (2009), and Derrida and Stiegler (2002) continue to urge, is increasingly critical.

Part I
The Database

1
The Emergence of Modulation

When two decades ago Gilles Deleuze claimed that we had shifted from a disciplinary society to a control society, he foregrounded a significant shift in the manner in which power was functioning. Already well before 9/11 it was clear that there was a mode of power emerging that was more modulatory in character, and much more focused on pre-empting contingencies. Foucault (1991; 2003) too, in his work on governmentality, had already recognized that there was something else at work that was clearly not disciplinary in character. This could be observed in various aspects of daily life, as well as in practices of government where increasingly the emphasis was on aiming to anticipate events in order to either prevent them from occurring or, indeed, try to encourage specific events to occur. What 9/11 and the subsequent War on Terror did was, as Dillon and Lobo-Guerrero (2009) phrase it, to give expression to that shift in politics, and, I argue, life more generally.

To be sure, Deleuze wasn't the first to have announced the end of panopticism and the disciplinary society. Baudrillard (1994), for example, had made that claim long before him only a few years after the publication of Foucault's *Discipline and Punish* (1979). The significant question that it raises, of course, is what a possible transition to a new mode of power that is not disciplinary in character means politically. If we accept the view that the disciplinary society has ceased to exist, then what happens to the main product of the disciplinary machine? In short, what happens to the production of the individual? This is the question Massumi poses when he asks, quoting Foucault, whether the transition in the mode of power means that 'politically "we are dealing with natural subjects" ' (2009, 155). This question is, in part, what I want to begin to address in this first, and the following, chapter, and is something I return to later.

It's somewhat pointless to ponder whether Foucault would today have shared the view that the disciplinary society had been replaced. At least in his later work his view was that a disciplinary society formed part of a wider arrangement together with a society of sovereignty and a society of government (Foucault 2003; Venn 2007). My view is that it is a mistake to claim the end of the disciplinary mode of power, as Deleuze and others have done. Instead, the digitization of the disciplinary machine's writing apparatus, in the form of databases, as well as the increased connectivity of our digital machines more generally, has significantly amplified the operation of the disciplinary machine, a point that Poster made when he argued that there is a superpanopticon in operation (1990; 1995). In my view, the mechanisms and instruments that Foucault identified as critical to the functioning of the disciplinary machine have not ceased to exist or broken down. In fact, the modes of observation by which discipline as a mode of power functions now operate more forcefully than ever, whether this be through the use of social media like Facebook, GPS location via mobile phone, radio-frequency identification (RFID), or the collection of consumer data in our day-to-day activities (Lyon 2006; 2009).

It is also clear, though, that there is something different at work, on a variety of scales, that is not disciplinary in character or rather, not necessarily only disciplinary in character. For example, when people make use of a digital machine, whether this be an app on a smart-phone that is free to download, or a 'stand-alone' computer game (such as *Assassin's Creed II*), that action is immediately visible and recorded, with the data produced often being connected to a specific individual's file. But interestingly, with many of our consumer actions, while there is clearly a file being produced and maintained about our consumption behavior, there isn't necessarily any requirement or expectation in place to behave according to any specific norm. As Deleuze stated (1992), there is no mold in place anymore for an individual to adjust to. Sure, you might be penalized if you don't pay a bill to maintain a service, which is clearly disciplinary. But in many cases, once you have purchased a product – as in the case of a game like *Assassin's Creed II* – you can only make use of it once you've logged onto a specific network (which is free of charge) that, while claiming to be necessary to prevent software piracy, also conveniently collects data about you as a player. These data are, in part, used to anticipate what you are likely to purchase in future. Aspects of a future like that described in the novel *Ubik* are therefore not so far removed from us, as Katherine Hayles (2009, 62) suggests with the example of the character Joe Chip: 'Perpetually short of cash, Joe must negotiate with the coffee pot, toaster, and even the door of his "conapt" to get them to perform routine services for which they demand instant payment.' That instant payment could obviously be information about our use of a product.

Of course, the non-disciplinary character of the emerging new mode of power that people such as Deleuze saw emerging can be observed in less seemingly mundane examples than computer games. Certainly since 9/11 and the War on Terror, but already well before that, there has been a clear shift to pre-emptive forms of observation, whether this be in the form of anticipating consumer behavior, risk analysis, or scenario planning (Cooper 2010). Indeed, the emergence and analysis of new forms of observation has been approached in a variety of ways (Lyon 2006). While some treated this as part of the development of what Foucault called biopolitics (Clough 2008; Thacker 2005), others, such as Massumi (2009), have suggested that instead it is part of an entirely new mode of power that has been emerging over the last couple of decades, preferring instead to view this as part of a broader ecology of powers. My approach is, in the first instance, to more clearly identify the specific mechanisms and instruments by which what I term modulatory power differentiates itself from other modes of power. Crucially what I am interested in is not only coming to an understanding of how new forms of observation are part of a new mode of power that actually functions as a coherent machine or assemblage, in much the same way that the disciplinary mode of power functions as a machine according to Foucault, but also, critically, I think, understanding how different modes of power act upon, and through, the same body or subject, at times in one and the same moment. This is critical because it forms part of considering the question of how we exist, or maintain an existence in a digital age. To ask that question differently, how can we understand the simultaneous operation of a mode of power like discipline, which is squarely aimed at producing 'useful individuals', while on the other hand there is a mode of power emerging that, to the extent it even recognizes individuals, has no care for them, with the notion of 'care' itself undergoing a significant transformation (Stiegler 2009b; 2010a).

My approach here, in other words, is to treat the possible emergence of a new form of control or new mode of power not as an either/or choice. As Venn (2007, 116) indicates, the 'anatomo-politics' associated with discipline and a biopolitics are not mutually exclusive. It is precisely the overlap between these possibly different forms of control and modes of power that interests me, though here, following Deleuze's approach, I focus mostly on the interaction between the disciplinary mode of power and the new modulatory mode of power. In what follows, then, it is specifically the engagement with Deleuze's approach to understanding this new mode of power, and what effects it has on how we exist, which Deleuze termed our 'dividuality', that drives this first part of the book. The reason for that is because it is precisely, against what Deleuze suggested, the ongoing production of an object that is molded and we recognize as an individual, and the simultaneous ongoing production of an objectile and an anticipation of flows, which has no form, and which, taking Deleuze's cue, I refer to in the second part of the book as a superject, that is at the core of dividuality and therefore at the core of what it means to exist in the so-called digital or control society.

The amplification of discipline

Foucault, in *Discipline and Punish* (1979), explained that discipline, as a mode of power, is a machine on a societal scale – a machine whose main function is to produce useful individuals, to produce useful forces out of subjected bodies. This it principally achieves by way of making things visible, and it is in that sense that Foucault saw discipline as a mode of power that is a 'political anatomy of detail' (1979, 39). This discipline, as a machine, achieves by way of four mechanisms, each of which is composed of specific techniques, and three instruments, using individuals 'both as object and as instruments of its exercise' (1979, 170). For the purposes of later on explaining how the modulatory mode of power differentiates itself from discipline, it is useful to briefly summarize these mechanisms and instruments here, as they are key to producing the specific form of individuality that Deleuze and others have suggested is no longer being produced.

The first mechanism of the disciplinary machine is that individuals are distributed in space, each space having a specific function (Foucault 1979, 141). This isn't simply the space of the factory, or the hospital, or school but, significantly, each individual within these spaces has a specific location. The second mechanism is that the activity of individuals in each of the spaces is controlled (Foucault 1979, 149). Again, this can involve several techniques, but typically involves at least the use of a timetable, for example, which can be used to divide an activity or process into smaller elements. The third mechanism – the organization of geneses (Foucault 1979, 156) – is basically a set of techniques or machinery used to organize an individual's training, and is critical to ensuring a standardization in the object produced – the individual – as well as in differentiating one individual from another in terms of her or his abilities. Finally, the fourth mechanism – the 'composition of forces' (Foucault 1979, 162) – organizes the various mechanisms, as well as each of the techniques that form part of them, in such a way as to produce the end product that we recognize as the individual. In effect it is this fourth mechanism that ensures the body becomes part of a larger 'multi-segmentary machine' (Foucault 1979, 164).

Effectively, it is these four mechanisms and the manner in which they function as a coherent assemblage – a machine – that produces the individual as a standardized object. Ideally this object is characterized by four features: it is cellular, organic, genetic, and, most significant of all perhaps, is combinatory. As objects they can in that regard be thought of as bricks, or 'plug and play' devices, in the sense that they have a defined form and are a known quantity, depending on their training of course. This means they are replaceable, and can be combined or rearranged depending on the requirements of work. In short, they are not fluid entities, even if they are mostly composed of fluids.

Some bricks can serve more specific functions, while others might have a wider use depending on the context in which they are placed. It is in this sense that individuals are molded to take on a specific form, and it is this that enables them to act with force. It is important to note that in order for the disciplinary machine to continue to produce its main product, the four mechanisms have to be intact. Without form, their capacity to act, and thereby their usefulness, is significantly reduced within a disciplinary context, and this is a point I will return to later, in both Part I and Part III, because it is precisely this production of form that is subject to interruption from the modulatory mode of power.

The three instruments by which the disciplinary machine operates – hierarchical observation, normalizing judgment, and the examination – are equally critical. So much so that Foucault credits discipline's success to these three instruments. This is mainly because they give the disciplinary machine the simplicity and modesty that it would otherwise not have. It is precisely in these instruments that not only the operation of Foucault's concept of power is most clearly visible, but it is here that it becomes clear what role and importance the 'apparatus of writing' (Foucault 1979, 189–190) has in the operation of the disciplinary machine overall. It is precisely the changes in the apparatus of writing, principally by way of databases (Poster 1990; 1995), that not only amplify the functioning and effects of the disciplinary machines but that, significantly, also produce effects that are not disciplinary in character.

That databases and the use of digital media more generally can amplify the effects of discipline is a relatively well-established point. In the first instance, by shifting to a more widespread use of digital media, the writing apparatus by which discipline operates is vastly expanded to incorporate more and more aspects of our life. We are no longer captured only by the apparatus of writing in clearly disciplinary spaces such as schools, hospitals, and offices, but increasingly outside of these spaces as well. In that respect, as our use of digital media grows, there are fewer and fewer spaces in which we are not made visible in some form (Abe 2009). Whenever we use our mobile phones, use a GPS device, look at a web page, post photos of friends or ourselves on social media, tweet something on Twitter, use our credit card to pay for groceries, the information is simultaneously recorded and sorted. As Mark Poster (1990) pointed out, we are now both the sources and recorders of information. In this sense, certainly in the past couple of decades, the field of visibility in which we could potentially be subject to the disciplinary gaze has vastly expanded (Lyon 2009). Indeed, especially when looking at the potential surveillance aspects associated with RFID tagging (Crandall 2010; Hayles 2009), the potential field of observation is expanding in quite significant ways.

Of course, the observation and recording of our actions does not always form part of a disciplinary mechanism, which I consider in more detail further on in this chapter. The point I make here is simply that in expanding the apparatus of writing we are thereby also potentially expanding, and, equally significantly, intensifying, the coercive function of observation as well as the network of relations that 'produces "power" and distributes individuals in [a] permanent and continuous field' (Foucault 1979, 177). For example, many people volunteer to offer information about themselves, their life outside of work, as well as their relationships to others, by way of social media like Facebook, Twitter, LinkedIn or MySpace. While these companies themselves might not necessarily collect the information as part of a disciplinary mechanism, this doesn't mean that the disciplinary gaze doesn't extend to these sites. As a host of incidences reported in the popular press have demonstrated, at times this information feeds into the disciplinary machine – when an employer, or prospective employer, discovers information about an employee, their activities, or their relations to others, which then subjects the individual to discipline, typically by way of a punishment mechanism rather than a reward mechanism. Indeed, there are numerous countries where people feel very much subject to a disciplinary gaze when it comes to their use of the Internet and communications more generally.

For example, it was widely commented on in the Western press more recently that outbursts of people in China on blogs and social media regarding accusations of government corruption in relation to the high-speed train network was very unusual because ordinarily people in China, especially journalists, are far more guarded about what they say on the Internet (Hutton 2011). At the same time, the people involved in organizing the London riots in 2011 were widely reported to have deliberately avoided the use of social media like Facebook and Twitter precisely because they were aware that the authorities monitor these sites, preferring to make use of Blackberries instead – the reason being that communications through the Blackberry are encrypted and more difficult to monitor. It's difficult to argue in the case of such examples that there is no disciplinary gaze at work, with, for example, the banning of the use of anonymous proxy servers in some countries sometimes leading to severe penalties, including the potential of death.

Equally significant in the amplification of discipline is that data can be relatively easily, and speedily, related and linked to other data that might exist on the wider network that forms the Internet. Prior to the use of our digital devices, and especially prior to the expansion of the Internet and the increased interconnectedness of these devices, there were still significant spatial as well as temporal restrictions in effect that limited the use and potential manipulation of data. In that respect a spatial annihilation of a very real kind both expands the network of relations established by the disciplinary machine, as well as brings the nodes in that network closer together. This is one of the reasons that in Australia, for example, there remains a lot of resistance to a shift to the use of networked patient records (Cresswell 2011), despite this bringing significant benefits to those working in the health sector, as well as potential benefits to patients.

One effect of the increased connectedness of the digitized writing apparatus, then, is that the instrument of normalizing judgment is significantly amplified. Indeed, through the use of digital media, it is possible to greatly extend the penal and reward mechanism by which discipline operates. As databases allow for the capture, observation, and recording of an ever greater amount and degree of detail of an individual's actions, so they also enable the 'discovery' or 'capture' of ever more detailed forms of 'incorrect behavior' (Agre 1994). In short, databases make it much easier to 'discover' ever more deviations from the norm. This in turn also enables an expansion of the rank or the grade in more and more areas of an individual's existence. One example of this is frequent flyer reward schemes, which aim to produce a loyalty to the company on the part of the customer, rewarding those who fly frequently with the company, while they simultaneously punish those who do not fly a lot, even if only by ranking them differently. Typically the schemes enable different ranks of frequent flyer to be 'rewarded' with a better or earlier choice of seat, or, for example, to be given a newspaper at the start of a flight. Again, databases allow for the constant observation of a customer's conduct, especially since, in the case of frequent flyer programs, there are often a host of other companies that form part of the program's network, automatically triggering rewards, or punishments, depending on the customer's behavior.

In that respect RFID tags can be used in disciplinary ways as well. They are used, for example, to 'deliver' so-called VIP care, so that when a VIP customer enters a shop or store they can be immediately greeted differently from other customers 'to make VIP customers feel like true VIPs' (Chen 2006). Indeed, while there are clear non-disciplinary aspects to the type of data that can be collected through RFID tagging, because it is site-specific, utilizing hardware and software, it can be set up to significantly amplify a disciplinary gaze in a specific space. In fact, an employer simply requesting an employee to sign onto Google Latitude with their phone already extends the disciplinary gaze in very significant ways. Indeed, in that respect, even GPS-enabled smart-phones can serve a very significant disciplinary function – especially handy for parents to keep an eye on their kids or for a manager to keep an eye on employees on the road. There is no need to separately tag people.

The third instrument of discipline – the examination – is also greatly amplified through the digitization of the writing apparatus. It is the amplification of this instrument that has an enormous effect on the operation of discipline as a whole, as it pervades the entire disciplinary system. The examination, critically, is for Foucault (1979) the site where the formation of knowledge is linked with the exercise of power. One very notable effect is that individuals, when using digital media, are always 'seen' and, as such, are subject to examination on a constant basis. In the case of a frequent flyer program, for example, a customer's actions – especially those that generate points such as grocery shopping, flying, using their phone through a specific provider, and so on – are constantly observed and recorded, and the customer is constantly tested to check if they pass the test for moving up or down a rank, of which they are constantly reminded. In the context of digital technologies, in other words, no action is not subject to constant examination in some respect.[1] This amplifies tremendously the effect of the examination as an instrument of objectification, and is key to the operation of discipline overall.

In short, it is primarily because of the increased connectedness between our digital machines that it is increasingly difficult not to be captured by, or engaged with, the writing apparatus that underlies discipline and by which it operates. It is increasingly difficult not to be observed in some way (Lyons 2006; 2009). Using a digital machine, even if it is a spoken conversation on a mobile phone or through Skype, is still a writing of binary code at least on the machine level. In my own workplace, for example, the moment I switch on a program like Skype I instantly receive an automated message that the use of programs like Skype generates large amounts of data, and that this may generate a charge if deemed 'excessive'. This not only indicates to me that I need to 'keep an eye' on my Internet usage and discipline my online behavior, as otherwise I might be penalized if I deviate from the norm, but it also indicates that what I do online at my workplace is potentially being monitored. In that respect, any action we perform by way of any digital machine is in some respects always a writing and recording of some kind, but critically, while at least some of these actions are subject to forms of observation that clearly are disciplinary in character, they are often also subject to forms of observation that are quite different in character.

The emergence of modulation

One of the earlier non-disciplinary effects that the use of databases had is that it altered the role of the expert (Castel 1991; Lyotard 1984; Miller and Rose 2008; Rose 1996). Much has been written about this, but in the disciplinary mode of power the expert is the person who holds and produces knowledge about their subject. Databases, however, enable ever larger amounts of different information about a subject to be held and for more and different relationships between those pieces of information to be 'discovered' than any expert or group of experts ever can. More importantly, much of this process of the storing, manipulation, and retrieval of information about a subject is often automated, and the complexities of these calculations are often far beyond the capacities of any human being (Crandall 2010; Henman 1997). One effect of this is that knowledge is decreasingly held and produced by 'the expert' and is increasingly held and produced by expert systems or programs (Crandall 2010), because only these can cope with what would otherwise be an overflow of information (recognizing that these programs are, of course, human constructs in the first place and that we need to consider these as actors as well).

Because knowledge is increasingly produced and held by databases, a shift occurs in which the expert is totally subordinated to their administrator or manager (Castel 1991, 291; Lyotard 1984, 50–3; Miller and Rose 2008; Rose 1996, 17). Experts are often considered less competent than the database, or 'expert system', in the production of knowledge. They are certainly slower in reaching a decision. Also they can be considered less precise and more likely to produce errors of judgment than the expert system (unless, of course, the program contains an error). This is either because they might be biased (and obviously the expert system can be biased too) or simply because they cannot deal with a similar amount of information in the same amount of time. In this context, the expert functions more as an adjunct to the manager or administrator (Castel 1991, 293; Rose 1996), merely collecting information in 'the field' to be entered in a database maintained by managers who do not necessarily need any extensive knowledge of the subject matter they are meant to administer. This subordination of the expert to the manager has, or rather reflects, very serious consequences for the operation of the disciplinary machine. Rather than leading toward an amplified function of the expert, the amplification of discipline in the form of, and by way of databases, leads to the very opposite (Castel 1991).

The changing role of the expert also reflects a different relation between those doing the observing and those being observed in the context of databases (Baudrillard 1994, 29–30; Castel 1991; Virilio 1986, 154–6; 1991). In the disciplinary mode of power, observation relies on the presence of those being observed. With the advent of databases and the digitization of the writing apparatus, however, the bodies of subjects are no longer required to be present 'in the flesh' (Castel 1991, 288). In that respect the observer has ceased to exist, though aspects of the human observer are obviously still in existence in the program that now does the observing (Crandall 2010). As such, the relation of immediacy between the expert and the subject that exists in the disciplinary mode of power, and which requires the presence of the subject, has disappeared, or rather, disappears in certain contexts. With that disappearance of the relation of immediacy comes a disappearance of the subject as well (Castel 1991, 21).

This disappearance of the relation of immediacy between the observer and the observed is reflective of an altogether different form of intervention (Castel 1991; Stiegler 2010a) – a form of intervention that is associated with a form of observation that is not disciplinary in character. Intervention in the disciplinary mode involves taking a specific individual as the target. This target or individual is cared for, and punished or rewarded, in order to be made to fit a specific mold, that is, to be (re)trained or (re)educated. Partly because of this requirement to 'care', discipline focuses on the internal state of individuals (Foucault 1979), correcting a person's behavior through reward and punishment, and thereby producing an awareness of being constantly observed for this purpose, which is what the panopticon achieves so efficiently. With the emergence of databases, however, the focus is increasingly on observing a number of different abstract factors in order to anticipate the emergence of deviant behavior (whether good or bad) so that it can be prevented before it even arises or, if good (such as the purchase of a product) be encouraged.

It is clear then that a form observation is emerging that does not function as part of any disciplinary mechanism or instrument. As I indicated above, this is not to say that databases are not used to amplify forms of observation that do form part of the operation of discipline. It is simply to say that databases also enable a non-disciplinary form of observation (Winokur 2008). Observation, which in discipline relies on the presence of the subject, is now more and more geared to recording information that does not necessarily directly relate to the internal state of any given subject. Stated differently, it is possible to record a very diverse range of information about the external relations, rather than the internal relations, in which subjects find themselves. Facebook and a host of other social media such as LinkedIn are perhaps the most obvious examples of this. In other words, the focus on the internal state of the subject – what one might term a 'soul' (Virilio 1986), which always requires a relation of immediacy between subject and expert – is removed (Feeley and Simon 1992; Rose 1999, 236). Instead, the collection and collation of factors external to the subject enables the production of various combinations that form sets of different profiles, with each profile essentially being a specific combination of factors. At the moment databases 'find' or produce such a specific combination of factors, a subject is placed into the profile that fits that combination. This new mode of observation, in other words, is pattern recognition, and aims at predetection or 'seeing before the event' (Bogard 1996).

This pre-emptive aspect to some of the new forms of observation goes well beyond the individual, across various aspects of life (Bailey 1996; Cooper 2010; Knorr-Cetina and Preda 2007; Massumi 2009). This new form of observation, manifested mainly through profiling and pattern recognition, but also through computer modeling and simulations (Bogard 1996; Crandall 2010; Hayles 2009), has several implications. The first is that, unlike hierarchical observation which forms part of discipline, it has no coercive function. Indeed, it can't have a coercive function. There are several reasons for this. First, subjects are not necessarily always aware of being observed in the context of databases. As Kiyoshi Abe (2009) points out, many users don't actually care about being observed, often taking the attitude that they simply have nothing to hide. The moment a person doesn't care about their actions being observed, the panoptic mechanism is either working very efficiently or, instead, has broken down entirely. The use of social networking sites like MySpace and Facebook are illustrative of this, but so is the attitude of many people toward being tracked through their GPS devices, whether this be their smart-phone or their car navigation system (Abe 2009). While in the disciplinary machine it is important that a subject has an awareness of being observed, or the possibility thereof, this is of no consequence for this new form of observation. Though, having pointed that out, it's worth reminding ourselves that many teenagers prefer not to have their parents as their online 'friends' and just as many, I suspect, prefer not to have their employer as 'friend' on Facebook or Google+. In short, there is something disciplinary at work when it comes to the observation enacted through many of our digital media, but at the very same time there is also something that has no disciplinary function.

A pre-emptive aspect of observation also means that subjects cannot adjust their behavior, mainly because they are not aware of the model they are meant to follow. The new form of observation, after all, 'sees' before the event occurs. In that respect, there is no model to which a subject must adhere. Even if there was one, the new form of observation simply doesn't require a subject to be aware of it. It's neither here nor there. Not only that, subjects cannot possibly be aware of, and have control over, the external factors of which, according to this form of observation, they are a product or expression. It is in this context that forms of control are emerging such as genetic screening, explored in movies like *Gattaca* (Niccol 1997), that are very insidious.

In other words, the new mode of observation – pattern recognition – that is enacted through databases cannot form part of any panoptic schema. Panopticism relies on four requirements, all of which need to be met in order for it to operate. First, panopticism relies on an awareness on the part of subjects that they are being observed or are likely to be observed. Second, panopticism relies on subjects being aware of the model toward which they have to adjust their behavior, otherwise any punishment or reward is pointless. Third, subjects actually have to care about being observed. Finally, there has to be a gratification-punishment mechanism in place. In the context of this new form of observation, with its focus on pattern recognition and simulations, the majority of these requirements are not and cannot be met. Again, this is not to say that databases and the digitization of the writing apparatus do not amplify panopticism, but simply to point out that another mode of observation operates through the digitized writing apparatus that supports discipline's operations, and which is not disciplinary. In that respect, as Baudrillard (1994) argued, there may well be a shift from a panoptic gaze to what he referred to as a pornographic gaze[2] – though a better term might be 'an anticipation', something I address in more detail in Chapter 2.

What is occurring, then, is a shift away from a mode of observation that is part of a mechanism that requires compliance, and instead to a form of observation that in many respects is simply content or risk analysis (Beck 1992; Braithwaite 2000; Castel 1991; Gandy 1993). Indeed, in addition to this, as Melinda Cooper (2010) indicates, the sort of modeling (typically in the form of scenario-planning) that is increasingly used to try and cope with what is understood to be a turbulent world, whether it be in the context of derivatives in financial markets, or planning against terrorist attacks in the post 9/11 world, doesn't even focus on risk anymore. Instead it focuses on

> [t]he radical uncertainty of unknowable contingencies – events for which it is impossible to assign a probability distribution on the basis of past frequencies. Instead, it develops a semantics of counterfactual propositions, opening up onto a pluriverse of alternative event-contingent worlds. If x were to occur, what world would we be living in? If x had occurred (or had not), what world would we be living in? [...] the spectrum of alternative futures is expanded beyond the logical possibilities of simple prediction [...].
>
> (Cooper 2010, 173)

This is precisely the post 9/11 world that Donald Rumsfeld was operating in when he made his comment about 'known knowns', 'known unknowns', and 'unknown unknowns'.

A similar shift away from a disciplinary gaze and toward a pre-emptive form of observation is also reflected in a 'superseding of the confession'. As Virilio argued some decades ago,

[i]f in these tests someone is still listening for a confession, it is evident that this confession is no longer the story of a crime by its author. This was completed notably by the mapping of heavy crime zones in urban planning systems, and beyond this by the 'criminostat' (computer-aided visualization of statistical fields) [...] We could imagine that at this level the gaps and hazards inherent in the ordering of materials should disappear, since with computers they could make the accusing discourse perfectly coherent, or at least approaching coherence, having to do both with the name of the subject and that of the object. At that point, they could do totally without the confession of the accused, who would be less informed about his [*sic*] own crime than the computer, and who, no longer being the one who knows 'the truth', would have nothing left to confess.

(Virilio 1986, 154–6)

In other words, instead of a molding, this is more in the nature of a tracing or tracking, even a programming (Bogard 1996, 33; Castel 1991, 294; Deleuze 1992). When the behavior of a subject, their weaknesses and strengths, their future(s), possible failures and desires can be detected long before they even occur, then one can 'order' those subjects, and their strengths and weaknesses in advance (Bogard 1996, 24; Castel 1991, 294). Movies such as *Gattaca* and *Minority Report* explore this in a variety of ways. As Bill Gates is reported to have stated (Kittler 2006, 179), 'In the future...we will treat the end user as we treat computers: both are programmable.' Most illustrative of this is the scene in *Minority Report* when the main character walks along the street and the environment, the various forms of advertising in the form of billboards, adjusts itself to his specific desires and tastes. His environment is programmed in advance of him, to create a smooth space, and to maximize the chances of him purchasing a product. This is the future, and companies such as NEC and Quividi – the latter claiming that 'the days of blind advertising are over' (Quividi 2011) – are well on their way to making it real.[3]

Profiling, as an 'observation before the fact' (Bogard 1996, 27), does not force a subject into a model, but makes any subject always and already an ideal, a model, a norm. As Baudrillard stated: '[t]here is no longer any imperative of submission to the model, or to the gaze "YOU are the model!" "YOU are the majority!"' (Baudrillard 1994, 29). The new forms of observation are associated, then, not so much with the imposition of an order, as is the case with discipline, as they are with the projection of an order (Castel 1991, 295). Control in such a schema, as Bogard points out, is more like discovering the algorithm of a computer game, enabling a player to anticipate all the surprises that, after all, are programmed in any case (Bogard 1996, 33; Wark 2007).[4]

This programming, which is administrated through management, implies 'the development of differential modes of treatment of populations, which aim to maximize the returns on doing what is profitable and to marginalize the unprofitable' (Castel 1991, 294). In that respect there are obvious connections with what Foucault identified in his lectures on security and governmentality (2007; 2008), though as Massumi (2009) suggests, this new mode of power is probably no longer biopolitics. The new forms of observation, in any case, are associated with a general shift toward a focus on performativity. Success – in the form of increased performance and efficiency – is increasingly tied to the ability to make more accurate predictions (Virilio 1995, 33). The emergence of these new forms of observation also ties in well with Lyotard's (1984) much earlier argument that databases, through the exteriorization of knowledge, reflect a general shift in which the production of knowledge is tied not into the production of truth, but instead is tied into making systems more efficient, and the past few decades have certainly demonstrated that Lyotard's argument, or at least some aspects of it, was 'on the money'.

The new forms of observation reflect not only a deregulation of the management of space, since where you are no longer matters (provided you are 'connected', of course), but they also reflect a similar deregulation of time. Time in the context of digital technologies is of a different order than that through which discipline operates. A good example of this is the fact that in simulations time can easily be sped up, paused, or slowed down. In other words, time (that is, the time of subjects) is organized very differently from that in the operation of discipline. In the context of digital technologies, time is not organized linearly in successive elements. There is, as Deleuze (1992) observed, no clear beginning or end to any specific task or element anymore. One no longer proceeds from mold to mold. Instead, a subject no longer ever finishes education and is always potentially at work. So while hierarchical observation is geared toward the distribution of bodies in space, one of the four main mechanisms of discipline, the new forms of observation instead aim toward what Virilio refers to as a populating of time (1991, 120). In such a context a person is potentially always at work, and potentially always at play, regardless of their location, and at the same time.

A trader's working life, for example, is determined by 'the market' as it makes its way around the planet in a 24-hour cycle and when the market moves to another time zone, they continuously stay in touch with it (that is, connected) through a variety of media and dealing screens (Knorr-Cetina and Preda 2007). This is an experience that is not dissimilar from that of gamers in massive online worlds such as *World of Warcraft, Eve,* or *Rift.* Indeed, this potential of always being at work in a digital world, in a 'connected' world (Shaviro 2003), is precisely why some people will travel to locations where there is no mobile network in order to properly disconnect, or, indeed, do not have an Internet connection in their home.

All of this suggests that the amplification of discipline, through the digitization of its writing apparatus, while able to produce an intensified normalization and individualization of subjects, at the same time also produces something quite different that is not of discipline. The existence of forms of observation that focus on a body's activities not as a subject as such, but merely on the patterns of code it generates, and treating these patterns of code as a resource, including, significantly, genetic code (Cooper 2008; Thacker 2005), suggests that mechanisms are operating that produce very different effects from those of the disciplinary mode of power. The new forms of observation operate by way of very different spatial and temporal structures. These are structures that require a very different relation, if a relation at all, between the observed and the observer. Indeed, the latter's relation to their observer, their 'manager', reflects a different operation of knowledge, which does not fit into the disciplinary schema. In effect, what is happening is that a very different reality is being produced through the new forms of observation, which is not at all the reality of 'the individual' with its four characteristics as discipline produces it. The production of this new reality must also be produced by different mechanisms and instruments than those that compose the disciplinary machine, and suggests that an entirely different machine or mode of power is in operation (Baudrillard 1994; Bogard 1996; Deleuze 1992; Galloway 2004; Massumi 2009; Rose 1999).

The mechanisms and instruments of modulation

[W]e're more focused and skilled than ever at providing the complete view of what consumers watch and buy through powerful insights that clarify the relationship between content and commerce.

(Nielsen 2011)

An unmeasured media is an undervalued media.

(Quividi 2011)

From the above discussion we can begin to delineate possible mechanisms and instruments of this new mode power, which, taking my cue from Deleuze (1992), I term the modulatory mode of power.[5] In part I do this because Deleuze saw the new forms of control as modulating. Equally important, however, is the fact that the term 'control' is, at least in my view, too broad to describe this mode of power, and Deleuze, at least in the postscript, is far too negative about control. While the latter point is developed further in Part II, for now I aim to differentiate the characteristics of modulation, before looking much more specifically at the production of the modulatory machine in Chapter 2.

One of the key characteristics of the new forms of observation, as pointed out above, is that they are pre-emptive (Massumi 2009, 167), that is, they are aimed at anticipating actions before they actually occur. In short, the new forms of observation are characterized by the fact that they aim to recognize patterns of code generated on the machine level. This code is produced whenever we do something, or are observed doing something, by way of a digital machine, whether this be our action as the action of an individual, or our action as part of a population, or, indeed, both.[6] It is significant that this form of observation does not operate in perspectival space, which is in direct contrast to how observation functions in the disciplinary machine. As I briefly touched on above, discipline organizes spaces so as to produce specific forms of conduct. One of the key elements in making spaces work – making them productive – is precisely the use of the instrument of hierarchical observation, as Foucault's example of the panopticon demonstrates so well. However, rather than looking through or behind something, the new forms of observation always project onto a screen (Bogard 1996, 21), and, indeed, when no humans are involved screens themselves are superfluous. In short, instead of focusing on bodies in space, the new forms of observation focus on detecting and predicting the emergence of specific patterns of code. Since they are not spatial, nor are necessarily aimed at modifying an individual's behavior, it suggests that they form part of a very different mechanism of power. For this reason that first mechanism can usefully be termed the recognition of patterns, and it is a key mechanism in the modulatory mode of power.

Of course, the patterns that are recognized, and the actions that are anticipated aren't spatial either. What is anticipated is an action that is yet to occur, that is, has not actually happened yet. These actions are in the first instance simply code on the machine level, and, indeed, the product of a program. This isn't to say that this code has no 'real' world consequences. In fact, this code, we need to recognize, is 'real', and, in that respect, not to be differentiated from physical actions, at least not in that manner. More significant, action itself, which forms the central focus of Part III, and, as a number of people have suggested, takes on the character of flow, that is, of a fluid (Hardt and Negri 2001; Knorr-Cetina 2003; Knorr-Cetina and Preda 2007; Parisi and Terranova 2000). The point I want to make here is that it is this non-spatial character of action that affects the second mechanism of discipline: the control of activity. This mechanism, in part, focuses on the efficiency of specific actions that the body must perform. As was pointed out above, however, with the new forms of observation actual bodies are not really an issue. Bodies are not forced to perform actions in a specific manner. As Deleuze (1992) indicated with the example of the marketing sample, there is no mold or norm to adhere to.

Equally significant when considering discipline's mechanism of the control of activity is that there is often no coercive instrument attached to the observation. Instead, the control of activity is replaced, as I tried to indicate above by way of the example of the scene in *Minority Report*, by something that involves the programming of activity. Rather than controlling the specific activities of individual subjects and forcing them to adopt a specific form or mold, they are now anticipated as a group or as part of an aggregate, as, for example, the emergence of a 'new penology' seems to reflect (Feeley and Simon 1992; O'Malley 2010; Rose 1999, 236). A generally increasing prevalence of strategies of risk management also reflects this (Rose 1999, 236–7). This suggests *the anticipation of activity* as a new mechanism. As a mechanism it operates in a variety of ways, whether it be through the use of cookies that enable a record of our past web-surfing behavior to be established, that can then be used to automatically have a web-site adjust itself according to our past uses of that site or whether it be in the form of software, such as Microsoft's latest installment of Word, setting up the interface according to what functions a person has most used in the past with the aim of encouraging a 'smooth' experience, a uninterrupted flow. Of course, if the activity isn't correctly anticipated, and the environment is not set up for the pattern or code being generated, it produces a very interrupted experience.[7]

This mechanism of the anticipation of activity is not only different from discipline in terms of how it affects the organization of the activities of subjects. As touched on before, it is also different in its use and construction of time. Where discipline constructs and organizes a person's time by way of timetables, partitioning a subject's time into increasingly specific segments, the subject's time is now set up as all potentially useful time instead (Nunes 1997). The mobile phone provides the most obvious example of this reorganization of time, ensuring that a subject is connected to the network as much as possible, and with devices such as smart-phones and tablets incorporating an increased amount of specialized actions in one and the same device, the 'resourcing' a subject can provide is increased as well. While there can be a clear disciplinary aspect to this, it is also precisely this different construction and use of time that is reflected in a third new mechanism of power.

The third mechanism of discipline, as described by Foucault (1979), is the organization of geneses or successive generations. This mechanism produces useful bodies by way of organizing their training into specific segments. Time, in this context, is broken down into specific threads or segments, which are then organized into a broader plan. Each segment has a very specific start and end point that requires that certain prerequisites, measured through examination, are met before the next segment can start. Increasingly, however, as pointed out previously, such segments with a clear start and end point are replaced through a constant training that has no endpoint (Deleuze 1992, 179). Rather than time being divided up into specific segments, which is central to discipline's mechanism of the organization of geneses, all of a subject's time constitutes one large segment that is subjected simultaneously to various forms of training, none of which have a clear end point. Deleuze referred to this shift as one from 'apparent acquittal' to 'endless postponement' (Deleuze 1992, 179). In that respect, one can refer to the emergence of a third new mechanism of power, which proceeds by way of the substitution of code, that is, it proceeds by way of the organization of antitheses.

This can be readily observed. Rather than engaging in the construction of generations and the construction of activities with a clear beginning and end, in the context of digital technologies, one is engaged in one of a whole series of activities, and at any moment one can swap, or rather, substitute one activity for another. As Deleuze explained,

> [i]n disciplinary societies you were always starting all over again (as you went from school to barracks, from barracks to factory), while in control societies you never finish anything – business, training, and military service being coexisting metastable states of a single modulation, a sort of universal transmutation.
>
> (Deleuze 1995, 179)

In that respect, one can characterize the difference between the organization of time, and therefore that of the subject, in discipline, as resembling a serial file, whereas the organization of time, and therefore that of the subject, in the context of digital technologies is more of the nature of a random access file. The former stores code in a serial manner, so that whenever any data need to be accessed the whole code, from beginning to end, has to be read through (Sinclair 1997, 392). With the latter, any given piece of data can be accessed at any time without needing to go through all of the code from beginning to end (Sinclair 1997, 357). Any data are instantly available at any moment.

Finally, the fourth mechanism of discipline – the composition of forces – is what combines and unifies the other three mechanisms into a functioning whole. It is an essential mechanism because it is that which enables the construction or constitution of the disciplinary mode of power as a unitary machine. Without this mechanism, discipline, as a mode of power, would not exist. Instead, some of the specific instruments of discipline might operate, as they did well before the development of the disciplinary mode of power, but they would form part of a different assemblage, if they formed part of anything at all. In short, this mechanism, like the others, relies on the use and production of specific spatial and temporal structures to make discipline into an efficient machine. The non-disciplinary effects of the amplification of discipline indicate, however, that other spatial and temporal structures operate that are not of discipline. This raises the question as to whether modulation, as a mode of power, has a similar mechanism. Such a fourth mechanism would still function to arrange the other mechanisms to operate as part of one machine or assemblage, but it would need to achieve this in a different manner. Stated differently, it would need to compose a very different set of forces that act upon and constitute subjects entirely differently from how discipline achieves this.

This is where the earlier point that action in a digital context is flow becomes significant. The reason for that is because the subject as such, or rather, the production thereof, doesn't appear to be a central concern in the new forms of observation. As Parisi and Terranova (2000) argued well before 9/11, and Cooper (2010), and Dillon and Lobo-Guerrero (2009) reminded us, there is something of a general mutation occurring in the operation of power that is not so much about the composition of forces, as being about the control of turbulence. In other words, there is no attempt to unify forces, as discipline does, in a mechanical, spatial, and solid form, but more an attempt to predict, to anticipate, or to calculate the emergence of patterns of flow or energy within an otherwise fluid system (De Landa 1991; Parisi and Terranova 2000), though as Massumi points out, to think of it as process is perhaps more appropriate than to think of it as a system:

> The coherence of a process is that of tendency, feeding back on itself in such a way as to generate always another difference. A process is fluctual. It is essentially unstable. A system, on the other hand, is an emergent, provisional stability arising at the cross-roads of processual tendencies whose formative force it siphons into its own self-organizing. A system feeds back on itself in order to settle things for itself: in order to settle a territory. Its mode of coherence is self-reproductive. Its operations feed back on themselves in the interests of their own conservation.
>
> (Massumi 2009, 168)

Stated more simply, process is flow, and therefore entirely fluid precisely because it has no stable shape, which is in direct contrast to a system, which reproduces itself, repeats itself, in order to be stable, in order to maintain a coherent form that persists over time. In short, a system has the characteristics of a solid entity. This is not to say, and it is critical to make this distinction, that solid and fluid, or rather flow, are opposite to each other, or somehow mutually exclusive (Jay 2010, 99). As Massumi makes clear in relation to system and process, the former is a mode of expression of the latter: 'A system embodies a processual tendency toward self-preservation (adaptive self-reproduction). Both process and system involve positive feedback. Thus neither a process nor a system can be accounted for without accounting for the nonlinearity of its causality' (Massumi 2009, 169).

Playing more liberally with the distinction Massumi draws here, ice, a solid that maintains form, and can for that very reason exert force, is in that respect a mode of expression of water, a fluid (that is, a substance that flows) and which therefore cannot act with force. Here, though, we need to be careful because (as I pointed out earlier) we shouldn't make the mistake that such flow takes the character of movement. Movement is something that occurs in perspectival space. Nor ought we make the mistake that flow is somehow unstructured or incapable of structuring (Knorr-Cetina 2007, 710). Flow, of course, is precisely what occurs on the level of the digital machine, though not in the sense of code moving around the global network infrastructure that enables the Internet. Flow occurs also on the screen in our interface or connection with our digital machines.

For now it is important to maintain the focus more specifically on what the mechanisms of the modulatory mode of power engage with and, what they, as a machinic assemblage produce. In the first instance they anticipate patterns of code. Once such flows are anticipated, one can order them and prepare for them in advance. In short, they can be pre-empted. What this requires is a fourth mechanism that functions similar to the composition of forces in discipline. This fourth mechanism is effectively the programming of flows,[8] and has most resonance with what Foucault dealt with in his lectures on governmentality as a mode of power (1991; 2007), in that this is the mechanism that is involved in determining how best to arrange things so as to maximize efficient economy as well as provide maximum security. It is important to point out, though, that modulation as a mode of power is not governmentality, but possibly operates as part of it in a similar manner to how Foucault suspected disciplinary power and sovereign power did (1991).

There are, then, at least four possible mechanisms in operation that form part of modulation as a mode of power. Looking at these in isolation, they don't have a disciplinary effect, or rather, none of them are deliberately aimed at producing disciplinary effects. Significantly, when operating as an assemblage, the reality that is produced by these four mechanisms is not the reality of an individuality endowed with its four characteristics as described by Foucault in the disciplinary mode of power (1979). Instead, their product is a very different form of subject, as far as this term is still appropriate here. Indeed, these mechanisms aim not at the production of identity, at individuality, but, instead, at its dispersal, though this too is not quite correct, because it doesn't do justice to modulation as a positive mode of power. In short, modulation doesn't aim to destroy the individual produced by discipline, but aims at producing something of an entirely different order, even if still of the same substance. In that respect, while some authors prefer to use the term 'fragmentation' to describe this production (Colwell 1996), or rather anti-production, of identity, 'dispersal' may be a better concept.[9]

Fragmentation refers to breaking up an originally whole object, and can only be done to entities that have form, that is, are solid. In the context of pattern recognition, however, one deals with many concurrently existing identities that I think is a mistake to think of as being fragmented. This 'subject' is not cellular but is composed of code. This code consists of the ongoing production of a variety of patterns, and has no clear beginning or end, apart from the switch that either connects or disconnects, though even disconnection is part of the generation of a pattern. My Internet service provider, for example, offers its customers a detailed, day-by-day, week-by-week, and month-by-month overview of my patterns of usage, and those patterns include information (that is, code) about when I am not connected. The code pertaining to my disconnections forms part of my pattern. Of course, as the latter example indicates, while flow of code in principle has no form, we can certainly take a snapshot, much like the cover image used for this book is a snapshot of flow. What this also suggests is that unlike the mechanism of the composition of forces, which is genetic, the programming of flows is antithetic. It is this product that Deleuze (1992) termed dividuality.

Like discipline, the modulatory mode of power uses a number of different instruments. The first of these is simulation, or computer modeling. Discipline's first instrument, in contrast, is hierarchical observation. Hierarchical observation is coercive and its structure is that of a pyramid. This means that it has a center and operates by way of relays. Observation in the context of modulation, however, has no center and, in one respect, is composed of nothing but relays. However, these relays are of a different materiality than the instrument of hierarchical observation, which, after all, operates in perspectival space. In a digital environment, however, everything a person does is simultaneously an action, a recording, a coding, and a sorting (Poster 1990; 1995). It is acted upon in one and the same moment, and at times even before the event ever occurs, all of which is automated. In other words, all the actions one performs in the context of digital technologies are open to anticipation. In that respect, any observation is always a simulation.

As indicated before, the modulatory mode of power doesn't have normalizing judgment as a mechanism. Such a judgment relies on a gratification-punishment mechanism and is aimed at making subjects become more like the norm. That isn't to suggest that modulation as a mode of power makes no use of norms, or does not establish norms, but instead no norm is put in place to which a subject has to conform and actively adjust their behavior. As explained above, even if such a norm or mold becomes clear, there is no gratification-punishment mechanism attached to it. Instead, modulation is an ongoing process of comparing, in order to determine which norm or profile you already are.[10] In that respect the norm has a significant role to play in both modes of power (Venn 2007). It is for this reason that categorical sorting forms a second likely instrument of the modulatory mode of power.

The lack of a gratification-punishment mechanism also indicates that the examination has no function in modulatory power. Instead, as Deleuze pointed out, the sample is one of the main instruments of modulation (Deleuze 1992). Marketing, as Deleuze suggested (1992, 181), is one of the principal forms of social control. The sample plays a key role in here, as this is, ideally, the only thing needed to discover the pattern of consumption to which one adheres. Of course, this use of the sample is also reflected in genetic testing and screening to see what profile your pattern of code fits. This is partly what makes the situation seem so hopeless for Deleuze and others when compared to how discipline functions. Discipline produces at least a capacity for action, even if it is reactive, in that you can at least try to fit a different mold, adopting a different form altogether, albeit within the confines of individuality. However, with modulation you either fit a pattern or you don't, and some patterns simply cannot be changed. This tension, produced by these different forms of regulation, is partly what is explored in the movie *Gattaca*, where the main character tries to escape from the life pre-determined for him by his genetic code, which in effect he can only achieve by hiding his own code and concealing it, through the use of biological material from another person, with a different code, a different pattern.

The modulatory mode of power, then, is composed of at least four mechanisms, and at least three instruments. Modulation proceeds by way of the recognition of patterns, the anticipation of activity, the organization of antitheses, and the programming of code. Its three main instruments are simulation, sorting, and sampling. Its product is an object, or as I'll argue in Chapter 2, an objectile (Deleuze 1993), that is characterized by its constitution as code. It has no form and is dispersed, keeping in mind that an entity in a gaseous state is fluid. It is also antithetic, and is programmable. From this point of view, discipline's and modulation's products are antagonistic to one another. Discipline is forever engaged in the production of form, that is, the individual, a stable entity that is capable of exerting force. Modulation, on the other hand, is only interested in the anticipation of flows. As a mode of power, the individual is not its aim. However, while modulation could be perceived as a successor to discipline, it is a major error to view modulation as replacing discipline. As Hardt and Negri pointed out, for example,

[t]he society of control might...be characterized by an intensification and generalization of the normalizing apparatuses of disciplinarity that internally animate our common and daily practices, but in contrast to discipline, this control extends well outside the structured sites of social institutions through flexible and fluctuating networks.

(Hardt and Negri 2001, 23)

Modulation and discipline in that respect often operate simultaneously, producing effects that are at times complementary and, at other times, can be very antagonistic to one another. It is precisely this simultaneous and antagonistic production, operating through the same database and working with the same body, that constitutes dividuality. Dividuality, in short, is not only the product of the modulatory mode of power. It is this dividuality that is at the core of the question of how we exist in a digital or so-called control society.

2
Dividuality

$$y(x, t) = y_1(x, t) + y_2(x, t)$$

Foucault was of the view that, besides there being a disciplinary mode of power that acted directly on the body, since the second half of the eighteenth century there was a new mode of power emerging that was applied to 'man-as-species'. While he later reformulated this mode of power somewhat in his work on governmentality (2007; 2008), already we could see a recognition that various modes of power exist, and produce, as part of a wider assemblage, even if they might operate on, as Foucault termed it, different levels, scales, and have different 'bearing area[s]', as well as make use of very different instruments (2003, 242). In Chapter 1, I aimed to identify and delineate more specifically the mechanisms and instruments as they might exist and relate to each other when examining the mode of power that Deleuze saw as replacing discipline. To be sure, there are clear points of connection between Deleuze's modulatory mode of power, and the mode of power that Foucault began to delineate in his work on biopower, and later governmentality. It is no coincidence, in that respect, that the tabulating machine, a digital device, was invented by Hollerith to compute data as part of the US census in 1890 (Strandh 1979). As indicated in Chapter 1, modes of power can function through the same writing apparatus. However, it is important to recognize that Foucault made his observations prior to the more widespread and everyday use of digital machines. Certainly, a similar claim can be made of Deleuze (Poster 2009), but Deleuze recognized that there was something significant and new in the use of digital machines more specifically, and that this warranted attention. Partly for this reason it is therefore useful to treat the modulatory mode of power as quite separate in its functions, recognizing, as Foucault did, that one mode of power can form a complex arrangement with another mode of power: 'It [can] dovetail into it, integrate it, modify it to some extent, and above all, use it by sort of infiltrating it, embedding itself in existing...techniques' (2003, 242).

It is precisely this dovetailing between modes of power that I now want to turn to, focusing specifically on how the modulatory machine operates in conjunction with the disciplinary machine. It is critical, therefore, to recognize that each mode of power can still function as a unitary assemblage (that is, as a machine) to produce effects that are specific to it, while at the same time recognizing there are significant points of connection between the two machines. As I indicated in Chapter 1, I want to argue that it is precisely this simultaneous operation that is at the core of dividuality, or rather, that constitutes dividuality.

This is a somewhat different take on it than, for example, that of Clough (2008, 18), and others. In part because dividuals, while 'statistically configured in populations that surface as profiles of bodily capacities, indicating what a body can do now and in the future... [and] statistically simulated as risk factors, can be apprehended as such without the subject, even without the individual subject's body' (Clough 2008, 18), are also (as I argue in this chapter) still treated as individual subjects. While Clough and others provide a sophisticated and useful approach to this in the context of examining biopower, Deleuze's dividual continues to be treated by most, including, notably, Deleuze (1992), as the sole product of a new mode of power. Stated differently, the operation of the disciplinary machine tends to be given a subordinate role to, indeed if any role in, the other modes of power, whether this be in examining biopower or, for those such as Massumi (2009) questioning whether it even is biopower, in examining pre-emptive power. At least in this chapter I want to add a corrective to this wider debate, by instead considering, as Foucault (2003; 2007; 2008) himself advocated in his later work, that discipline continues to operate. This I do as part of approaching the broader question of how modes of power can operate in one and the same moment, through the same digital media device, while producing differential, antagonistic, and complementary effects that, ultimately, involve the same body at some point. Before suggesting a mechanism by which we might understand this operation, it is first necessary to delineate more clearly the product produced by way of the mechanisms and instruments of the modulatory machine. This product I want to foreground here is not an object in the sense or form that the individual produced by way of discipline is an object. Instead it is what Deleuze refers to in *The Fold* (1993) as an objectile, and has quite a different status from an object. However, I'll begin by delineating some of the characteristics of dividuality.

The objectile

The individual, as Deleuze pointed out, is always identified as a position in a mass; it is always an individual and part of the mass (Deleuze 1992). This individual is also constructed by way of dualities. As Colwell states, it is

> either feminine or masculine, mad or sane, good or evil, in a manner that assigns this identity as a continuous structure that permeates the individual's entire existence and extends through the various spaces through which one moves.
>
> (Colwell 1996, 212)

The dividual, on the other hand, is not constructed by way of such dualities (Colwell 1996, 212; Deleuze 1992, 179–80). The dividual is constructed out of code (Deleuze 1992, 179–80), and 'finds itself aligned with any and all of these identities (among others), depending on the vicissitudes of the immediate situation' (Colwell 1996, 212). Hardt and Negri, for example, make clear that

> in disciplinary society each individual had many identities, but to a certain extent the different identities were defined by different places and different times of life … In the society of control, it is precisely these places, these discrete sites of applicability, that tend to lose their definition and delimitations. A hybrid subjectivity produced in the society of control may not carry the identity of a prison inmate or a mental patient or a factory worker, but may still be constituted simultaneously by all of their logics. It is factory worker outside the factory, student outside school, inmate outside prison, insane outside the asylum – all at the same time.
>
> (Hardt and Negri 2001, 331–2)

Another key difference between individuality and dividuality in that regard, as Colwell points out, is that '[d]ividuality is a different form of repetition than individuality' (Colwell 1996, 212).

From an electronically discursive standpoint, dividuals are constructed in databanks, each aspect of the person assembled in separate computer files, each file available for a different purpose, the parameters of each file organized around that purpose. This is quite different from Foucault's conception of the creation of an individual via the construction of a file that assembles the entire genealogic history of a person in order to make h/er an object for scientific study and intervention.

(Colwell 1996, 212)

This means that the individual, as a product, is always made into an identity; whereas the dividual, in some respects, is a constantly deferred identity – that is, it never is an identity. So, while one of discipline's main aims is the production of identity, of a specific type of subject, modulation has no such aim. Indeed, if anything, modulation can be said to be an anti-production of identity, though as I indicated in Chapter 2, this is not quite correct. It is an anti-production in the sense that it does not aim to produce identity and has no interest in identity as such. Again, in this respect (as noted earlier) the individual is more like a serial file or serial memory, whereas the dividual is more like a random access file or random access memory, and always available on call.

Discipline is also forever interested in making visible what is invisible (Bogard 1996, 21; Colwell 1996, 215). It is forever interested in a subject's desire, wills, and intentions. It is primarily interested, in other words, in the internal state of the subject, and it coerces this internal state precisely by way of making it visible (Colwell 1996, 215). Modulation, on the other hand, has no interest in the actual internal state of its 'subject'. Indeed, to use the notion of a subject in the context of modulation is quite problematic. Modulation is only interested in the desire and intentions of subjects in so far as these are outwardly manifested (Colwell 1996, 215). As Massumi, for example, indicates, these are a 'subject[s] of interest' (2009, 157), and no longer 'subjects of right' (Terranova 2007). In that respect, modulation is only interested in the patterns of code that are generated. Modulation is only interested in the actual and immediate vectors, or rather, flow lines of code that actions generate. Another way of saying this is that discipline is aimed at producing specific outward manifestations of behavior, whereas modulation is aimed at predicting them. As Deleuze stated, discipline operates by way of molds, while modulation 'is more like a sieve whose mesh varies from one point to another' (Deleuze 1992, 178–9).

This difference between the mold and the sieve is clearly reflected in the different apparatuses of discipline and modulation. Discipline's mechanisms distribute individuals in specific spaces, controlling both their activities and the use of their time, and make it all function as a whole machine. Modulation's mechanisms operate through the recognition, derivation, and generation of the patterns that different activities generate, constantly substituting, copying, and pasting strings of code. Discipline's and modulation's mechanisms operate in, or rather through, very different spatial and temporal structures. While discipline operates in actual space in real time, modulation does not operate spatially. One might say that discipline's main dimension is space, whereas modulation's is speed or time (Virilio 1986; 1991). Indeed, digital media more generally are increasingly recognized to construct time differently, requiring a different sensibility (Hansen 2006; 2009).[1]

This difference can also be observed when comparing the instruments of discipline and modulation. Discipline, for instance, operates by way of observation, using a perspectival gaze, whereas modulation uses simulations. Both space and time are of a very different order in each instrument. Discipline operates on actual or physical bodies in space, whereas modulation operates on the code that these bodies generate and, as such, does not operate spatially. This can also be observed in the difference between the instruments of normalization and sorting. Discipline constantly aims to make subjects conform to the mold, to adopt a specific form, whereas modulation is always already a mold, always already one or other pattern of code. This is also reflected in the difference between the examination and the sample. The examination is a test to determine whether you have conformed to the mold, and can move up a rank. The sample has no such interest and does not even require your awareness. Indeed, whether you are aware of it or not makes no difference.

Discipline and modulation are two very different modes of power then. They produce very different realities, proceed by way of very different mechanisms and instruments, employ and construct different spatial and temporal structures, and, to an extent, express, or are the expression of a different relation between power and knowledge. The following table summarizes some of the more specific differences that exist between discipline and modulation.

The main difference between discipline and modulation, then, is that the former operates spatially, whereas the latter operates temporally, or as flow, which is in part a function of the digital machines we use (Hansen 2004; 2009).[2] While for discipline the location of the body

Table 2.1 Characteristics of discipline and modulation

Disciplinary schema	Modulatory schema
You must be aware of the gaze.	The sample requires no awareness.
The gaze operates spatially.	The gaze, or rather trace, operates virtually.
Spaces matter.	Code matters.
Multiple gazes collapse into one through relays.	Multiple traces exist independently of one another.
You must care about the gaze.	You do not have to care about the trace or sample.
You must be aware of the purpose of the gaze.	You do not have to be aware of the purpose of the trace or sample.
You must be aware of the mold to which to conform.	There is no mold.
Conformity is important.	Conformity is not an issue.
There is a clear punishment-reward system in place.	There is no punishment-reward system in place.
Observation is always in real or past time.	Observation, or rather, detection is both in real time and before the event.
Discipline is reactive.	Modulation is pre-emptive.
The focus is on bodies.	The focus is on patterns of code.
Not all actions are recorded.	All actions are always recordings.
Discipline is vertical – networks enhance central control and are of the form of a pyramid.	Modulation is horizontal – there is no central control in the network form of organization.
Discipline focuses on what cannot be seen – observation is internal.	Modulation focuses only on what can be 'seen' – observation is external.
You are produced.	You are anticipated.
Distance matters – your location in relation to the center matters.	There is no distance – you have no physical location.
Discipline produces by way of differentiating.	Modulation operates by way of reducing everything to code.

is important with respect to what specific subject is produced, in the context of modulation a body's location, as long as it generates code in one form or another, is to some extent irrelevant. Modulation is certainly very effective in determining your physical location, provided you are connected, and produces different effects depending on a body's location. Mobile phones that are GPS-enabled are a good example of this. Even when many of these phones are turned off, or have a different SIM card inserted, you can locate them if they are lost or stolen. Indeed, even if you don't carry a digital media device, a body's location can still be registered, as the use of facial recognition technology in billboards referred to in Chapter 1 illustrates. As Crandall points out, we are increasingly being tracked by our environment:

> Architectural elements of physical space, as well as social architectures, often frame and cue actions – some very minute and instantaneous. As calculation, action and materiality intertwine, gestures, objects and environments can 'speak', however seductively or violently, in ways that are not always addressed to humans or known by them. To use a portable GIS device for real-time traffic information is a performative and declarative act. The question is the *program* at work in the environment within which these acts register and congeal.
>
> (Crandall 2010, 71)

In other words, it matters less and less whether you are physically connected to the network. Your body itself, certainly in the case of facial recognition technology, generates the code. So, increasingly, when a person might want to 'access' something, irrespective of whether that is a physical space or an electronic site, your body, and not some password you have to remember, or a card you have to carry with you, will determine whether that access is granted or not. In that respect, bodies that do not generate code, at least from the perspective of modulation, do not exist. The more wired the world becomes, the more code bodies will generate, including on the biological level. So while in discipline you are subject to different techniques and instruments depending on the spaces in which you find yourself, with modulation no such barriers exist. In the context of modulation it is the code that you are assigned, and the code you generate as you live your life, that determines whether you are accepted or rejected, and what sort of actions are effected upon you – how your environment responds to you and sets itself up for you. It is this code that determines whether or not you receive the message 'access denied' on the screen, or whether or not the password protected door to a building opens for you, regardless of whether that code is genetic or binary (Parisi and Terranova 2000). Genetic code is in that respect simply information, and, as code, forms part of the same continuum of information (Clough 2008; Thacker 2004). The move to an increased use of biometric technologies (as with passports, for example) is illustrative of this. However, these technologies are also increasingly being used in the technologies people use day-to-day. Many laptops, for example, can offer the option to make use of facial recognition to determine whether a person can make use of the machine or not. In such a context, as Rose pointed out,

> a politics of conduct is designed into the fabric of existence itself, into the organization of space, time, visibility, circuits of communication. And these enwrap each individual life decision and action – about labor, purchases, debts, credits, lifestyle, sexual contacts and the like – in a web of incitements, rewards, current sanctions and forebodings of future sanctions which serve to enjoin citizens to maintain particular types of control over their conduct. These assemblages which entail the securitization of identity are not unified, but dispersed, not hierarchical but rhizomatic, not totalized but connected in a web of relays and relations. But in policing the obligatory access points to the practices of inclusion, they inescapably generate novel forms of exclusion.
>
> (Rose 1999, 246)

More than a decade on from Rose's observation, and our digital technologies have taken on an ever more critical role in that fabric of existence. This is taking a variety of forms, such as with radio-frequency identification (RFID) tagging (Hayles 2009), but also with smart fabric:

> Smart fabric is, in this sense, serious fun. Serious, because what it demonstrates is an environment that is both material and informational, with the environment being internal to the material; and funny, because it touches a raw nerve in a society that believes its working relations to be a matter of its own choosing, not least because it is dominating matter through machinery.
>
> (Küchler 2008, 101)

The mobile phone is equally significant here, as it is a device that many see as an essential item, with smart-phones enabling people to surf the Web, check their e-mails, post on their Facebook page, tweet and skype their friends, all with a single device that fits in the palm of a hand. But, as indicated before, any action performed by way of a digital media device generates code, and this code is a valuable resource, including for telecommunication companies that can gather a large amount of information about each of their customers, including their daily movements (Abe 2009; Crandall 2010; Lyon 2006; 2009).

Of course, while according to Featherstone (2009) these 'new ubiquitous media offer greater possibilities for surveillance and recording by the state and other agencies, [and] not just benign and friendly "wireless environments"', we also need to recognize that they enable a new capacity for action that, as Hayles (2009) and Küchler (2008) argue in different ways, might actually enhance life, which is a point that I return to later in the book.

Discipline and modulation are modes of power that, though often operating through the same digital media devices and databases, do very different things from one another. Discipline's product or effect, individuality, is very much an object in a material sense. Individuals have substance. Individuals can be observed or watched. They are objects that are moved, separated, and acted upon so that they take on a specific form, depending on what a given situation requires. Individuals have a specific, recognizable, structured, and standardized form, and subjects that have no such form are certainly made into that. This is part of what 'care' is about in a disciplinary context, whether this be medical care or education. More importantly, as standardized objects of substance, individuals have an essence, and much of discipline's energies are aimed at laying bare, or rather, producing this internal essence. Individuals are distinct material objects, or entities, that are made of the same substance. Their equality in that regard, at least on one level, is important.

Modulation's product, on the other hand, is very different. A crucial characteristic of modulation is that production never actually ceases. With modulation, there is no specific beginning or end to production, or rather, the anticipation of identity. As pointed out earlier, what one might term the production of identity is always deferred in the context of modulation (Colwell 1996; Deleuze 1992). There is no product as such, or more appropriately, there is no object produced by the modulatory apparatus. Instead, there is a constant, varying production, with no definitive beginning or end, which does not have the subject as its aim. Indeed, a population in such a context is 'a dynamic quasi-subject constituted by a great number of variables' (Terranova 2007). Modulation's product, in other words, is formless, it is variable, and by definition therefore fluid (Hardt and Negri 2001, 197; Parisi and Terranova 2000). Deleuze already hints at this when he points out that the corporation is 'gaseous' (Deleuze 1992). In that respect modulation's product is the actual ongoing process of production itself. Indeed, the very nature of 'production' is different because it does not so much aim to produce some 'thing' as it anticipates or attempts to predict an activity.

It is for this reason that the product of modulation is more appropriately described as an objectile, rather than an object. Deleuze explains in *The Fold* (1993) that an objectile

> refers neither to the beginnings of the industrial era nor to the idea of the standard that still upheld a semblance of essence and imposed a law of constancy ('The object produced by and for the masses'), but to our current state of things, where fluctuation of the norm replaces the permanence of a law; where the object assumes a place in a continuum by variation... The new status of the object no longer refers its condition to a spatial mould – in other words, to a relation of form-matter – but to a temporal modulation that implies as much the beginnings of a continuous variation of matter as a continuous development of form.
>
> (Deleuze 1993, 19)

The 'subject' produced by modulation, in short, is an objectile. As Deleuze (1993) argues, it is a form, or rather, a manner of identity (for as far as 'identity' is an appropriate term to use in this context). It is characterized by having no specific or definite form. Instead, this 'form' is in 'continuous development' as well as about the 'continuous variation of matter'. In short, the main characteristic of this 'identity' is that it is formless. For that very reason it is fluid, irrespective of whether it manifests itself in a gaseous or a liquid state. Being fluid means that 'identity', in the context of modulatory power, is of the nature of a flow. In this context, 'identity' has no beginning or end. It is neither 'here' nor 'there'. As an entity it does not move in any spatial sense. Indeed, the very concept of 'identity' as 'absolute sameness', as a 'continuous unchanging property throughout existence' (NSOED 1997), does not exist in the context of modulatory power. In other words, the subject produced as objectile by modulation is not something of substance. More importantly, this objectile has no essence. Instead, the subject as objectile becomes what Deleuze terms an event (Deleuze 1993, 19).[3]

The disciplinary and modulatory modes of power, then, produce very different effects. Discipline produces distinct, relatively stable or static entities of a standardized form: subjects as individuals. Modulation, on the other hand, does not produce any subjects as objects. The modulatory mode of power is not interested in subjects, in essences.

Nor is it interested in making subjects behave in a specific manner, in making 'good subjects'. Instead, it produces objectiles, or more appropriately, it produces subjects as objectiles. It is not interested in the actual subject, but in the effects, the patterns of code that are continuously generated by 'subjects' as they use their mobile phone, twitter, check their Facebook and MySpace pages, drive their car, do their shopping, or surf the Web. What causes subjects to behave in a specific manner, or what causes them to generate certain effects, is not an issue that holds immediate interest in the modulatory mode of power (which is not to say that such information is not useful).

In comparing, then, the product of the disciplinary mode of power with that of the modulatory mode of power, one has to deal with what Deleuze pointed to as a profound change in both the status of the object and that of the subject (Deleuze 1993, 19). This profound change is a shift from object to objectile, from subject to superject, from essence to event. This shift also reflects, produces, and is the product of a significant political change. In other words, in looking at databases and the emergence of digital technology more broadly, and the emergence of this new mode of power called modulation, we are also looking at the emergence of a new politics very different from that to which the disciplinary mode of power belongs.

As a mode of power, discipline is of modern politics, emerging with the Enlightenment and its centerpiece of 'the individual' (Kirby 1996). Much of modern political thought, whether it be of a liberal, socialist, or feminist variety, takes the individual and its well-being as the central goal of its theorizing (Cohen 2008). The individual's relationship to other individuals, its ability and capacity to maintain its existence or form in a reasonable state vis-à-vis others, and its ability to propagate itself are issues of key importance in modern politics. In this respect, discipline, for Porter especially in terms of the development of statistics (Porter 1986; Rose 1999, 200–1), is very much a machine of modern politics. If discipline would have only one aim or end – one desire – it is care for the individual. To this end, in combination with other modes of power such as biopower or governmentality (Burchell et al. 1991; Rose 1999), discipline painstakingly gathers information about and 'guides' or, indeed, constructs each and every individual in order to secure that individual's well-being. Ultimately the aim is that each individual will 'care' for, that is, govern its own behavior, and conduct itself in an appropriate manner.

Modulation, as a mode of power, holds no such interest. Modulation's desire is not care for the individual. One main reason it holds no such interest is because, as discussed before, it literally does not 'see' 'individuals'. From the perspective of modulatory power, individuals do not exist. All that exists are patterns of code, flows of code. Modulation does not deal with or produce entities for which it cares. Indeed, in that respect, 'care', as a notion itself, does not appear to be a part of modulation, certainly not as the notion of care is used in the context of discipline. To describe this difference between discipline and modulation in terms of being a 'lack' is inappropriate, however, for while modulation may not have the individual as its main aim or interest, it does have another interest.[4]

The difference in the status of the object between disciplinary power and modulatory power also reflects, I think, an important difference in the concept of function. As noted above, discipline's main function or aim is to produce an object. Its main function is to produce an entity of a well-defined form that is capable of acting with force, that is, capable of 'work'. Modulatory power, on the other hand, does not produce or effect such an object. Much like Leibniz's mathematics, the modulatory mode of power 'assumes variation as its objective' (Deleuze 1993, 18).

With variation as the objective of modulatory power, the consequence is not only that 'the notion of function tends to be extracted, but the notion of objective also changes and becomes functional' (Deleuze 1993, 18). In other words, the aim of modulatory power, instead of 'being defined by an essential form', 'reaches a pure functionality, as if declining a family of curves, framed by parameters inseparable from a series of possible declensions or from a surface of variable curvature that it is itself describing' (Deleuze 1993, 19). In short, whereas the function or aim of disciplinary power is the production, as efficiently as possible, of an object, that is the individual, the function or aim of modulatory power, of the operation of power in context of digital technologies, is pure functionality.

In some respects, this difference in function between disciplinary and modulatory power can be conceptualized and described as an increase in control, as Deleuze (1992) has done. Indeed, the general shift to digital technologies is often characterized as one of increased control (Beniger 1986). It is also a change that many theorists, including those of the Frankfurt School, have taken to be a key characteristic of societies in a capitalist mode of production, including their politics (Habermas 1971; Marcuse 1964).[5] While certainly pointing to an important element of any digitization of politics, this view ignores a subtle but important change in the nature of control. In part, perhaps because it does not view digital technologies as being substantially different, but rather, as more of the same. However, control in the context of modulatory power is of a different order when compared to control in the context of disciplinary power.

With disciplinary power it is always an object that is controlled. Discipline is all about shaping matter into a specific form. The aim of discipline is to make good individuals out of bad or useless subjects. This process of production requires a constant regulation, a constant control, ideally performed by the individual itself, in which subjects are frequently measured, by way of an examination, to determine whether they have reached a required standard. Depending on how closely they approximate that standard, subjects may either be punished or rewarded. In the context of discipline, control is something that subjects experience and, indeed, ideally impose upon themselves, so as to make themselves into good individuals. Control, both in the sense of regulating by way of checking against a register and in the sense of exercising influence, is central to discipline.

Control is not experienced in such a manner in the context of modulatory power. The main reason for this is that modulatory power is not engaged in making specific forms out of matter. Modulatory power has no interest in making 'good' individuals. It does not produce a standardized object in the way that disciplinary power does. Instead, events are anticipated. This is why Massumi (2009) can refer to it as pre-emptive power, though this term only highlights one key aspect of modulation. The anticipation of these events is the objectile. The objectile is not made or controlled in the manner that an object is. It has a different status in that regard. In many respects, the actual *anticipation* of the event is precisely what constitutes the objectile. Modulatory power operates to recognize a specific pattern of code or flow being generated and then anticipates or predicts the possible continuation/s, as well as the emergence of that pattern or flow. Modulatory power, or more precisely, the objectile that is generated, as Deleuze explains, is very much 'the trace of the same line' (Deleuze 1993, 19).

Derivatives and foreign exchange trading are often used as instances of this form of anticipation, as well as examples of a broader shift to what is treated, and constructed, as a turbulent world. This is no coincidence, given that it is banking's encounter with digital machines that made derivatives trading possible in the first place, and created an entire industry in the form of financial risk management (Arthur 2010, 155). Critically, as Melinda Cooper points out, 'where the neoclassical economist discards the unexpected event from his calculus of the future, the trader in derivatives focuses on the fluctuation itself and the critical points at which an unexpected event might happen to occur' (2010, 177–8). Traders operate as part of an environment that is pure flow (Knorr-Cetina and Preda 2007) – an environment, produced by way of digital machines, that requires a very different sensibility in order to be capable of effective action. As Knorr-Cetina and Preda point out in relation to foreign exchange traders,

> Understanding speculative behavior requires, we claim, that we move away from the decision-making frameworks that dominate the economic and some of the sociological literature on market behavior. In currency spot transactions, trading tends to be a form of *informed tracing* – a form of following and anticipating the flow, grounded more in a structure of feeling than in modes of calculation.
>
> (2007, 132; emphasis added)

It is precisely this constant anticipation of 'the event', the 'emergency of emergence' (Dillon and Lobo-Guerrero 2009, 10–11) that many argue characterizes a broader political shift. As Cooper indicates, following Peter Gowan's work in *The Global Gamble* (1999),

> The production of monetary and financial turbulence, whether threatened or real, exercises an undeniable political leverage. It enables the international financial institutions to force through the privatization of state industries, welfare and infrastructure, and to further impose forms of debt-financing (securitized debt and short-term loans, for example) that are most volatile and most profitable to the institutional investment funds. In the current context, there is something both strategic and accidental about this form of political intervention, since it relies for its effects on a market-generated turbulence that can materialize in any place at any time and whose unfolding is essentially unpredictable.
>
> (Cooper 2010, 168)

This produces a politics that is, at least in part, about a governing through both contingency and emergency (Dillon and Lobo-Guerrero 2009). As Massumi extends the argument,

> in a crisis-prone environment, threat is endemic, uncertainty is everywhere; a negative can never be proven. Positive military response

must then be ever at the ready. The on-all-the-time, everywhere-at-the-ready of military response operatively annexes the civilian sphere to the conduct of war.

(2009, 158)

It is important to recognize that this process is productive, even if one of the products, just like in the game *Rift*, is a near-constant state of anxiety about what might happen next.

To return to modulatory power more specifically, there is no matter that is produced or molded into a specific form. There is, rather, a continuous anticipation of events in an otherwise turbulent environment, irrespective of whether these events or flows may constitute a specific identity or 'form' at any given moment. The event, or rather the objectile, is not controlled or produced to be of a specific form. In such a context, there can be no control in the same sense that one uses the word when discussing disciplinary power. Instead, what emerges is a form of control that operates almost solely by way of anticipation, at times inviting events to happen. It is in that sense that with modulatory power objectiles are prepared for in advance.[6]

Crandall (2010), when commenting on 'dwell-time' analytics, makes the point that we should not only think about this in terms of identifying objects that have been in one place too long (such as parked cars, or packages or people) that might suggest a violent event:

When used for marketing purposes, analytics applications such as 'dwell time' are useful not in gauging danger so much as desire: to identify whether customers stop at product displays and how long they remain there, absorbing the seductive messages conveyed therein. Here the event is not something to be prevented so much as courted: the object left stationary too long is none other than the spellbound shopper, dwelling in the image of an idealized world.

(Crandall 2010, 73)

At first sight this suggests there is a contradiction at work with these technologies, in that they both aim to anticipate an event, but can also aim to prevent it from occurring (2010, 73). As Massumi explains,

An anti-accidental exercise of power, at whatever setting on its operational continuum, can only counter the event-driving force of the accident if it catches it in the before of incipience. To do this, it must move into that proto-territory. It must move as the accident moves, to where it may irrupt, catching it 'before it actually emerges' (as the

Bush doctrine of preemption instructs). It must come as 'naturally' as the enemy. It must give of itself just as insistently. It must mimic the accident, in operative anticipation of the actual playing out of its potential effects.

(Massumi 2009, 167)

From this perspective, the form of control that occurs with modulatory power is of a very different order from that which occurs with disciplinary power. With disciplinary power, you are always made into something, and ideally make yourself into something. With modulatory power, the environment is adjusted to and adjusts itself to suit your behavior. The former involves a regulation that is far more directly experienced. The latter involves a regulation that is not experienced in the same way. It is far more subtle and indirect. With modulatory power you are not required or forced to behave in a specific manner. When social media such as LinkedIn or Facebook recommend a new list of friends, or when Amazon recommends books or music you would like, or, indeed, when your mobile phone predicts the next word you are about to type, it may give the impression that modulatory power is not really about control. Indeed, in some respects modulatory power can be presented as increasing choice, even freedom, as it relates to how one lives and consumes. Negroponte, for instance, describing living in the 'post-information age', argues that the manner in which machines will be able to anticipate each individual will enhance the quality of people's lives (Negroponte 1995, 164–5).[7] In that respect it aims to set up an increasingly smooth space of flows, aiming to reduce interruption to these flows.

In other words, in the context of discipline, the environment is the mold and, as the panopticon shows, it is literally a spatial mold. In the context of modulation, however, the environment is continuously adjusting itself, something over which you, as a subject, have no control. One example of the manner in which the environment comes to adjust itself in the context of the operation of modulatory power is that you (that is, your physical body) are increasingly becoming the environment itself. This is occurring in terms of the nature of the interface with digital technologies, but also in terms of genetic engineering (Clough 2008; Cooper 2010; Parisi and Terranova 2000; Thacker 2004; 2005).

Modulation, or control, never ceases then (Deleuze 1992; 1993). Modulation, in other words, 'is molding in a continuous and perpetually variable fashion' (Deleuze 1993, 19). The control that occurs in the context of modulatory power is not something to which a subject can either positively or negatively adjust its behavior. The reason it cannot adjust its behavior is because it is fully anticipated. The control, especially in the case of genetic engineering, has already occurred prior to a subject's arrival or eventuation. It is, after all, an objectile. One is always already prepared for or ordered in advance. With modulation, in other words, control may appear to be more subtle, even presenting itself as 'choice', but the control is actually more insidious and total, and of a very different form than that of discipline. It is in that context that the form control takes in the context of modulatory power is more in the nature of a programming and anticipation of flows within a turbulent system. As Parisi and Terranova state, 'control emerges as an immanent process of rechanneling of turbulent flows' (Parisi and Terranova 2000).

This differentiation in control, as suggested above, is a product or reflection of the difference in function between disciplinary and modulatory power. Disciplinary techniques of control are aimed at objects of substance. As argued above, the function of disciplinary power is the making of objects. In the context of modulatory power, however, such objects do not exist. Instead, modulatory techniques of control are aimed at variation. They are aimed at objectiles, events, flows (Hardt and Negri 2001; Parisi and Terranova 2000). Indeed, the anticipation of the event is what constitutes the actual objectile. This difference in status of the object (as noted earlier) suggests a different notion of function. It suggests a pure functionality as the aim or function of modulation.

Such a concern with 'pure functionality', in part reflected by a new form of control – modulation – may very well be another key feature of politics in the digital. Tonn and Feldman, for example, have argued that new non-spatial forms of government may be emerging (Tonn and Feldman 1995). These are forms of government that will not concern themselves with spatial entities (such as nation states) but with highly specific functions (Tonn and Feldman 1995). Early examples of this are multinational corporations and some educational institutions that concern themselves with entirely different, non-territorial, populations (Tonn and Feldman 1995). Indeed, when you consider that the company Blizzard had over 12 million paying subscribers at one point for *World of Warcraft*, just one of its online games, that is quite a population to be concerned about, which makes the governance of this population a significant issue.

Indeed, the view that politics would increasingly concern itself with the efficient functioning of the system – or performativity – and be accompanied by a dramatic increase in techniques of control was established much earlier, albeit in a different context, by a number of different authors, most notably Habermas and Lyotard (Habermas 1971; Lyotard 1984). Habermas, for example, argued that

> [i]nsofar as government action is directed toward the economic system's stability and growth, politics now takes on a peculiarly negative character. For it is oriented toward the elimination of dysfunctions and the avoidance of risks that threaten the system: not, in other words, toward the *realization of practical goals* but toward the *solution of technical problems.*
>
> (Habermas 1971, 102–3)

In a game like *World of Warcraft* – indeed, in most massively multi-player online role-playing games (MMORPGs) – the governance of the population is treated precisely as a technical problem.

Lyotard (1984) conceptualized this new politics as a new language game. Central to this game, so Lyotard argued, is a transformation of knowledge, and hence of power. Knowledge, according to Lyotard, and its legitimation as the production of truth are increasingly tied to questions concerning performance or efficiency. In this context, one is no longer concerned with questions of whether or not something is 'true', but whether it increases performance. Also, knowledge is decreasingly held by experts, and instead by databases. In such a situation, issues of access and knowledge of how to use databases well (that is, the moves in the new language game) become crucial political issues.

Habermas (1971) approached the question of politics in this situation differently. Habermas, like Lyotard, was concerned that politics would increasingly concern itself not with questions concerning the 'good life', but with questions of the functioning of the system. Central to Habermas' argument is the view that technology is the expression of a specific form of rationality that is becoming increasingly dominant. This form of rationality, he argued, against others such as Marcuse, is not of the form of an ideology (Habermas 1971, 111). The reason for this is that, unlike ideologies, it does not 'express a projection of the "good life"' (Habermas 1971, 111). In other words, unlike an ideology, a concept that only holds up with a specific understanding of knowledge (Valentine 2000, 31), the database does not express any 'interests'. The only things this form of rationality, and by extension politics, concerns itself with are issues that relate to the efficient functioning of the system – that is, performance or pure functionality. As Deleuze similarly remarked, communication is now precisely the problem, it having become 'corrupted', as he terms it in an interview with Negri (Deleuze

1995, 175). In that respect Deleuze's concern that we've lost belief in the world and that we need to become creative to some extent echoes Habermas' concern about there being a lack of engagement with the question of what constitutes the 'good society'.

The database, or rather the modulatory mode of power, certainly reflects a politics increasingly concerned with efficient functioning. As argued above (and this is probably the key difference between the politics of which discipline forms a part and that of which modulation forms a part), with the modulatory mode of power there occurs both a dispersal and a dissipation of the individual. Modulatory power simply does not concern itself with individuals, or even issues of identity for that matter. Fines, for example, no longer function in the way they used to (O'Malley 2010). In the digital realm the individual is increasingly dissolved in the flux of patterns of code, emerging, if at all, only momentarily. A central element, in other words, of the digitization of politics is this dissipation of the individual, as well as a dissipation in a care for the individual (Stiegler 2010a). The emergence of modulatory power suggests that politics in the digital is concerned, instead, with the discovery of patterns, of algorithms and flows, in order to act before the event even takes place; with the central aim becoming the performance of the system in all its detail and the identification of potential dangers to that performance.

The politics of the digital is not concerned with questions concerning 'the good'. As Chung (2006) argues, what were at one point political problems are increasingly reduced to technical problems. One can see, in other words, a very different production of a very different reality taking place when comparing the disciplinary with the modulatory mode of power. On the one hand is a reality of objects and essences and their organization in space, with each and every object having its place. This is a reality, and a politics, in which the construction of objects, forms, and essences – of individuals – is primary. On the other hand, there is also a new politics of fluids, a reality of flows and objectiles, concerned with the 'management of flows', which is equally an attempt not only to manage turbulence (Parisi and Terranova 2000) but also to produce turbulence (Cooper 2010; Massumi 2009). I explore this politics in greater detail in Part III.

At this point, it should be emphasized that these two productions of reality occur simultaneously (Hardt and Negri 2001, 23). While one can certainly see a crisis in the institutions of discipline (Deleuze 1992; Hardt and Negri 2001), there is certainly not enough evidence to claim that discipline and panopticism have declined to the point that they no longer constitute useful categories (Boyne 2000, 285). There remains, then, a constant production of individuality. A person is, at the same time, made into an object and constituted as objectile; made into an essence and constructed as an event; made into a solid form and dissolved into a flow; to be partly uncoded or deterritorialized, as Deleuze and Guattari might argue. Indeed, it is this twin antagonistic process, and not the production of the objectile alone, that constitutes what Deleuze termed 'dividuality'. Dividuality is the end product, not solely of the modulatory mode of power, but of the simultaneous productions of disciplinary and modulatory power – to, on the one hand, be made into a useful force for production (a useful worker), and at the same time be turned into a line of flight for potential profit to be made.

The principle of superposition

As I argued in Chapter 1, the digitization of discipline's writing apparatus strengthens the overall operation of discipline. It amplifies discipline and its effects. As Poster (1990; 1995) and others have pointed out, databases extend discipline to the social totality (Mehta and Darrier 1998). That this amplification also pushes discipline beyond its limits (Bogard 1996), producing non-disciplinary effects in the process, does not mean that discipline has come to an end. It is not an either/or situation, in which either discipline or modulation operates. Indeed, databases, and digital media more generally, act both as part of the disciplinary machine and as part of the modulatory machine. Both modes of power operate by way of the same digital machines at times, and often do so in one and the same moment.

Effectively what the two modes of power express are two different ways that people are acted upon in the context of digital technologies. People are subject to both these modes of power, even though these operations might produce antagonistic effects. The contradictory production of individuality and dividuality is an example of this antagonism. Discipline is all about the formation of identity, while modulation is about its continual postponement, or rather, its ongoing and constant dispersal. However, the fact that these two dominant effects are antagonistic to one another does not mean that they cancel one another out, nor that only one of them can be effected upon the same person in any given moment or environment.

Indeed, this constant antagonism is produced through the concurrent operation of both discipline and modulation, and is precisely what dividuality is (Colwell 1996). This constant push to be made into a subject, into an individual on the one hand, while at the same time never being quite that, is exactly what the experience of dividuality is. It is the individual constantly divided against itself, and divided among an ever-increasing number of patterns and files. With the concurrent operation of discipline and modulation a person is, in one and the same moment, both produced as whole, as a distinct and solid form, while on the other hand is always multiple, always more than one, an infinite dispersal of patterns or flow lines of code. It is this seemingly contradictory nature, between neither being this nor that, of being formless and fluid, that is the defining characteristic of dividuality. It is precisely this that Deleuze perceives as a weakness of dividuality (Deleuze 1992). After all, it is difficult to imagine how you can act with force in an environment composed of flows. Not much happens when you try to punch a gaseous entity like a corporation.

In any case, before I begin to address in Part II the question of how to conceptualize being, and in turn doing, in what is an environment of flows, one crucial issue with respect to the concurrent operation of the two modes of power I described above remains. How do we conceptualize how these two modes of power, and indeed, other modes of power, act on, and through the same bodies at the same time? How can they operate simultaneously and still maintain their independent productions upon the same body, or more precisely, upon the same being or entity? One answer is that being subject to these two different modes of power is comparable to listening to music, in that a number of different sounds, different waves, act upon the body at the same moment. In that regard, discipline's and modulation's instruments are merely two among a whole range of instruments that subject a body to their different effects.

Foucault (2003, 249) suggests this is a superimposition of one mode of power upon other. But a less static and more dynamic approach, which I think is apt and necessary for the modulatory mode of power, especially given its speed, is to recognize how modes of power – in this case discipline and modulation – behave in the manner of waves. This can explain with more precision how what appears as one event or moment actually constitutes two or more events at once, as well as over time. This is explained by what is known as 'the principle of superposition'. This principle, used by Fourier to analyze non-sinusoidal wave forms, states that 'a wave function describing the resulting motion…where a wave combines with a reflected wave, is obtained by adding the two wave functions for the two separate waves' (Sears et al. 1987, 499). This principle is expressed by the following equation:

$y(x,t) = y_1(x,t) + y_2(x,t)$ (Halliday and Resnick 1988, 403). Essentially, what this principle describes is how two, or more, sets of phenomena, whether waves or motions, coincide as independent influences on one system.

The principle of superposition, then, can provide a model of the manner in which two waves of differing amplitudes and frequencies can travel through one another to form one standing wave where they may appear as one, yet each retain their respective characteristics and effects. It is this principle that explains, for example, how one can hear the different sounds of instruments that fall simultaneously on the same eardrum (Halliday and Resnick 1988, 402). This principle explains how both discipline and modulation, through one and the same database, through one and the same profile, can simultaneously produce totally different effects.

In that respect, discipline and modulation can be understood to behave like two different waves operating on a different register. Each has a different amplitude and frequency, and each produces its own distinctive effects. These effects are often enacted on the same surface or substance, and sometimes at the very same moment through one and the same instrument. This is useful to remember when examining any operation of power. Power is always an orchestra and hardly ever a well-conducted one, if it is ever conducted at all (Foucault 1991, 103). Indeed, at times, the instruments (in this case those of discipline and modulation) may produce a harmony, while at other times they may produce a very inharmonious result. It is in the moments of unharmony that the possibilities for constituting oneself, for folding the force as it were (Deleuze 1995), exist. It is in that context that the interface becomes important, because it is at the point of interface, and the consequent emergence of a new human-machine assemblage, that new forms of subjectivity and new forms of existence can emerge.

In his postscript Deleuze was quite negative about our future in control societies. How do you act as a fluid, and 'against' other flows, when fluids, regardless of whether they are liquid or gaseous, are incapable of acting with force by definition? It is for this reason that Hayles' approach, questioning whether the surveillance capacities of RFID tags are an enhancement to life or not (2009), is vital. As she indicates, it is a matter of rethinking human subjectivity, for which, as Hayles emphasizes, Deleuze's work is ideally suited. It is a matter of thinking differently about the relations between 'human, animal, and thing' (2009, 49), which the rapid developments in both digital technology and biotechnology (the latter to a large extent made possible by the former) have brought into question in recent decades. In short, how do you exist as part of a societal assemblage that has as its components, among others, a mode of power that on the one hand is intent on producing people as individuals, as objects that are capable of acting with force that can be arranged for the purposes of 'work', while on the other hand there is a mode of power – modulation – that aims to anticipate your every thought, before you even encounter it, to produce a seemingly smooth being of flow/s, while at the very same time arranging those flow/s in a state of permanent anxiety as to their capacity for action in the world.

At least, from the point of view of an individual, dividuality appears to be, and is, a very inharmonious form of existence. The opposite point can be made, of course, by a dividual. It is in this context that discipline and modulation, with their productions of two very different types of subject, seem to reflect a different politics. Discipline, with its production of individuality belongs to the machinery of modern politics. Indeed, the construct of the individual (as Part II explores in a different context) is central to the modern construct of the political. Modulation, on the other hand, is reflective not of the management and governance of individuals and populations of individuals (which belong to a different mode of power altogether), but is instead more engaged in the generation and anticipation of flows in order to either avoid or predict, and create (Massumi 2009), moments of turbulence and crisis. In short, there is a very different construction of the political in operation in such a context. Part II examines more closely the different configurations or expressions of being within the context of the interface, because it is at this site that the production of new forms of being produces a different construction of the political. It is also at this site that we can begin to think differently about action itself in a digital world.

Part II
The Interface

3
The Human-Machine Assemblage

Figure 3.1 A human-machine assemblage (artist unknown, in Strandh 1979, 196)

> No production possible without an instrument of production, even if this instrument is only the hand. No production without stored-up, past labor, even if it is only the facility gathered together and concentrated in the hand of the savage by repeated practice.
>
> (Marx 1973, 85–6)
>
> It comes as a connection, always a connection, because it connects a problem with a principle that can handle it.
>
> (Arthur 2010, 116)
>
> And … and … and …
>
> (Deleuze and Guattari 1987, 25)

Many of us treat technological objects as if they are something separate from human being. Technologies, whether they are simple tools, like hammers, or complex machines, such as computers, or, indeed, the applications people use on their smart-phones, are often treated as if they are somehow outside of us, and separable from what it means to be human. Instead, I adopt a view that all forms of human being are forms of technological or machine being. To imagine a human being that is not technological is in my view impossible.

Equally significant is that different types of technologies and machine can be grouped together to constitute an 'assemblage' or 'ensemble'. It is these technological ensembles, I argue, principally following theorists such as Marx, Mumford, Guattari, and Deleuze, that express or manifest specific forms of human existence, both in terms of people's day-to-day lives, and how they relate to each other, as well as how a society is organized more broadly. To phrase that differently, each of these ensembles express, and are the expression of, very specific needs and interests – needs and interests that are in many cases specific to the ensemble in question. As Stiegler phrases it, '[h]uman society is always founded on a technicity to which psychic functions are delegated and by which they become social apparatuses' (2009b, 34).

This question of technology, or technics as Stiegler (1998) refers to it, is one that in many respects only came to be seen as important in the past two decades. Until then it was treated as a secondary concern (Stiegler 1998, ix). As I indicated in the Introduction, the lack of critical engagement in thinking about technology, in the humanities and social sciences more broadly, but in political theory more specifically, is what formed the initial impetus for this book. In recent years there has been a recognition by many, in part because of the use of digital machines and the emergence of what I call the digital ensemble, that technology needs to be addressed more directly. Central to this recognition is that digital technologies both enable, and require, a different sensibility, both in terms of recognizing new differences when considering the use of these machines, and also in terms of being capable of effective action. While, for example, Stiegler (1998; 2009a; 2010b) and Hansen (2004; 2006; 2009) focus more specifically on how our experience of time is constituted differently by digital machines, others such as Galloway (2006), but also Brown and Fleming (2011), focus more specifically on new forms of action that are enabled, and how to recognize them. Here, I am principally interested in how our connection to digital technologies affects how we come to constitute ourselves as actors in the world. Before I do that, however, first I want to offer a more detailed explanation of the view that human being and technology cannot be disentangled from one another.

All forms of human being are forms of technological or machine being. Different machines, in that respect, enable and express different possibilities for action, or rather, for doing. As such they manifest different interests and capacities for human action and human being, and, while they might solve some problems, in turn they can create entirely new problems and new possibilities. These problems and possibilities can manifest themselves equally in the development of new medical techniques that might cure specific forms of cancer, as well as in new forms of communication and media entertainment. Mobile phone radiation, for example (at least according to some (Davis 2010)), may result in entirely new large-scale health problems in some societies.

Equally important, in order to be capable of acting within a technological ensemble, I argue that people have to constitute themselves as a specific form of subjectivity, or more precisely, a specific 'unicity' as Deleuze and Guattari phrase it. So that while Part I can be characterized as focusing on how people are acted upon, in Part II I want to focus on how we come to constitute ourselves as actor within specific technological ensembles. Important in this is the role of the interface, because it is precisely our connections with our machines that enable us to act differently, and exist differently.

Human being

Heidegger, as Stiegler reminds us (1998, 13), offers one of the ways forward in beginning to think more critically about technology. Indeed, phenomenology more generally has always stressed a close and dynamic relation between subject and object. So much so that the very concepts of subject and object are considered problematic because they are argued to distort the nature of the human experience of the world (Moran 2000, 13). For this reason, phenomenology points to the significance of the human body in humans' perception of the world. Humans, from such a perspective, are not outside the world, but rather, they are of the world. As Heidegger and others pointed out, '[h]umans are always already caught up in a world into which they find themselves thrown' (Moran 2000, 13).

For Heidegger, this sense of human being as 'being-in-the-world', this sense of always being caught up in the world, is what is termed *Dasein* (Mansfield 2000, 23; Moran 2000, 238). The significance of this insight is that human being or human existence, which more traditionally is understood by way of terms such as subjectivity, the self, consciousness, or identity, cannot be separated from the world. In other words, whereas more traditional models of subjectivity define human existence as having 'an interiority that is set off against the exteriority of the objective outside world' (Mansfield 2000, 23), according to, for example, phenomenology '[s]ubjectivity must be understood as inextricably involved in the process of constituting objectivity' (Moran 2000, 15). What we call the subject, identity, or the self, in other words, is not a naturally occurring thing, but emerges within, and in some sense is a product of, 'particular contexts of practical engagement' (Coyne 1998).

From this perspective the objects and things people make use of, the technologies they use, are not separate from what it means to be human. As Heidegger pointed out, when we initially make use of objects it 'is in terms of their use and availability to us for certain assigned tasks, tasks generated by our interests' (Moran 2000, 233). Stated differently, in our immediate and day-to-day use of objects, we don't think of objects as separate from us. Initially, we don't see objects, tools, or machines, as 'things in themselves, as things standing on their own, available for inspection' (Moran 2000, 233). Such a view of objects is a product of a separate act of intention, one more theoretical (Moran 2000, 233). Instead, objects initially present themselves to us in terms of what Heidegger referred to as *Zuhandensein*, or 'readiness to hand' (Moran 2000, 233).

Heidegger's (1977) approach therefore points to a very close relationship between being and doing. From his point of view, technology is not a means to an end (Stiegler 1998), but rather, as Heidegger phrased it (1977, 37), a 'coming to presence' of human being. Technology is 'the way that human subjectivity reveals the truth and potential latent in the world' (Mansfield 2000, 156). Technology, in other words, whether it be in the form of simple objects or complex machines, is an expression or manifestation of how people live. On the most immediate level, it is the expression of a specific act, a specific activity and a specific form of doing, whether that is using a plane to travel, or posting a comment on Facebook. It is these immediate acts, these concrete and material expressions of what people do, that, as Marx (1973) pointed out, say something about how people live and exist. Technology is an expression or manifestation of the sorts of people we are and how we relate to others and ourselves.

This is obvious when looking at archaeology (Stiegler 1998, 2), which makes use of material remains. When archaeologists go to work they use the material objects they find to analyze how people might have lived and related to one another. These objects express specific actions or, at least, the possibility of certain types of action. Objects, in other words, are the material expression of specific forms of action, or of specific ways in which people relate to one another and their environment. The objects archaeologists find are manifestations of specific ways of doing. Archaeology as a discipline very much rests on the idea of a close relation between being and doing. Indeed, one would be hard pressed to come to an understanding of how people were and are should such objects not be available for study.[1]

Given this simple fact, it becomes difficult to maintain a view of technology as something that is different, or rather, separable from what it means to be human. Not only that, it becomes difficult to understand how anyone can be against technology per se (Arthur 2010; Harraway 1991; 1995; Stiegler 1998). Indeed, as Habermas pointed out, this is the main problem with Marcuse's one-dimensional man [*sic*] thesis (Habermas 1971; Marcuse 1964). Marcuse took the view that the only way one could emancipate modern individuals, and free them from what he called a technological rationality, was for people to renounce modern technology and invent an entirely new technology. As Habermas pointed out, however, that is simply not possible. The reason it is not possible is that technology is what we are. Technology, Habermas argued, 'follows a logic that corresponds to the structure of purposive-rational action regulated by its own results, which is in fact the structure of *work*' (Habermas 1971, 87). From this point of view, it becomes 'impossible to envisage how, ... we could renounce technology, more particularly *our* technology, in favor of a qualitatively different one' (Habermas 1971, 87). Or, as Guattari, taking Heidegger to task, put it,

> [p]eople have little reason to turn away from machines; which are nothing other than hyperdeveloped and hyperconcentrated forms of certain aspects of human subjectivity, and emphatically not those aspects that polarize people in relations of domination and power.
>
> (Guattari 1992, 18)

Technologies, then, express or 'reveal' who people are. They are an expression and manifestation, a revealing, of people's actions, and are a manifestation of being-in-the-world, more specifically, of what Heidegger termed *Dasein*. In effect, technologies *are* the link between being and doing. More importantly, they are both the expression and manifestation of a possibility of certain forms of action. Technologies, in that respect, constitute both limits to action and thought, and the possibility or potential for forms of action and thought. Technologies constitute, express, and make possible the expression and manifestation of specific forms of action, or rather, of specific forms of doing and therefore of being. Stated in a more Heideggerian fashion, technologies are a revealing of new practices (Coyne 1998; Heidegger 1993a; Stiegler 1998). Guattari states,

> technological transformations oblige us to be aware of both universalizing and reductionist homogenizations of subjectivity and of a heterogeneity and singularization of its components. Thus 'computer-aided design' leads to the production of images opening on to unprecedented plastic universes ... or to the solution of mathematical problems which would have been quite unimaginable a few years ago.
>
> (Guattari 1995, 5)

Computation, in other words, 'is a world within which certain things can be done' (Arthur 2010, 80). Technologies both enable and disable. They open up possibilities concerning the construction of what can be termed a particular field of action (Chesher 1997, 79), or more significantly, a specific way of doing and being-in-the-world. They also close off other ways of being-in-the-world, of existing.

This, however, does not mean that technology should be understood to be neutral or controllable. Technology, as Heidegger pointed out, is not only a means to an end. Indeed, to view it simply as such, at least according to Heidegger, 'conditions every attempt to bring man [*sic*] into the right relation to technology' (Heidegger 1993a, 313). Technologies, precisely because they express and delineate specific fields of action and practice, and disallow other actions, practices, and forms of thought, cannot be considered to be neutral. In that respect, technologies function very much in a similar manner to the way discourse functions, at least as Foucault (1970) understood it.

Certainly Arthur (2010) makes this argument quite strongly, arguing that groupings of technology (and for him, significantly, all means are technologies, whether they be organizations, methods, musical instruments, or scientific concepts or legal codes) form 'a language within which particular technologies – particular devices and methods – are put together as expressions within that language' (2010, 69). Arthur terms these groupings 'domains' (such as, for example, the digital domain):

[a] new device or method is put together from the available components – the available vocabulary – of a domain. In this sense a domain forms a language; and a new technological artifact constructed from components of the domain is an utterance in the domain's language. This makes technology as a whole a collection of several languages, because each new artifact may draw from several domains. And it means that the key activity in technology – engineering design – is a form of composition. It is expression within a language (or several).

(Arthur 2010, 76)

For Arthur (2010, 84) a technology can enlarge our capacity to act – our power – which is partly a function of the new statements that can be made, as well as a function of how existing statements can be combined and applied in new ways, acting like 'pre-formed blocks of commonly used expressions kept at hand for ready use by old-fashioned typesetters (the French printers of the 1700s called them clichés), except that they are conceptual and not necessarily premade' (Arthur 2010, 75–6). While some domains (such as that of 'canal building') allow only a limited set of possibilities, a limited range of utterances, other domains (such as the digital domain for Arthur (2010)) encounter and connect to existing domains and the economy at large in very significant ways.[2]

If technologies, if our machines, are a reflection or revealing of who we are, as, for example, Harraway argues (1991, 180), then we have to stop treating technology as if it is something outside of us. Indeed, the very manner in which technology is often conceptualized and talked about is to some extent problematic. For the very construction of technology as something fundamentally different from what one may term 'nature' or 'human' makes no sense (Harraway 1991; Mansfield 2000, 161; Stone 2001, 188). As Stone points out,

> Francois Dagognet suggests that the recent debates about whether nature is becoming irremediably technologized are based on a false dichotomy: namely that there exists, here and now, a category 'nature' which is 'over there', and a category 'technology' (or, for those following other debates 'culture') which is 'over there'. Dagognet argues on the contrary that the category 'nature' has not existed for thousands of years... not since the first humans deliberately planted gardens or discovered slash-and-burn farming. I would argue further that 'Nature', instead of representing some pristine category or originary state of being, has taken on an entirely different function in late twentieth century economies of meaning. Not only has the character of nature as yet another co-construct of culture become more patent, but it has become nothing (or nothing less) than an ordering factor – a construct by means of which we attempt to *keep technology visible* as something separate from our 'natural' selves and our everyday lives. In other words, the category 'nature', rather than referring to any object or category in the world, is a *strategy* for maintaining boundaries for political and economic ends, and thus a way of making meaning.
>
> (Stone 2001, 188)

The very conceptualization of technology as something that is separate from being human means that it can be treated as some sort of independent, or even autonomous, force. Much thinking about technology therefore revolves around arguments as to whether this force is beneficial to human existence and nature, or whether it produces mostly negative effects. Such a conceptualization of technology, as something clearly separable from human being or 'nature', also forms the basis of disputes concerning technology's determinist or indeterminist status, and about whether technology functions as cause or effect. It is not that such views are incorrect or unimportant. As Arthur (2010, 216) points out, 'our consciousness makes a distinction between technology as enslaving our nature versus technology as extending our nature'. But this dichotomy dominates thinking on technology to such a degree that even the process of writing differently about technology is permeated by it.[3]

Technologies, then, are an expression, a revealing as Heidegger termed it, of what it means to be human or, more precisely, of human being. To exist within the context of certain types of technologies means you exist in a specific manner. This explains why '[t]he technology to which we have been acclimatized for decades, centuries and millennia seems to us to be perfectly in tune with what we imagine to be our true selves' (Mansfield 2000, 148; Smith 1986). The emergence and use of different types of technology (that is, of different ways of doing), in that respect, can both effect and reflect major changes in how we imagine our selves to be, or in how we perceive or produce the world and our selves.

The technological ensemble

As pointed out above, technologies, whether they be stone tools or a combustion engine, express and make possible specific forms of action. This means that they open up specific possibilities for action (that is, have a certain potential for action), while at the same time they also place a limit on what can be done (Arthur 2010; Chesher 1997, 79; Guattari 1995, 5). For example, one can perform a whole range of actions with a typewriter, from typing a letter to using it as a paper-weight, but one cannot use it for transporting oneself between two different locations. Importantly, this applies to action in a physical or corporeal sense and also to action in terms of thought or conceptualization. Stated differently, technologies, in part because they enable different forms of physical action or different ways of doing, also express and, potentially, open up different avenues for thinking. In short, they are the expression of new human practices, and can enable entire new universes of thought (Arthur 2010; Coyne 1998; Guattari 1993).

Any technology or tool, because it expresses a specific human practice, forms part of a specific context, part of a delineated range of practices. It belongs to a universe of action or human practice, and a discursive field (Arthur 2010). Consequently, technologies or 'objects-for-use' often have little use when removed from their context. As Heidegger made clear in his explanation of the ancient Greek conception of cause, objects are indebted to a number of different things: the matter out of which they are made, the form that gives them their shape, that which gives the objects their bounds or *telos*, and the participant who makes the objects ready for use (Heidegger 1993a, 314–16). It is particularly the third thing to which objects are indebted, their aim or *telos*, that is of interest here. In short, one cannot remove objects or technologies from their context and still expect to be able to use or even understand them in the same manner one did previously.

Take, for example, the pyramids in Egypt. These objects, or perhaps more appropriately these machines (Mumford 1995a), certainly do not produce the same set of effects today as those they were intended to produce at the time of their construction. Indeed, even in today's so-called age of great technological know-how, experimental archaeologists still debate how these objects or machines could possibly have been constructed. Even using the latest engineering techniques and technologies, engineers and architects would have a difficult time producing a replica of these pyramids, let alone those built by the Aztecs and Incas in the Americas where no use was made of the wheel. That they would not, or could not, recreate these objects or machines suggests that they formed part of a specific cultural context, a specific range of human practices, in which alone they could be produced and could have functioned. To put that in a more Deleuzian phrase, it's simply a matter of some connections not always being possible.

Any object, machine, or technology then, whether it be of a material or abstract form, constitutes part of a specific context or culture; though a more useful way of describing this is to say that it forms part of what can be termed a 'technical ensemble' or assemblage. This is not quite the same as Arthur's use of the word 'domain', noted above, but instead reflects Deleuze and Guattari's use of the term:

> We will call an assemblage every constellation of singularities and traits deduced from the flow [of matter and energy] – selected, organized, stratified – in such a way as to converge...artificially or naturally.... Assemblages may group themselves into extremely vast constellations constituting 'cultures', or even ages...We may distinguish in every case a number of very different lines. Some of them, phylogenetic lines, travel long distances between assemblages of various ages and cultures (from the blowgun to the cannon? from the prayer wheel to the propeller? from the pot to the motor?); others, ontogenetic lines, are internal to one assemblage and link up its various elements, or else cause something to pass...into another assemblage of a different nature but of the same culture or

age (for example, the horseshoe which spread through agricultural assemblages).

(Deleuze and Guattari in De Landa 1991, 140)

When a technological object is taken out of its ensemble or the context to which it belongs, it means nothing, or rather, it means something very different. Indeed, the machine or the technical object literally does not exist when it is taken out of its context or assemblage. Any machine, including a simple one like a wall or knife, is 'the ensemble of the interrelations of its components, independent of the components themselves' (Varela in Guattari 1993, 16). One could not, in other words, take a television, a blog or Facebook, or, indeed, a car outside of their context and place them in another, as they would literally cease to exist as that technology, that is, as that human practice (much like as has occurred with the pyramids). In short, when one takes an object out of its context, it ceases to be an expression of the specific human practice for which it was intended. As Guattari points out, the materiality of a machine and the organization of a machine have little to do with one another (Guattari 1993, 16). What constitutes technology, then, is not just the technological objects, as these are simply material components but also the entire set of practices, and the various human and machinic needs and interests they serve (Guattari 1995, 36; Heidegger 1993a, 312; Mumford 1995c, 305).

This is well illustrated by experimental archaeology whose main aim is to understand how objects and machines from other assemblages functioned in their respective assemblages. Here objects and techniques (such as Roman bridge building, the hanging gardens of Babylon, and Archimedes' 'ship-shaker' (Strandh 1979)) are found or talked about in texts, but the knowledge that went into their production and use no longer exists. The attempts to reproduce such objects and techniques, even using present-day engineering techniques often fail. This suggests that the knowledge of one technical ensemble or assemblage is no less or more advanced than that of another. They simply constitute different forms of knowledge, different responses to different problems, that function only within the specific assemblage that they produce, reproduce, and express.

This does not mean that different assemblages can be clearly distinguished from one another. Some types of assemblage exist over long periods of time in many different cultures, whereas others are very much culturally and temporally specific (Arthur 2010; Deleuze and Guattari

1987). In some cases components of one assemblage may exist and form part of another assemblage, or they may simply be leftover fragments that continue to produce specific effects (Deleuze and Guattari 1977, 42).[4] As Mumford pointed out,

> [o]ur mechanical civilization represents the convergence of numerous habits, ideas, and modes of living, as well as technical instruments; and some of these were, in the beginning, directly opposed to the civilization they helped to create.
>
> (Mumford 1995b, 324)

This means that you can use different criteria in constructing or identifying different assemblages. One option is to use specific types of technique or technology. Mumford, for instance, used a more classic definition of the machine to identify what he called the megamachine, examples of which, he argues, are the labor machine and the military machine:

> To call these collective entities machines is no idle play on words. If a machine be defined more or less in accord with the classic definition of Reuleaux, as a combination of resistant parts, each specialized in function, operating under human control, to transmit motion and to perform work, then the labor machine was a real machine: all the more because its component parts, though composed of human bone, nerve, and muscle, were reduced to their bare mechanical elements and rigidly restricted to the performance of their mechanical tasks.
>
> (Mumford 1995a, 315–16)

Indeed (as noted earlier), Mumford argued that the pyramids were a product of such a machine. This was

> a machine of a hundred thousand manpower, that is, the equivalent, roughly, of ten thousand horsepower: a machine composed of a multitude of uniform, specialized, interchangeable, but functionally differentiated parts, rigorously marshaled together and coordinated in a process centrally organized and centrally directed: each part behaving as a mechanical component of the mechanized whole: unmoved by an internal impulse that would interfere with the working of the mechanism.
>
> (Mumford 1995a, 318)

Another way to identify such machinic assemblages is by way of the types of machine or technological object by which they operate:

> Types of machine are easily matched with each type of society – not that machines are determining, but because they express those social forms capable of generating them and using them. The old societies of sovereignty made use of simple machines – levers, pulleys, clocks; but the recent disciplinary societies equipped themselves with machines involving energy, with the passive danger of entropy and the active danger of sabotage; the societies of control operate with machines of a third type, computers, whose passive danger is jamming and whose active one is piracy and the introduction of viruses.
>
> (Deleuze 1992, 6)[5]

Such a focus on machines, however, does not mean that they explain anything in themselves about a society and the people that form a part of it. As both Deleuze and Guattari pointed out, 'you have to analyze the collective arrangements of which the machines are just one component' (Deleuze 1995, 175; Guattari 1995, 35). These components include:

> [m]aterial and energy components; semiotic, diagrammatic and algorithmic components (plans, formulae, equations and calculations which lead to the fabrication of the machine); components of organs, influx and humors of the human body; individual and collective mental representations and information; investments of desiring machines producing a subjectivity adjacent to these components; abstract machines installing themselves transversally to the machinic levels previously considered (material, cognitive, affective and social).
>
> (Guattari 1995, 35–6)

It is the above-mentioned component of the subjectivity produced adjacent to the other components that is important in discussing the political effects of changing one's sense of being in the world. In other words, different assemblages, expressed through and by way of different types of technique and machine, are composed of, among other things, different forms of subjectivity. In order to be capable of operating or simply existing within a given assemblage, a subject has to conduct itself in a manner specific to that assemblage. Changes in the type of technology both effect and reflect changes in people's mode of perception and, therefore, in their sense of identity, collective or otherwise (Smith 1986). In short, people have a different sense of the world depending on the technologies they use. As Mumford argued, no two cultures, in this case no two machinic assemblages or ensembles, live conceptually in the same kind of time and space (Mumford 1995b, 329).[6]

Of course, this does not necessitate that machines or technologies directly affect the production of subjectivity, that is, that technology is determinist in character. Instead, it is a question of certain components being 'essential for a given setup to take consistency in space and time as a function of technical, scientific and artistic transformations' (Guattari 1992, 21). As Turkle puts it,

> there is no simple causal chain. We construct our technologies, and our technologies construct us and our times. Our times make us, we make our machines, our machines make our times. We become the object we look upon but they become what we make of them.
>
> (Turkle 1995, 46)

Not only that, but (as pointed out earlier) without the component of subjectivity there is no such thing as technology. Technology, in other words, and more importantly a technological ensemble, is not only the actual technical or material object. The technological ensemble is the entire set of components that includes the material machinic components,[7] abstract machines, the conceptualization of space and of time, the range of practices, and the various manifestations of what is termed subjectivity. Subjectivity is only one of these components, though without it the technological ensemble as such does not exist.

Machines, in that respect, are, on the one hand, nothing but an expression of people, or parts of people (Crandall 2010; Guattari 1992, 18). On the other hand, they make it possible for people to express themselves, or to act, in a specific manner. In that sense, one can view types of machine as forming part of a specific discourse, each of which operates by way of a specific production of subjectivity, or more precisely, by way of the production of a specific form of existence or being. This means that in order to be capable of expressing and functioning within a specific machinic assemblage, one has to operate with a specific sense of being in the world, that is, a specific sense of what it means to be a subject, a specific sense of identity. In short, different machinic assemblages operate with and by way of different forms of subjectivity.

Machine being

As pointed out above, both the subject and subjectivity are essential components in any machinic assemblage or ensemble. The various machines with which one interfaces, whether they are simple proto-machines such as knives (Guattari 1993) or complex machines such as computer networks, allow for, or make possible, a specific range of actions, just as they disallow other actions. More importantly, how one is interfaced within the overall ensemble and the types of machine one interfaces with, affects, and is expressive of, a specific form of subjectivity. In short, the component of subjectivity is different depending on the type of assemblage of which it forms a part.

From such a perspective, any form of human being or human existence (that is, subjectivity) is always part of some technological ensemble. The machine or technological object, whether of a simple or a complex form, or a material or abstract form, has always been a central element in processes of subjectification. Guattari points out, for instance, that even 'pre-capitalist' or 'archaic subjectivities' were 'already engendered by a variety of initiatory, social and rhetorical machines embedded in clan, religious, military and feudal institutions' (Guattari 1992, 18). According to Guattari, these are machines which function as 'collective apparatuses of subjectification' (Guattari 1992, 18).

Subjectivity can be defined in a number of ways (Heller 1990). One definition is provided by Guattari who argued that subjectivity is 'the ensemble of conditions which render possible the emergence of individual and/or collective instances as self-referential existential Territories, adjacent, or in a delimiting relation, to an alterity that is itself subjective' (Guattari 1995, 9). Subjectivity, in short, refers to a relative sense of unicity that people maintain despite and because of the 'diversity of components of subjectivation' (Guattari 1995, 16) that pass through a person. More broadly, subjectivity is a question, as Deleuze put it, of how one exists or maintains a form of existence in a given context or ensemble (Deleuze 1995).

From such a perspective, the form that unicity takes, or the manner and form of existence one attempts to produce and maintain, differs depending on the different components of subjectivation that exist at any given moment. Subjectivity, in that respect, is not something that has a natural or universal form. It changes depending on the various forces and pressures by which it is produced and by which it produces itself. One of these components (focused on in this chapter), which at the same time is an expression of subjectivity, is the actual machine or technology.

Machines and technologies alter how one can act in the world (Arthur 2010; Mansfield 2000, 149; Smith 1986, 156). They affect, and are an expression of, how one experiences the world (Stiegler 2009b). They do so on both a large and a small scale (Arthur 2010), depending on whether they are large-scale social machines, as described by Mumford (1947) and Deleuze and Guattari (1977; 1992), or whether they are simple proto-machines like a knife (Guattari 1993). One's entire perception of how one can act in the world, one's entire sense of action, of doing and being in the world, and therefore one's sense of self, is both affected and effected by different types of machines and technology.

While others (such as Stiegler and Hansen) emphasize the importance of time in coming to an understanding of how digital media affect us and our broader politics, Kirby, for example, has pointed to the importance of the conceptualization of space in the constitution of subjectivity (Kirby 1996). The importance of the conceptualization of space in subject constitution wasn't always clearly recognized (Kirby 1996), and shouldn't be neglected at this point. The basic argument is that '[i]f an essential element of a given sociocultural space-time continuum undergoes change, this will affect the entire structure; our perception of space-time will also lose its accustomed orientation' (Schivelbusch 1986, 36).[8] The use of different technologies, in short, can both effect and reflect a change in people's mode of perception. Stated differently, the use of different technologies expresses a change in one's sense of being-in-the-world. The introduction of the railway, for example (Schivelbusch 1986), brought about a very different sense of doing, a different perception, and therefore a different sense of being, or existing, in the world.

> Any artificial means of motion – horseback riding, for example, or travel by horse-drawn carriages – would dictate new strategies of perception, but the phenomenological adjustment required by railway movement proved to be far more extreme. In walking, running, and riding, the perception of the landscape has a physical correlate in human muscular activity. To a lesser extent, the same is true of animal propulsion...there is a sense of bodily displacement that matches one's actual spatial displacement. Older transport technology preserved the traditional space-time continuum.
>
> (Kirby 1996, 74)

Space, like time, then, is in many ways a product of each respective technological ensemble (Castells 1996, 376–469; Harvey 1989). As Castells has pointed out, '[s]pace is a material product, ... a concrete expression of each historical ensemble in which a society is specified' (Castells in Soja 1989, 830).[9] More importantly, as Lefebvre's work shows, 'space and the political organization of space express social relations but also react back on them' (Lefebvre in Soja 1989, 81). There is, therefore, a very close and dynamic relation 'between the kind of space occupied by a subject and the form the subject takes' (Kirby 1996, 7), and technology is a crucial element in that relation and the production of one's sense of being in the world.

Technological shifts, in other words, produce and express quantitative shifts that can result in qualitative shifts in people's perception, and experience, and sense of being in the world (Benjamin 1969; Smith 1986). An example of this is found the construction of the human megamachines described by Mumford (1947; 1995a), which introduced and constituted an entirely different field of action and limit of possibilities. Even such a simple thing as a difference in speed (Virilio 1986; 1991) or, indeed, vision (Romanyshyn 1989) can profoundly alter the ways in which one can act in the world and imagine oneself. Consider, for instance, the simple difference experienced between walking or riding a bicycle and how this affects one's sense of how one can act in the world and thereby how one can situate and constitute oneself. Technologies, therefore, are both the expression of specific forms and aspects of subjectivity, and they enable the production of specific forms and aspects of subjectivity (Guattari 1992; 1993). Again, it doesn't matter whether we consider this on the level of individual technologies (such as Google's Goggles application) or whether it be on a larger societal scale.

This also suggests that if certain types of machine or technology are approached with a particular sense of unicity or subjectivity, they simply will not work, or at least, they will not work as they may have been intended to work. Certain forms of subjectivity may develop over long periods that often cannot cope when introduced to new forms of technology, that is, new ways of doing things as well as doing new things. Take, for example, all the effort put into the massive retraining schemes of an 'old' work force, or the effect of the introduction of a word processor on a person who has always worked with a typewriter. In many cases the word processor continues to be used as if it was simply a more efficient typewriter, preventing one from performing an entirely different range of actions with it.

Different types of technology, then, require, produce, and are the expression of specific forms and aspects of human subjectivity, or human ways of being and doing. Different types of technology, and the machinic assemblages of which they are an expression, are therefore associated with different forms of subjectivity. Indeed, as stated before, different assemblages or ensembles require very specific components of subjectivity that form a constituent part of them. In order to be able to exist within a specific ensemble, or be capable of action within any given ensemble, one has to constitute oneself, and be constituted, as a specific form of unicity. The components of subjectivity have to be arranged in a specific manner. One has to have a specific sense of being an actor in the world in order to be capable of existing in each respective technological ensemble.

Guattari's 'three zones of historical fracture' express, among other things, specific individual and collective forms of subjectivity (Guattari 1992). More important, for this and the following two chapters, is his argument that each of the zones of historical fracture contains a material apparatus specific to it that enables the emergence of specific forms of (self-) expression, or of specific ways in which forms of subjectivity can emerge.[10] It is at this point, especially when considering the issue of different forms of subjectivity and the politics of different technological ensembles, that some of Marx's arguments become relevant.

Marx pointed out that '[p]roduction . . . is also immediately consumption, consumption is also immediately production' (Marx 1973, 91). In his view, there is a very close relation between production, the object produced, and the manner of consumption, both objectively and subjectively (Marx 1973, 91). For example, following Marx, '[h]unger is hunger, but the hunger gratified by cooked meat eaten with knife and fork is a different hunger from that which bolts down raw meat with the aid of hand, nail and tooth' (Marx 1973, 92). It is this close relation between production, consumption, and both the object and subject produced as a consequence of each that is important in the production of the political for each specific technological ensemble. It is important because what each ensemble effectively produces or reproduces are very different needs and interests, that is, a different construct of 'the political'.

A similar point is made by Stiegler (2009b, 35), when he places digital technology as central to the question of where our politics, and our construct of 'the political' is heading. As he explains it, digital communication technology 'allows each and every one of us to be at a distance always and everywhere', leading to a broader question 'of knowing what "being" can mean here'. For Stiegler, the political

> is the space where the authority of the law constitutes itself, as a public space and time established in and by the distance that opens up between distant citizens, and as a distance that brings them closer

precisely to the extent that they can be distinguished within its perimeter. This distance thus opens up possibilities: those made possible, for example, as legitimate yet new interpretations of the law. These possibilities, which open the city to its future, shape the desire of the city: as the desire to be together, the desire of a becoming-together, where philia is formed, this philia without which, says Aristotle, no city is possible.

(Stiegler 2009b, 36)

A shift to the use of digital technologies, at least according to him, might further open up 'the possibility of democracy', but 'it is also that which makes possible democracy's destruction, since, to the extent that it makes remote control possible, as the power of the distant, it constantly threatens this democracy, of which it is the possibility' (Stiegler 2009b, 36).

Objects that we make use of in the world are practices. They reflect and express specific ways of doing and being in the world. They are an expression of people's needs and interests (Arthur 2010). They reflect specific ways of existing, or of living. As such, the politics of each technological ensemble, or rather, the construction of the political in each ensemble, is specific to that technological ensemble. Each technological ensemble produces specific needs and interests, and, therefore, is also a very specific political organization.[11] This organization is expressed not only spatially (Harvey 1989; Lefebvre 1991; Soja 1989; Stiegler 1998; 2009b), but also in the relations between people and between people and things. The technological ensemble of which the pyramids in Egypt are an expression requires a very different political, and thereby economic, organization, and construction of the political from, for instance, the factories of the industrialized mechanical ensemble. In each respective ensemble there is a very specific organization of people, both in terms of the relations between them and in terms of their organization of subjectivity, or of how they exist. As Marx stated: '[production] is always a certain social body, a social subject, which is active in a greater or sparser totality of branches of production' (Marx 1973, 86).

In many respects, a point is now reached at which it is possible to more clearly demarcate the functions that technology can have in processes of subjectivation. The reason for this is that digital technologies are in the process of introducing and effecting entirely new ways of acting, or rather, possibilities for thinking differently about how one can act in the world (Arthur 2010; Crandall 2010; Guattari 1992; Hayles

2009; Smith 1986). This is not to suggest that digital technologies should not be seen as, in some ways, continuing already existing fields of action. In some respects, they are very much the continuation of long existing assemblages, but, at the same time, they constitute a radical change in terms of how people can act and, therefore, how they think of themselves as actors in the world. In short, they constitute a change in the way people do things in the world, a change in how they construct themselves as actors and, therefore, a change in the conceptualization of the political. I now turn to this Chapters 4 and 5, in comparing the politics of the motorized ensemble with that of the digital ensemble, which in the first instance has to be a question of asking how we exist and constitute a sense of unicity in each respective ensemble.

4
Mechanical Being

> Were we required to characterize this age of ours by any single epithet, we should be tempted to call it, not an Heroical, Devotional, Philosophical, or Moral Age, but, above all others, the Mechanical Age.
>
> (Carlyle 1984, 32)

So Thomas Carlyle, in the early nineteenth century, described the times in which he lived. Carlyle, being a conservative, lamented the dominance of the machine and what he called 'Mechanism'. He especially criticized the dominance of 'Mechanism' in the newly emerging politics of his time. This was a politics expounded by theorists such as Adam Smith and Jeremy Bentham, who, so Carlyle argued, saw politics as being about the arrangement of mechanisms that would work toward improving people's physical and economic condition, rather than people's spiritual and moral condition (Carlyle 1984, 40–1). Indeed, Carlyle criticized these theorists for believing that people's happiness, strength and dignity of mind were a product of mechanisms such as the structure of legislation, checks upon the executive, and a 'wise arrangement of the judiciary'. What Carlyle lamented most of all was not simply the change in people's modes of action but the change in their mode of thought; in short, the change in their entire mode of existence (1984, 37).[1]

Especially for a generation that hasn't known life without being connected, life without the mobile phone and the Internet, it is increasingly difficult to imagine what life is in a 'disconnected world'. The specific sense of unicity, the specific sense of being as a fragmented individual, as I will explain in this chapter, that characterizes life in Carlyle's mechanical age, is one that seems increasingly foreign to many people. Indeed, for the generation that grows up with games like *World of*

Warcraft, Facebook, and the instantaneity of Twitter, when disconnection comes, especially when it comes in the form of losing the mobile phone, it is often experienced as a profound loss. Most often, when I speak with people about their experience of losing their mobile phone or their connection to the Internet, they describe it in terms of suddenly being isolated, being alone, in much the same way that the drones in *Star Trek*'s Borg collective become functionless when they are disconnected from the collective. Indeed, like the Borg drones that become disconnected from the collective, the sole task after being disconnected is to become connected again, because without connection to our networked digital machines we are, quite simply, incapable of action in a digital world. Connection for people who live and work in the digital ensemble is essential to their sense of being in the world.

This same desire to be connected to machines doesn't exist in the same way in the industrialized or motorized mechanical ensemble. Indeed, connection to mechanical machines is often perceived to be quite limiting, and, worse, as being subject to the machine in question. The machines of the industrialized age appear more autonomous, as well as separate from us in a way that our digital machines aren't. In the motorized mechanical ensemble, the principal expressions of which are the combustion engine and the factory, a very specific construct of self is required in order to be capable of effective action. With this comes the generation of needs and interests – a politics – that is also very specific to the motorized mechanical ensemble. It is this sense of self, and the politics associated with it, that I want to delineate more clearly before discussing digital being.

The motorized mechanical ensemble

The tools, machines, and technologies that express the industrialized mechanical ensemble are levers, pulleys, gears, linear perspective, steam and internal combustion engines, the railway, and the factory (Arthur 2010, 212–13; Castells 1996, 38–40; Deleuze 1992; Forbes 1958; Küchler 2008, 104). Of all these, the steam engine is without a doubt the most critical expression of the mechanical ensemble. The steam engine expresses a specific production, use, and distribution of energy, as well as a standardization and uniformity in the use of materials and the output of power, a great concern with quantitative precision, functional differentiation, and, significantly, a new-found mobility. In other words, as Deleuze and Guattari might state, the steam engine expresses, and is capable of producing, a radical deterritorialization. This deterritorialization is expressed on a number of different levels, producing and reflecting a sense of independence and autonomy that did not exist before its invention. As Marx observed,

> [n]ot till [*sic*] the invention of Watt's second and so-called double-acting steam-engine was a prime mover found which drew its own motive power from the consumption of coal and water, was entirely under man's control, was mobile and a means of locomotion, was urban and not – like the water-wheel – rural, permitted production to be concentrated in towns instead of – like water-wheels – being scattered over the countryside and, finally, was of universal technical application, and little affected in its choice of residence by local circumstances.
>
> (Marx 1990, 499)

In some respects one can argue that there was nothing qualitatively new about this mechanical ensemble. Many, if not most of the steam engine's principles, had existed for a long time. Heroes and Archimedes, for instance, had long considered the idea of harnessing the power of steam (Strandh 1979, 113), but had neither the materials nor the science or metallurgical techniques to do so. The ancient Egyptians also had long made use of large-scale machines (Mumford 1995a, 318). Clearly, many elements from earlier forms of technological ensembles, including the Middle Ages in Europe (White 1962) and China, continued to be used, and necessarily so.

One major characteristic that distinguishes this ensemble from other ensembles, however, is in terms of its modes of power or, more precisely, its use of energy (Castells 1996; Deleuze 1995; Marx 1990). At its 'core there was a fundamental innovation in the generation and distribution of energy' (Castells 1996, 38). Previous forms of mechanical ensemble operated by way of muscle, wind, and water power. These ensembles relied heavily on the flow of rivers, the strength, direction, and consistency of wind, and the use of draught animals. Indeed, these ensembles were very much dependent on these sources of energy. A consequence of this was that territory, one's locality, whether it be in the form of land or water, was a critical element in the forms of action available to people as individuals and the larger assemblages of which they formed a part. Not until the widespread use of the steam engine, whether it was in the form of factories, trains, or ships, did people become less reliant on animals, wind, or water. As Carlyle lamented, '[o]ur old modes of exertion are all discredited, and thrown aside' (Carlyle 1984, 34).

The sources of energy for this new mechanical ensemble were, and still are, coal and oil (Yergin 2008). However, it is not simply the sources of energy that are different. More significantly, it is in the use of energy that this mechanical ensemble distinguishes itself (Deleuze 1992, 6; 1995, 121; Heidegger, 1993a). The use of different prime movers, in short, is effectively what makes possible entirely different and new forms of action or, rather, new forms of doing. Of course, in principle, many of the mechanical principles stay the same between the mechanical ensemble operating by way of muscle, wind, and water power, and that operating by way of steam and combustion engines. Both operate by way of an energetic conception of motion, where individuals are the source of a specific movement or action (Deleuze 1995, 121). One critical difference, however, is expressed in terms of the mobility and speed at which various components operate (Beniger 1986; Virilio 1986).

These new sources and uses of energy enable forms of acting or doing that no longer rely on the territory. No longer is there a reliance on the direction and speed of the wind in shipping, or on the stamina and will of horses or people, or on the volume of water in rivers (Schivelbusch 1986, 9). In short, steam and combustion engines produce an entirely different sense of mobility and possibility.

> As the motion of transportation was freed from its organic fetters by steam power, its relationship to the space it covered changed quite radically. Pre-industrial traffic is mimetic of natural phenomena. Ships drifted with water and wind currents, overland motion followed the natural irregularities of the landscape and was determined by the physical powers of the draught animals.
>
> (Schivelbusch 1986, 9)

Instead, the steam engine produces a constant and reliable source of power that does not depend on anything but the supply of fuel and water. Territory, whether it be the degree of the slope of a hill, the amount of water in rivers, or the direction of the wind, ceases to play as significant a role as it does in the previous form of the mechanical ensemble. When people travel in the industrialized mechanical ensemble, of which rail travel is most symbolic, there is a degree of separation from place and a sense of mobility not experienced before (Schivelbusch 1986). In some respects, following Virilio's thought, one might just as easily refer to the industrialized mechanical ensemble as the motorized mechanical ensemble.

Not only does the steam engine by and large eliminate a regard for territory, it also introduces a new and different consideration of human bodies, as muscular power ceases to be such a significant factor in work. As Marx pointed out,

[i]n so far as machinery dispenses with muscular power, it becomes a means for employing workers of slight muscular strength, or whose bodily development is incomplete, but whose limbs are the more supple. The labor of women and children was therefore the first result of the capitalistic application of machinery! That mighty substitute for labor and for workers, the machine, was immediately transformed into a means for increasing the number of wage-laborers by enrolling, under the direct sway of capital, every member of the worker's family, without distinction of age or sex.

(Marx 1990, 517)

In short, the steam engine, on different levels, both produces and expresses a tremendous degree of standardization and uniformity, another key characteristic of the industrialized mechanical ensemble. So that, while it produces a very significant deterritorialization, it also produces an equally significant reterritorialization.

Standardization and uniformity pervade the entire industrialized mechanical ensemble. This is expressed in cartography and representations of space and territory (Kirby 1996, 44), in the imposition of a metric system and the importance placed on quantitative precision (Nef 1960, 6–17), in the use of more reliable and uniform building materials such as iron (Beniger 1986; Schivelbusch 1986, 2), in the standardization of time (Hansen 2009, 303; Kern 1983),[2] and in the uniformity and standardization of the production and delivery of power and energy. Indeed, standardization and uniformity are especially important in a mechanical ensemble central to which are the production, distribution, and consumption of goods on a mass scale. These processes are organized not only to reduce costs, but also to eliminate as much as possible the occurrence of errors and discrepancies (Beniger 1986; Marx 1990, 537).

Key elements in such standardized production are techniques that make use of a high degree of differentiation of function. Standardized production, especially on a mass scale, requires an intense division of labor. Of course, a division of labor is not something peculiar to the industrialized form of the mechanical ensemble. Marx, for instance, pointed out the importance of the division of labor and its effects on work and workers in manufacturing (Marx 1990).[3] The introduction of machinery, however, 'had the effect of making manufacturing more efficient, uniform, and intense' than it was before (Marx 1990, 537). In other words, industrial machinery affected the division of labor so as to increase the functional differentiation of work, thereby increasingly standardizing and reducing both work and workers to the same level. This was manifested most explicitly in the factory.

> The factory, through the machines, destroys the technical foundation on which the division of labor in manufacture was based. Hence, in place of the hierarchy of specialized workers that characterizes manufacture, there appears, in the automatic factory, a tendency to equalize and reduce to an identical level every kind of work that has to be done by the minders of the machines.
>
> (Marx 1990, 545)

As noted earlier, this standardization and uniformity is expressed on a number of different levels. Very significant to, and a key feature of, the industrialized mechanical ensemble is that processes of production, distribution and consumption are standardized and uniformalized. More importantly, these are processes that, in the industrialized mechanical ensemble, take place on a greater scale than they ever did before. For these processes to take place on such a scale in a smooth manner and on a uniform level requires a high degree of control and a sophisticated form of the organization of people (Beniger 1986; Dandeker 1990; Gendron and Holmstrom 1979, 122). This is a form of organization and control that is centralized, hierarchical, efficient, and capable of adjustment and correcting errors. In short, the industrialized mechanical ensemble requires a bureaucratic form of organization (Beniger 1986; Dandeker 1990; Weber 1978).

These, then, are some of the main distinguishing features of the industrialized mechanical ensemble, the 'Age of Mechanism', to which Carlyle reacted. This is an ensemble in which things and people are increasingly standardized and made uniform, ranging from the work people perform, to the products they produce and consume. More importantly, it is an ensemble in which, due to the steam engine, and exemplified in rail, car, and plane travel, a new sense of mobility exists. This sense of mobility is no longer associated with the actual territory in which one finds oneself. Indeed, this new-found mobility, in combination with an enormous increase in speed (whether it be in the form of rail travel (Schivelbusch 1986), or whether it be in the form of the mass production, distribution, and consumption of goods (Marx 1973, 533–4)), results in a need for ever greater degrees of control and more efficient forms of organization (Beniger 1986; Dandeker 1990). In short, everything within this ensemble is now done by way of machinery, both material and abstract. As Carlyle commented,

> [n]ot the external and physical alone is now managed by machinery, but the internal and spiritual also. Here too nothing follows its spontaneous course, nothing is left to be accomplished by old natural methods. Everything has its cunningly devised implements, its preestablished apparatus; it is not done by hand, but by machinery.
>
> (Carlyle 1984, 35)

This dominance of 'mechanism', to which Carlyle refers, pervades the entire industrialized or motorized ensemble on all levels, the most crucial manifestation of which is the production of a new sense of space and time (Castells 1996; Kern 1983; Kirby 1996; Lefebvre 1991; Mumford 1947; Schivelbusch 1986; Virilio 1986). This new sense of space and time, or new 'spatiality' (Kirby 1996, 73), is effectively a product of an increase not only in speed, both of physical mobility and of communication, but is also a product of the standardization and uniformity effected by processes of industrialization and motorization (Schivelbusch 1986). Indeed, the production of this new spatiality, or this 'spatial condition' as Marx suggested (Marx 1973, 533), is very much a key element of the production process in the industrialized ensemble (Schivelbusch 1986, 40), especially in its capitalist manifestation.

> *Circulation proceeds in space and time.* Economically considered, the spatial condition, the bringing of the product to the market, belongs to the production process itself. The product is really finished only when it is on the market... [T]his spatial moment is important in so far as the expansion of the market and the exchangeability of the product are connected with it. The reduction of the costs of this *real* circulation (in space) belongs to the development of the forces of production by capital, the reduction of the costs of its realization... *Secondly, the temporal moment.* This is an essential part of the concept of circulation... The abbreviation of this moment is likewise development of productive force.
>
> (Marx 1973, 533–4)

This shortening of the spatial and temporal moment, as Marx calls it, is not the only spatial effect of processes of industrialization and motorization. Space and time in the industrialized and motorized mechanical ensemble – and the railway reflects this very well (Schivelbusch 1986) – also become fully standardized and uniformalized, indeed, nationalized. In other words, space and time are no longer different depending on one's locality, but are now the same regardless of the location one is in. Space and time also become centrally organized and maintained, key examples of which are the timetable and the map (Kern 1983; Kirby 1996; Schivelbusch 1986).[4]

Effectively, then, the industrialized mechanical ensemble produces and organizes a specific space within which people exist. In doing so, it also expresses a specific organization of people. This can be observed both in terms of the collective organization of people, and in their organization in relation to one another and themselves (Foucault 1991; Gordon 1991). To be capable of existing, of functioning, within this ensemble, one must be capable of connecting with and using various machinic components, those of both a physical and an abstract form. Unless one is capable of operating or functioning within these machines or assemblages one cannot act. To operate these machines effectively requires a specific understanding or sense of being an actor in the world. It means one has to have a specific sense of perspective and a specific understanding of self.[5] As Arthur (2010, 198) points out, 'factories created not just a new organizational set of arrangements but called for a new kind of person.' In short, a different construction of subjectivity is required for effective action and existence within this ensemble. Indeed, in some respects it does not so much require a different construction of the subject, so much as it requires *a* construction of the subject (Heller 1990).[6]

Within the context of the industrialized mechanical ensemble one is connected to, acts by way of and acts through machines that are organized, and organize, very differently. A prime example of this is the assemblage we call the factory. This is an assemblage each of whose components, abstract and material, human and machinic, is differentiated and organized in terms of a highly specific function. Not only that, but this functional organization is also expressed in terms of a specific spatial and temporal organization. Also important is the continued, or rather, the emphasized importance placed on the body and how it functions within the overall assemblage (Mumford 1995a). The disciplinary mode of power, for instance, is all about the organization of individual bodies,[7] in relation to both themselves and others. Indeed, the disciplinary mode of power, much like the steam engine, is very much about a harnessing and concentration of energy.[8]

The industrialized ensemble, then, is distinguished from other machinic ensembles by the manner in which it harnesses, organizes, and distributes energy. The machines that express this ensemble (such as the steam engine) enable the performance of forms of action entirely different from that found in other ensembles. In some respects, one could argue that these actions, or ways of doing, and these machines, because they are highly functionally differentiated, are relatively inflexible. When understood from the point of view of the industrialized mechanical ensemble, however, this inflexibility is a strength. After all, without standardized and highly regulated processes of production, mass production and consumption cannot exist. To again emphasize, any technological ensemble (a 'world' as Arthur (2010, 83) terms it) offers different possibilities that it excels at.

The industrialized or motorized mechanical ensemble, then, is an ensemble that operates by way of an understanding of time and space very different from that of other technological ensembles. The fact that it is a time and space that is organized very differently from the time and space of other technological ensembles enables entirely different forms of action and thought. Being of this technological ensemble, then, involves a very specific sense of doing – a sense of doing that relies on, or rather, involves, among other things, a very different sense of mobility, an increased sense of independence from one's place and, importantly, an increased sense of separation from what one produces. Indeed, this increased sense of separation between one's actions as producer and the product produced seems to place an ever greater emphasis on one's actions as a consumer. The industrialized mechanical ensemble, in other words, constructs, and requires, a very different sense of being as doing. In short, it requires a very specific sense of existing and constituting oneself as subject as a function of existing within a very differently organized space and time.

The mechanical subject

These things, which we state lightly enough here, are yet of deep import, and indicate a mighty change in our whole manner of existence. For the same habit regulates not our modes of action alone, but our modes of thought and feeling. Men [*sic*] are grown mechanical in head and in heart, as well as in hand. They have lost faith in individual endeavor, and in natural force, of any kind ... Their whole efforts, attachments, opinions, turn on mechanism, and are of a mechanical character.

(Carlyle 1984, 37)

There was a time when people grew naturally into the conditions they found waiting for them and that was a very sound way of becoming oneself. But nowadays, with all this shaking up of things, when everything is becoming detached from the soil it grew in, even where the production of soul is concerned one really ought, as it were, to replace the traditional handicrafts by the sort of intelligence that goes with the machine and the factory.

(Musil in Hardt and Negri 2001, 284–5)

A primary characteristic of human existence in the industrialized mechanical ensemble, indeed, in any ensemble, is that one is a body. 'Being a body', as Heim states, 'constitutes the principle behind our separateness from one another and behind our personal presence. Our bodily existence stands at the forefront of our personal identity and individuality' (Heim 2001, 81). It is the fact of being a body that constitutes a possibility for differentiating between an inside, that which is 'me', and an outside, that which is other than 'me'. As Cohen (2008, 106) explains, 'in order to imagine the "sameness" of "the body", let alone to imagine "the body" as a thing, a possession or a kind of property, one must first take another conceptual leap and imagine "the body" as circumscribed within a well-defined perimeter.' One's existence, in other words, or rather, one's sense of being, is bounded in a very specific manner, even if it is a fiction (Cohen 2008; 2009).

The sense of being a body is, of course, not something specific to existence in the industrialized or motorized mechanical ensemble. It applies to all forms of human existence, regardless of the technological ensemble one is situated within, including the digital one (Hansen 2006; Munster 2006). Indeed, as Heidegger made clear, corporality is 'a characteristic of *Dasein* that is prior to the notion of the body' (Coyne 1998). The way in which being a body differs in the industrialized mechanical ensemble is first in terms of how it is situated in the world or, more specifically, in terms of the space in which and through which it exists, and second, and consequently, in terms of a notion of the body that is constructed (Kirby 1996).

As stated above, in the motorized and industrialized mechanical ensemble a sense of space is produced that is very different from that of previous mechanical ensembles. A first difference is that, on an unprecedented scale, it is a space organized as a system of magnitudes rather than as a hierarchy of values (Mumford 1995b, 330; Romanyshyn 1989). As such, it is very much a more standardized and uniform space. Indeed, in some respects it is a more homogenous or isotropic space (Poovey 1995; Rose 1999, 38), crucial to which is the dominance of linear perspective, as a way or technology of understanding and seeing the world (Harvey 1989; Romanyshyn 1989).

> One of the indications of this new orientation was the closer study of the relations of the objects in space and the discovery of the laws of perspective and the systematic organization of pictures within the new frame fixed by the foreground, the horizon, and the vanishing point. Perspective turned the symbolic relation of objects into a visual relation: the visual in turn became a quantitative relation.
>
> (Mumford 1995b, 330)[9]

Another crucial difference in the space, and time, of the industrialized or motorized ensemble lies in one's capacity for physical mobility in this space. As explained in the Section 'The motorized mechanical ensemble', with the introduction of the steam engine, exemplified in rail travel, there occurs what is often referred to as an 'annihilation' of space and time. With the technology of the industrialized ensemble, the distance between geographical locations, which was previously an important aspect in travel, seems to vanish (Kirby 1996, 72; Schivelbusch 1986). The effect of the new technologies (such as the train, the bike, and the car) and including new communication technologies like the telegraph and later the telephone, is to both expand or open up space, in terms of bringing more places closer together, while at the same time also destroying it, by eliminating the distance between places (Harvey 1989; Kirby 1996, 72; Schivelbusch 1986, 38).

The industrialized mechanical ensemble, then, constructs, or is constructed of, a space in which one's sense of being a body, unlike previous technological ensembles, is very much separated from the landscape, from one's place. Consequently, '[w]hereas once location may have seemed a dependable, stable thing – one's body, one's place, gets its sense of groundedness by a long-standing attachment to locale – at this time "location" becomes a matter of investigation and negotiation' (Kirby 1996, 72). Indeed, this process of what Kirby refers to as a 'liquidation' of space (1996, 72), or a loss of a sense of groundedness to one's place, occurs with the quantification of time as well: It loses its reality, and we find ourselves in an exceedingly difficult position in our efforts to orient ourselves in the time process, to find out 'where we are' and where are the other social phenomena on 'the bridge of time' (Sorokin in Schivelbusch 1986, 36–7).

The space and time of the industrialized mechanical ensemble is not annihilated, then, as people in the nineteenth century often described it (Schivelbusch 1986), but is constructed entirely differently, producing, and being a product of, a very different perception.

> Thus the idea that the railroad annihilated space and time must be seen as the reaction of perceptive powers that... find suddenly that technology has been replaced by an entirely new one. Compared to the geotechnical space-time relationship, the one created by the railroad appears abstract and disorientating, because the railroad – in realizing Newton's mechanics – negated all that characterized geotechnical traffic; the railroad did not appear embedded in the space of the landscape the way the coach and highway are, but seemed to strike its way through it.
>
> (Schivelbusch 1986, 37)

The mechanical uniformity of machines, in short, replaces the previously dominant mimetic relationship between one's sense of being and geography (Kirby 1996, 74; Schivelbusch 1986, 9–14) and alters the relationship between one's sense of being and one's capacity for physical action. 'Nothing is now done directly', as Carlyle (1984, 34) commented, 'or by hand'.

The industrialized ensemble produces, or at least enables the production, of a sense of being that is very much independent from the body. More precisely, compared to earlier technological ensembles, it enables a sense of being the production of which does not rely on one's geography and limits for physical action, though these are only perceived as limits within the industrialized mechanical ensemble. The sense of being it enables is very much a strengthening of a sense of self. In some respects, following Hegel's line (Hegel 1971), it is a sense of being that is increasingly aware of an increased consciousness of self. A consciousness of self as being far more independent, at least in some respects, from the spaces it inhabits, including, importantly, the construction of that space called the body (Cohen 2008; 2009; Kirby 1996; Romanyshyn 1989).

In some ways, this sense of being, and of being a body, as independent from the world it inhabits, is very much a continuation of the Enlightenment individual (Kirby 1996, 38). A being that is very much separated, or rather, isolated from the world, as Marx puts it (Marx 1973,

84) – a world, according to Descartes, 'in which objects appear within their own bubbles, self-contained and separate, but largely irrelevant to this autonomous, self-sufficient Ego' (Kirby 1996, 38). The industrialized mechanical ensemble, with the new-found mobility it produces, very much accentuates this sense of being, or this sense of individuality, if it does not represent its coming to fruition. It is a sense of being that, very much as a function of the technologies it uses (from the increased mobility of the railway to the increased power of the steam engine), has or reproduces a heightened sense of autonomy. Indeed, as shown below, this sense of autonomy is central to the construction of the political. However, while the industrialized or motorized mechanical ensemble seems to accentuate the production of autonomy in the production of self, on the one hand, at the very same time, it destabilizes this production of autonomy. It is especially here that the sense of being a body in the industrialized mechanical ensemble is very different from pre-industrial or pre-motorized mechanical ensembles.

First, while the space and time of the industrialized mechanical ensemble is very much homogenous, it is also an extremely fragmented space. It is a space that is always differentiated into smaller spaces (Deleuze 1992; Foucault 1979). Space in the industrialized mechanical ensemble is a Cartesian space. Unlike the space that existed in the Middle Ages in Europe, it is a space that operates by way of a grid and grids operate by way of a precise division of spaces (Chesher 1997; Romanyshyn 1989). This fragmentation is partly a function of the way that increased speed opens up an increased number of locations. Indeed, in some respects, this shortening of distances destabilizes linear perspective vision because it blurs distinctions between near and far (Schivelbusch 1986, 42).

More important, however, is the fact that space in the industrialized mechanical ensemble (more so than that of any other ensemble) is functionally differentiated. Spaces become organized differently depending on the function they are to serve in an assemblage. This functional differentiation of space, in the form of specific assemblages within the ensemble, exists on larger scales and smaller scales. The separation of space on a functional basis is obvious on a number of different levels. One can see it on a smaller scale in the internal organization of factories, while on a larger scale it exists in terms of a separation between spaces such as the factory, the school, the hospital, and the family home (Deleuze 1992; Foucault 1979), as well as the zoning of cities more generally. The largest space of all being the space of the nation state.

Another level at which this fragmentation is expressed – and the fragmentation of space is very much organized through this, certainly at its micro levels – is in terms of a person's actual 'doing' in the form of work. Production is now divided

> into its various detailed operations, and each single operation crystallize[s] into the exclusive functions of the specific worker, the manufacture as a whole being performed by these partial workers in conjunction.
>
> (Marx 1990, 456)

The term Marx used to describe this person – the 'partial worker' – is significant because it points to how their existence, at least their existence as a working being, is literally fragmented and divided into various components. These components are distributed and organized into specific times and places – places such as the factory floor, the territory of the nation-state, and even on a planetary scale.

More importantly, with the further intensification of this division of labor, one's sense of being, at least as a working being, becomes totally separated and alienated from the bodily acts in which one engages (Gendron and Holmstrom 1979, 132; Marx 1973, 704). According to Marx,

> [i]t converts the worker into a crippled monstrosity by furthering his [*sic*] particular skill as in a forcing house, through the suppression of a whole world of productive drives and inclinations, just as in the states of La Plata they butcher a whole beast for the sake of his hide or his tallow. Not only is the specialized worker distributed among the different individuals, but the individual himself is divided up, and transformed into the automatic motor of a detail operation, thus realizing the absurd fable of Menenius Agrippa, which presents man as a mere fragment of his own body.
>
> (Marx 1990, 481–2)

As Deborah Levitt (2008, 205) points out, referring to Agamben's work on gesture, '[i]n this world, study becomes the experience of piecing oneself together from fragments, performing a kind of reconstitution of alienated objects'. In fact, not only do the division of labor and its necessary fragmentation of time and space produce, and require, an alienation from the bodily acts one performs. It also produces, and requires, an alienation from the general processes of production

(Gendron and Holmstrom 1979, 132). This is an alienation that even the capitalist, as owner of the means of production, experiences, because they are simply another component in the overall process of production (Marx 1990, 423).

Space in the context of the industrialized mechanical ensemble or, more precisely, space as it is produced by this ensemble, is a very much fragmented space. As one moves from one space to another, from one location to another, one exists and operates within different machinic assemblages. Whenever one links up with one of these machinic assemblages, whether that be the physical machines of the factory floor or the more abstract machines of the education system, one is always engaged in the production of, and more importantly, always produced as, a different object.[10] The subjective component of the machinic assemblage, in other words, is never identical in every space.

Being, or certainly one's sense of being, then, is very much fragmented. Crucially, in the context of the industrialized mechanical ensemble, this fragmentation is of a specific form. The reason for this is that, at least in Cartesian space, one cannot exist in two spaces at the same time. Thus, at any given moment one can only function as an active component of one specific machinic assemblage. This means that the fragmentation of space and function, and the resultant multiplicity of identity this requires and produces, has a linear character. Identity, being composed of multiple subject positions, at least in the context of the mechanical ensemble, has a 'linear multiplicity'. One can never exhibit two identities, two forms of existence, at one and the same time in the serial logic of a Cartesian universe. (See Figure 4.1) Indeed, any such schizophrenic manifestations of identity are usually considered to be unhealthy and subjected to treatment (Deleuze and Guattari 1977).

Such a fragmentation of identity, as a product of having to exist in sometimes very disparate functional spaces, produces an overall sense or experience of disunity in one's sense of being an autonomous embodied entity. From this perspective, one could see the emergence of the subject

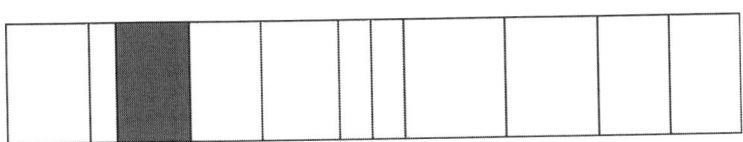

Figure 4.1   The individual

(Heller 1990) and the sense of self as a detached spectator (Romanyshyn 1989) as mechanisms for trying to deal with the overall feeling of a fragmentation of identity that exists in the industrialized mechanical ensemble. In that respect, subjectivity can be seen as a mechanism for attempting to exist as a more unitary, coherent form of being within the context of a world that operates by way of a fragmentation of existence. Subjectivity is the attempt to integrate one's experience of fragmented being into a harmonious whole. It is to produce a sense of unicity and to be capable of acting in the world.

The emergence of subjectivity as something that is separate from the body is in some ways very much a product, though not necessarily a calculated one, of the industrialized mechanical ensemble. Indeed, this split between the subject and the body has only increased over the duration of the industrialized mechanical ensemble (Stone 2001, 187), and can be understood as a defining characteristic of modernity (Heller 1990), as is the notion of the unitary self. In that respect, the concept of the individual, and individuality, is also a product of the mechanical ensemble. After all, two different bodies cannot occupy the same Cartesian space. Therefore each body must be, or rather must harbor, a unique individual. Such an understanding of subjectivity is central to concepts such as alienation (Jameson 1991) and the separation of product and producer, actor and action.

Connection to the various machines and assemblages of the industrialized mechanical ensemble produces a number of effects in one's sense of being. On the one hand, these technologies produce and express a heightened sense of independence and autonomy. Things that previously would have been considered unquestionable parts of life (such as the features of the land, the speed at which one travels, or the strength of the wind) now (if considered at all) become expressed as limits that can be, and are, transcended. Tourism is the most obvious example of this, with both Mount Everest and the Antarctic now being increasingly 'available' for a greater number of people. On the other hand, these very same technologies produce an extreme degree of fragmentation on a number of different levels. A fragmentation that produces, as shown above, a separation of one's being and one's work. Being connected to various technological assemblages, therefore, becomes not only a possibility for a specific form of action and form of existence. It also becomes an extreme limitation on one's capacity for action and, consequently, an extreme limitation on one's sense of being, and on one's capacity for constructing a meaningful form of existence. Existence in the industrialized mechanical ensemble, then, is affected, or rather effected, by at least two major processes: increasing autonomy and increasing fragmentation.

Furthermore, the increased fragmentation that is a feature of the industrialized mechanical ensemble requires one to be connected to an ever-increasing number of assemblages to an ever-greater degree. Without connection there is little capacity for autonomous action within the context of the industrialized mechanical ensemble. At the same time, however, connection to its various assemblages produces a fragmentation of existence and develops a degree of dependency on other subjects that is unparalleled in any previous technological ensemble.

> The more deeply we go back in history, the more does the individual, and hence also the producing individual, appear as dependent, as belonging to a greater whole...Only in the eighteenth century, in 'civil society', do the various forms of social connectedness confront the individual as a mere means towards his [*sic*] private purposes, as external necessity. But the epoch which produces this standpoint, that of the isolated individual, is also precisely that of the hitherto most developed social relations.
>
> (Marx 1973, 84)

Mechanical being and the political

> Nowhere...is the deep, almost exclusive faith we have in Mechanism more visible than in the Politics of this time.
>
> (Carlyle 1984, 40)

> It is very characteristic that the enthusiastic apologists of the factory system have nothing more damning to urge against a general organization of labor in society than that it would turn the whole of society into a factory.
>
> (Marx 1990, 477)

As pointed out above, the new sense of space expressed in and produced through the use of new motorized and industrialized technologies is both a much more homogenous space and a very much fragmented space. It is a space in which one seemingly exists as a far more independent and autonomous entity, with a far different capacity for action than that experienced previously. The production of such a space as homogeneous and fragmented, and as a space that one occupies as a body, is expressive of specific material conditions – a specific politics – and reflects a specific construction of the political in the industrialized mechanical ensemble.

> As Lefebvre points out, and Poulantzas, Foucault, Giddens, Gregory, and others repeat in different ways, spatial fragmentation as well as the appearance of spatial coherence and homogeneity are social products and often an integral part of the instrumentality of political power. They do not arise from material spatiality or the mode of production in some simple, deterministic fashion, nor do they reflect back on society, once established, with simplistic determinacy of another kind. But conceptions or representations of space in social thought cannot be understood as projections of modes of thinking hypothetically (or otherwise) independent of socio-material conditions no matter where or when they are found, whether they emanate from the collective minds of a band of hunters and gatherers or from the institutionalized citizenry of the advanced capitalist state.
>
> (Soja 1989, 126)

This politics of the industrialized mechanical ensemble and, more importantly, the construction of the political in this ensemble is first expressed by theorists such as Descartes, Hobbes, Locke, and Rousseau. Of course, the industrialization of the ensemble had not yet occurred when these theorists expressed their ideas. They are, however, expressing the beginnings of a new construction and organization of material and political space. Locke's thinking about politics, for instance, is very reflective of this (Locke 1963), as he is trying to make sense of a change in the material conditions of seventeenth-century England, which is moving 'from a kinship society toward a society organized around economic markets' (Kelly 2002, 363).

The primary event of this new politics is the production of a sense of being as autonomous and independent from the world it inhabits (Cohen 2008; 2009; Kirby 1996, 37–8). As Hardt and Negri point out, '[b]odies and brains were fundamentally transformed. This historical process of subjectivization was revolutionary in the sense that it determined a paradigmatic and irreversible change in the mode of the life of the multitude' (Hardt and Negri 2001, 74). This is a sense of being that, gradually, no longer grounds its sense of self in its location or in its kinship ties (Kirby 1996, 38) but, instead, in itself. It is a sense of being that constructs itself, and is constructed, as a space (Kirby 1996). This space is uniform, coherent, complete, and totally separate from its environment (Cohen 2008; Kirby 1996, 38). As pointed out earlier, subjectivity, or rather its construction, can be seen as an attempt or strategy for coping with a fragmented existence that is produced as a result of connecting to and disconnecting from the various machinic assemblages and spaces in which one exists. Subjectivity is therefore an attempt to form a coherent unity of being through various processes of subjectivation, an attempt to produce a unitary sense of self (Guattari 1995). A sense of self that, necessarily so, is separate from the body and the various assemblages to which it finds itself connected.

The self can be seen, then, as something of an enclosure against the world (Foster 1997, 26; Heim 2001, 81), or a fortress, as Heidegger described it (Mansfield 2000). This construction, albeit an ongoing one, of a form of subjectivity as a unique and enclosed space in some degree separate from the body and functioning as a detached spectator (Romanyshyn 1989), has a number of consequences. The production of subjectivity, the construction of this enclosed and fortified space that is called the self is, as Guattari states, not something that is given as in itself (Guattari 1995, 7). Rather, subjectivity is nothing less than a process 'of the realization of autonomy' (Guattari 1995, 7). It is, in other words, about staking out one's own territory as 'mine'. It is most immediately about the construction of a space that is relatively independent from what are perceived to be 'external' influences, that is, that do not originate from within one's own space. In short, the maintenance of the autonomy and independence of these spaces, these individuals, is a characterizing feature of the politics of this ensemble, especially so since these spaces are considered to be universal, equal, and unique (Kirby 1996, 44). Unique because each of these identical spaces is considered to contain a unique self as a function of its experiences in the world.

Importantly, however, mechanistic existence or mechanical being relies on a strong connection between body and sense of self. Stated differently, there is a recognition of the importance of the body in one's doing. Indeed, this connection between the autonomous self and its body is very much the grounding for the concept of property in the motorized mechanical ensemble.

> Though the Earth, and all inferior creatures be common to all Men [*sic*], yet every Man has a *Property* in his own *Person*. This no Body has any Right to but himself. The *Labour* of his Body, and the Work of his hands, we may say, are properly his. Whatsoever then he removes out of the State that Nature hath provided, and left in, he hath mixed his *Labour* with, and joyned to it something that is his own, and thereby makes it his *Property*. It being by him removed from the common state

Nature placed it in, hath by this *labour* something annexed to it, that excludes the common right of other Men. For his *Labour* being the unquestionable Property of the Labourer, no Man but he can have a right to what that is joyned to, at least where there is enough, and as good left in common for others.

(Locke 1963, 328–9)

According to Locke, it is what one does with one's body that forms the basis of property in this ensemble. The work one performs does not belong to some local lord, nor, ultimately, to some king or queen, nor to the state, but to one's self. Property and ownership are gradually no longer defined by one's place within societal relations based on kinship but are defined by one's own doing.

This concept of property and ownership forms, together with the notion of the autonomous and independent self, or individual, the central organizing principle in the construction of the political and the organization of politics, including today (Cohen 2008; Kelly 2002). Indeed Locke, as Kelly points out (2002, 361), is one of the first liberal theorists who addresses the issue of the public/private distinction, which is critical to our construction of politics. In Locke's work there are two different models of this distinction. First, Locke opposes the notion of divine right by creating a division between paternal power – the private sphere – and political power – the public sphere – thereby separating the family from politics (Kelly 2002). Second, Locke also argues that individuals can agree to government without having to relinquish their autonomy and independence, thereby separating the private individual from the public state (Kelly 2002). Indeed, according to Locke, government is a necessity, as it alone can preserve the property of individuals (Locke 1960, 395).

The idea, or fiction (Cohen 2008), that a subject is an autonomous and independent entity and the idea that its body and the work performed by way of that body belongs to it, indeed, is *of* it and defines its very being, is at the core of the construction of the political in the industrialized mechanical ensemble. More importantly, the idea that these entities, these individuals, pursue their needs and interests, and that such a pursuit could jeopardize the needs and interests of other individuals is at the core of the organization of politics in the industrialized ensemble. These are ideas with which all modern political theorists engage, from Smith (1976), to Wollstonecraft (1992), to Marx (1973). All modern political theorists explore issues related to the preservation of the autonomy of the individual, the definition of who belongs to that category, and the notion that their doing is *their* doing, performed by way of *their* body, and properly belongs to them and is of them.

Of course, many of the basic elements of this conceptualization of politics precede the processes of industrialization and motorization discussed in the Section 'The mechanical subject'. These are elements of a politics that was already beginning to reflect the production of a newly emerging sense of space and time (Kirby 1996), of new material conditions, and of a new understanding of political power (Hardt and Negri 2001, 73). With the development of manufacturing and the space of the economic market, and the start of industrialization and motorization, however, many of these earlier political concepts, of the autonomy of the individual, of one's doing as one's property, and, especially, of the need to regulate or to govern the relations of those autonomous individuals, come to be expressed on a mass scale. As Kirby points out,

> [w]ith industrialization, great numbers of people were thrown together in the growing urban centers. More importantly, perhaps, with modernism the site of cultural consciousness shifted from country to city as the population did. An identity once founded on solitude in open space, privacy, and centrality relative to an unpopulated environment had to redefine itself in relation to masses of obtrusive, impinging 'others' who could be ignored only at one's own peril.
>
> (Kirby 1996, 75)

More significantly, the earlier liberal views of the autonomous and independent individual and its government come to be challenged (Kern 1983; Schivelbusch 1986, 27). With industrialization, and especially with the increasing differentiation of function with the division of labor, as well as the fact that no single individual can lay claim to the ownership of any whole product, including the capitalist (Marx 1990, 423), there comes an increasing perception of society as a construct of a multitude of smaller components that all depend on one another and require central government. Indeed, as Schivelbusch points out, the railway is a very good example of how earlier laissez-fair views came to be challenged, as trains are not amenable to notions of individualism in transportation (Schivelbusch 1986, 28).

Processes of industrialization and motorization, then, increase already existing tendencies toward making spaces more homogeneous, fragmented, and measurable. Politically, this is especially reflected in the increasing concern with a leveling of traditional hierarchies and how 'the contraction of social distance assaulted a variety of social orderings' (Kirby 1996, 72). As Kirby points out,

> [r]eal transformations in space interlocked with...modifications in the aesthetic and scientific perception of the real and with political and popular conceptions of the self. The emerging visibility, the 'presence', of numerous distinct, coexisting, equal areas corresponds well with the nonhierarchical 'democratic' philosophy of governance gaining ascendancy in Europe at this time.
>
> (Kirby 1996, 72)

The politics of the industrialized ensemble, then, is a politics concerned with the autonomy of independently minded individuals. This autonomy is constantly jeopardized by the actual interactions, and need for interaction, between these individuals. In short, as stated earlier, the chief end of government is the preservation of property, defined broadly by Locke as including people's lives, their freedom to act, and their actual estates. This concern is reflected in the development of philosophies of governance and an increasing concern with the health of individuals and their conglomeration in the form of the population (Foucault 1991). Indeed, as Marx pointed out (1990, 484), an entirely new industrial pathology with a whole new range of diseases and illnesses develops as a consequence of manufacturing and industrialization. These too are the new problems and possibilities, the new utterances, of the industrialized mechanical ensemble, and are issues that are central to the governance of both individuals and populations (Foucault 1991).

It is in such a context, then, that there develops a science of the state, or statistics (Foucault 1991; Hacking 1991; Rose 1999). The entire space that is the industrialized mechanical ensemble is open for investigation in the interests of maintaining healthy individuals and healthy relations between individuals. Indeed, not only is the space of the industrialized mechanical ensemble as a whole made visible and open for inspection, but so are the plurality of spaces that constitute it, including the space that is the individual. All of this is done in the interests of good governance, including in the interests of how individuals govern their own production and maintenance as healthy individuals who are capable of working and existing within the highly fragmented space of the industrialized mechanical ensemble.[11]

Making spaces visible in the interests of good governance suggests that the whole of society comes to be seen as a machine constructed of various components requiring maintenance and regulation (Carlyle 1984). The very processes of government itself, or a restricted notion of politics, come to be treated as somehow open to scientific investigation. Hobbes and his conceptualization of the 'Body Politique' as a mechanical machine, including his view that this machine can be, and must be, scientifically examined, is probably the earliest example of this (Hobbes 1968). Another good example of this is the 'new political science' of the American Revolution, with its focus on checks and balances, and the splitting up, or fragmenting, of political power (Hardt and Negri 2001, 161).

Great concerns arise in the industrial mechanical ensemble when certain spaces are not transparent or visible. Spaces that cannot be seen are troubling, especially those that cannot be made available for observation. A lack of transparency of any given space prevents the identification of the specific cause of an effect. It prevents the identification of who, or what, is responsible for any given action. This can range from a lack of transparency in 'spaces' such as 'the market', the corporation, the factory floor, the police, or even government itself. A lack of transparency of the public space affects accountability and the ability to effectively govern a space.[12] More importantly, a lack of transparency affects the legitimacy of authority (Porter 1996; Rose 1999, 208). It is for this reason that politics, or government, comes to be composed as a series of mechanisms.

> In the very outset, we might note the mighty interest taken in *mere political arrangements*, as itself the sign of a mechanical age ... A good structure of legislation, a proper check upon the executive, a wise arrangement of the judiciary, is *all* that is wanting for human happiness. The Philosopher of this age is ... a Smith, a De Lolme, a Bentham [who argue] that our happiness depends entirely on external circumstances; nay, that the strength and dignity of the mind within us is itself the creature and consequence of these. Were the laws, the government, in good order, all were well with us; the rest would care for itself! Dissentients from this opinion, expressed or implied, are now rarely to be met with; widely and angrily as men differ in its application, the principle is admitted by all.
>
> (Carlyle 1984, 40–1)

Politics as it is produced in the industrialized mechanical ensemble, then, is very much about the governance of fragmented spaces and their relations. The very construction of the political itself, as it is produced in the industrialized mechanical ensemble, is a product of the ongoing construction of a sense of autonomy of self, itself a product of being a body and having to operate within a functionally fragmented space. Politics, therefore, is also about how these selves, these individuals, can maintain themselves without interrupting each other. Politics in the industrialized ensemble, in other words, is not only about the governance of the public spaces in which individuals find themselves, but is also about the governance of their private space, that is, about how individuals govern themselves. Indeed, it is this construction of themselves as autonomous individuals that enables them to act within, and as part of, the industrialized mechanical ensemble.

At the same time, for any individual to connect to any other component of the industrialized mechanical ensemble endangers their sense of autonomy. The reason for this is that the components are organized into highly specific, and differentiated, functions. The extreme degree of the division of labor and the sense of alienation this produces in its human components is one example of this (Gendron and Holmstrom 1979). Indeed, the very organization of society as a factory that is owned only by a handful of individuals jeopardizes the production of a sense of autonomy, as in some respects these are very much organized like 'mitigated jails' (Marx 1990, 553). Yet, at the same time, this very connection of the human component to the machinic component enables entirely different forms of action, not only greatly increasing productive capacities, but also one's mobility. In other words, connection to the various components generates very different needs and interests on the part of individuals, and it is the regulation or, rather, the governance of these very different needs and interests, including the sense of autonomy of self, that defines much of the politics of the industrialized mechanical ensemble.

5
Digital Being

> Technology reveals the active relation of man to nature, the direct process of the production of his life, and thereby it also lays bare the process of the production of social relations of his life, and of the mental conceptions that flow from those relations.
>
> (Marx 1990, 493)

The digital ensemble has no clear beginning. As Deleuze and Guattari point out, it's a question of connections, and the connections that produced the difference that we recognize as the digital ensemble are many. Certainly the late 1940s can be identified as a point of emergence, though already before this the general expansion of control technologies in the century preceding it certainly forms part of its trajectory (Beniger 1986). More significant is the current merging of biology and technology by way of the digital ensemble (Arthur 2010; Clough 2008; Thacker 2004), which perhaps indicates that it's difficult to understand the digital ensemble as anywhere else than in its early formation. The digital ensemble's encounter with all aspects of the industrialized mechanical ensemble, its politics, economics, and culture has been nothing short of revolutionary in many respects. The possibility of doing new things, whether positive or negative, stating new things in all areas of the economy, whether in medical science, engineering, finance, and areas such as biotechnology and nanotechnology, was only enabled by the use of digital technologies and the new connections they made possible. Even those who are seemingly far removed from having to deal directly with any such machines (whether by choice or not) are to some extent regulated and constituted by them. As Shaviro (2003, 4) points out, 'escape is nearly impossible'.

These machines, and the forms of action that they enable, are part of the construction of a new universe of action (Arthur 2010; Coyne 1998; Finneman 1999; Guattari 1995; Winner 1999; Winner and Brien 2005). To be sure, the institutionalization of this universe is a political event in its own right, but to exist in that universe, to be capable of acting in it, requires an even more dramatic shift. It requires a shift in one's understanding of self, or in one's understanding of being in the world, similar to the way that the industrialized mechanical ensemble required it. This change in the production of a sense of unicity when we become increasingly networked, or connected, in the digital ensemble is what I now turn to. We can see this reflected in the manner in which we make use of social media, in the games people play, in how people work. Indeed, we see it in the very things that we produce and how we do so. We also see it expressed in people's use of digital media in responding to major disasters, as with the use of crowdsourced information in the 2011 Christchurch earthquake, but also in the use of social media in political events, as reportedly occurred with the Arab Spring, or the use of, for example, Ushahidi in the Kenyan elections (Crandall 2010). This is precisely the point that Marx's quote, opening this chapter, makes.

In order to arrive at a discussion of what possible understanding of the self and the political is expressed by digital machines, this chapter does several things. First, it offers a brief description of the digital ensemble and some of the important characteristics expressed, and enabled, by the machines that compose it. Then I argue that in order to use these machines we connect to them differently from the machines that express the industrialized mechanical ensemble. This different connection – our interface to these machines, and the actions they make both possible and impossible – requires and produces a different understanding of self. More accurately, this is a construction of a sense of unicity that is different from the unicity required in connecting with the machines of the industrial or motorized ensemble.

Important in all of this, as hopefully should be clear from Chapter 3, is that I don't see digital machines as somehow disembodying people or dehumanizing people. Far from it. These machines are 'us', irrespective of whether they are the best or the worst of us. Instead, I view digital technologies as a different doing, and therefore as expressive of a different being. Our digital machines, and the media environment that they produce, form part of what is our second skin (Morse 1998). In a very real sense, as people such as Hayles (2009), Hansen (2006; 2009), Galloway (2006), and Munster (2006) have explored in different ways, they offer us a different capacity for action in the world. Indeed, they enable the constitution of a different world or aspect thereof, and with it an ability to begin to experience, sense, and manipulate that world in a way that people couldn't before. It is precisely in that respect that the digital ensemble opens up a new world (Arthur 2010; Guattari 1993).

As part of this I argue that being in, and of, the digital ensemble produces a construct of the political very different from that of the industrialized mechanical ensemble. It is a construct of the political central to which is the interface and a constitution of being as flow/s. As I foregrounded earlier in the book, the reference to flow here is not intended as a metaphor. When people are connected to their digital machines, when people act by way of or through their digital machines, they constitute themselves in a very real sense as code – code that flows – indeed, code that in many respects cannot do anything other than flow, which is in some respects a function of how our digital machines operate, at least as some experience it. In the first instance (in this chapter at least), my interest is much more in the immediate sense produced, and required, when people connect. This sense can, for example, be usefully explored in areas like foreign exchange and derivatives trading (Cooper 2010; Knorr-Cetina 2003; 2007; LiPuma and Lee 2004), but also in computer gaming (Galloway 2006). The unicity required in such contexts, I argue, takes the character of the superject.

At this point, it should be noted that any discussion of the political in the digital is very much limited, mainly because the digitization of politics is still in its formative stages. The following discussion, therefore, is still very much underpinned, and necessarily so, by the continued existence of the industrialized mechanical ensemble. What I think we do need to be mindful of is to see any wider process of digitization, and especially a digitization of politics or 'the political', as somehow necessarily being of a negative character. Stiegler (2010b), for example, leaves us with a less than positive view to state the least (Hansen 2004; 2009).

Any technology opens up possibilities, as Karl Marx and Lewis Mumford made clear so well, and while, yes, we do need to be mindful of those productions that are negative, we also need to consider how technologies might enhance what Spinoza termed our *potentia* – our capacity for action or power. But before I consider action, and how we might conceptualize it (which forms the focus of Part III), I first want to consider the specific constitution of the unicity that takes the character of the superject (that is, of flow/s) – a superject that is generated by, and generates, needs and interests, which I want to suggest are part of a different construction of 'the political' than that of the subject of the industrialized mechanical ensemble.

The digital ensemble

It is generally accepted that, certainly from the 1970s onward with the creation of the microprocessor, we have been undergoing a drastic transformation of our material culture, and that central to this transformation are information or digital technologies (Castells 1996, 29). Different processes that form part of this transformation have been examined by a number of different authors, indicating different institutional positions and different conceptions of this transformation. These include post-industrialism (Bell 1976), the 'network society' (Castells 1996), post-modernity (Lyotard 1984), the 'second media age' (Poster 1995), the 'information society' (Webster 1994), the 'age of planetary computerization' (Guattari 1992), the 'Third Machine Age' (Mandel 1978), 'the virtual age' (Stone 1995), and 'the digital domain' (Arthur 2010). Central to this transformation, however, are machines and principles that express very different forms of action, or doing, than those that exist in the industrialized or motorized mechanical ensemble.

These digital machines came into being as part of a process to make the industrialized mechanical ensemble more efficient (Beniger 1986), the driving force behind this process being the State (Castells 1996). Digital machines are so different from the machines expressive of the industrialized mechanical ensemble, however, that we can well and truly state that they form a new technics (Mumford 1947), or, at the very least, a part thereof. They are still, unlike the machines of the industrialized mechanical ensemble, something of which people are conscious or aware. This is a result of the fact that the technologies that express it are still treated as something other than us.

Picking up a book or opening the fridge, for example, are actions most of us who own fridges don't immediately think about. These actions are very much an extension of what we do and are. In some respects this is what allows us to identify and recognize some of the digital ensemble's key effects, as well as how it differs from other technologies. At the same time, though, when we now consider that there is at least one, if not two generations in some sectors of some societies that didn't experience a world without the World Wide Web, mobile phones, and digital media, we need to recognize that what was new for some, is for others increasingly the way the world has always been. To imagine myself writing a book on a typewriter in the 1960s, for example, without the use of a word processor or, even worse, without 'the Internet', would require not simply a change in the logistics of the process of research and writing, but, even more significant, a change not only in the way I think about my capacity for action, but in my very structure of thought, I suspect. The suggestion that people used to literally 'cut and paste' text seems almost weirdly 'unnatural' somehow. As Kittler points out, it is important in that respect to not ignore questions of ontology when considering media technologies (2009).

In the above example, it is easy to recognize that '[t]he future is shaped far more by practical inventions that subtly alter the infrastructure of life than by paradigm shifts in scientific knowledge' (Küchler 2008, 104). This isn't to say that over the past couple of decades there hasn't been something of a paradigm shift occurring (Castells 1996; Dibbell 1994, 256; Guattari 1992; Virilio 2001), but it is perhaps more in the games people play, how they entertain themselves, and how they change their daily habits, including in their work, that we can recognize how we come to think differently of each other, as well as ourselves and the world we live in. In subtle and significant ways, just the use of e-mail in the workplace has altered the daily working lives of many people, as well as how they relate to each other, which should be immediately obvious to anyone who has seen a misunderstanding via e-mail spiral out of control.

Central to this shift – what Virilio (2001) refers to as a disturbance of people's perception of what reality is – are the principles on which our digital machines operate. These machines express, and embody, very different practices. They are very different forms of doing than those expressive of the industrialized mechanical ensemble. Even activities that on the surface may look quite similar (such as the typewriting versus word-processing example above) in that they involve the same bodily activity, punching keys, are actually very different from one another. As Poster explains,

> [t]he shift from the typewriter keyboard to the computer keyboard is ontological: the former instantiates and reinforces a subject-object. The paper page receives the mechanical blows of the keys as the writer presses on the machine to produce the inked page. The typewriter merely improves the legibility of the page over the hand-manipulated quill, ink pen, or pencil, where one scratches inscriptions into the paper. The computer keyboard, by contrast, sends digital signals to the central processing chip through the word processing program, producing letters on the screen that lack the material properties of the typed paper page. The letters on the screen are fluid, easily changeable and moveable.
>
> (Poster 2002a, 754–5)

Not only that, but with the word processor it is not just that the typing in itself is different. There is also a near-instantaneous access to a host of other files (Poster 2002a, 755). A word processor, in other words, is not simply a more efficient form of the typewriter. This point is strengthened even further when taking into account the use of hypertext and the ways in which information can be linked.

One of the key characteristics of the digital ensemble, compared to other machinic ensembles, lies in its use of energy. While the industrialized mechanical ensemble is by and large characterized by its generation and distribution of energy, the digital ensemble is not engaged in the production of energy at all (Castells 1996; Jameson 1991). In many respects the machines of the digital ensemble are instead engaged in the reproduction of energy. As Jameson pointed out, the machines of the digital ensemble are no longer machines that have anything to do with motion, with kinetic energy, but, rather, are machines that are engaged in 'reproductive processes' (Jameson 1991, 37). More specifically, the machines of the digital ensemble are engaged in 'the action of knowledge upon knowledge itself as the main source of productivity' (Castells 1996, 16–17). As Jameson (1991) pointed out so well, it is for this reason that the machines of the digital ensemble don't have the same capacity for representation as those of the industrialized mechanical ensemble (as, for example, the steam engine or smokestacks do).

One of the key distinguishing characteristics of the practices or the doing expressed by the machines of the digital ensemble, then, is that they are not engaged in motion. There is no mobility. When you post a comment on Twitter, load something up on Tumblr, fly with your avatar in an online game such as *World of Warcraft*, or are engaged in a financial transaction with people on the other side of the globe, you don't actually go anywhere. Yet, at the same time, many have commented that digital machines operate at the 'speed of light' (Harraway 1991; Virilio 2001, 23). This is certainly correct in the sense that the entire digital ensemble is powered by electricity – which, it is worth remembering, is still generated by the machines of the industrialized mechanical ensemble. In any case, at least so Virilio dramatically states, to have achieved this, '[t]o have reached the light barrier, to have reached the speed of light, is a historical event which throws history in disarray and jumbles up the relation of the living being towards the world' (Virilio 2001, 23). It is precisely this 'jumbling up', this reconfiguration of us and our relation or connection with our world, that we need to come to terms with.

This twin process of, on the one hand, having reached the speed of light, while, on the other hand, no longer being engaged in physical motion is often expressed in terms of an annihilation of time and space. In many respects this process of so-called 'annihilation' is a continuation of the same process observed by Marx, who argued that the shortening of the temporal and spatial moment was a product of the development of productive forces, that is, of capitalism (Marx 1973, 533–4). Rather than refer to it as an annihilation, however, it would be much better to argue that the digital ensemble is expressing a sense of time and space very different from that of the industrialized mechanical ensemble (Hansen 2006; Harvey 1989; Soja 1989) – which is not to say that this new sense of time and space is not a product of the continued development of productive forces. What the use of the term 'annihilation' does seem to indicate, as it did when the industrialized mechanical ensemble came into being (Schivelbusch 1986, 10), is that 'we do not yet possess the perceptual equipment to match this new kind of hyperspace [...]' (Jameson 1991, 38–9; Morse 1998).[1]

Just as the use of the machines of the industrialized mechanical ensemble creates its own spatiality (Schivelbusch 1986, 10), so the use of the machines of the digital ensemble are creating theirs. In the first instance, the machines of the digital ensemble, because they have nothing to do with the generation of energy and mobility, make much of the space of the industrialized mechanical ensemble irrelevant. For one thing, digital technologies enable actions to be performed on a truly global, or rather, planetary scale. Geographical location and the distance between locations is, in that sense, at least in the use of digital technologies, made irrelevant. Space, as understood in the industrialized mechanical ensemble, at least in the context of the digital ensemble, ceases to be an issue for human existence (Mansfield 2000, 14).[2]

However, while the machines of the digital ensemble do not produce a space in the same sense as that of the industrialized mechanical ensemble, they do produce a very different sense of space in its stead, though to refer to it as 'space' is not correct (Baudrillard 1994; Chesher 1997, 80; Knorr-Cetina and Preda 2007; Mihalache 2002; Nunes 1997). What is produced instead is often referred to as 'virtual reality', 'cyberspace', or 'hyperspace'. This reality is very different from that produced by the mechanical ensemble. The main reason for this is that in the machines of the digital ensemble what we understand as space and time are collapsed. Space in this context is time (Chesher 1997; Mihalache 2002; Virilio 1991; 2001). In this so-called 'space' there is no sense of depth (Jameson 1991). At most, at least for now, there is the surface of the screen. As Virilio argues, '[w]ith acceleration there is no more here and there, only the mental confusion of near and far, present and future, real and unreal [...]' (Virilio 1995, 35). In short, it is not a space in which one moves from location to location. It is not a space one physically inhabits with one's body. If anything, it is a space that inhabits us rather than us inhabiting it – this is especially so with the advent of nano- and biotechnology (Küchler 2008; Virilio 1995, 99–100).

Instead, the 'spatiality' of the digital ensemble is information (Knorr-Cetina 2007; Nunes 1997). Information has no perspective in the manner that the spatiality of the industrialized mechanical ensemble does. Information is not something one can inhabit nor, for that matter, is it a place one can visit (Nunes 1997) – though a number of authors have certainly tried to conceptualize the spatiality of the digital ensemble as a collection of places (Chesher 1997; Mihalache 2002). This information world is one that, at least for people, exists on screens.[3] Derivatives or foreign exchange traders especially inhabit, or maybe rather, are inhabited by this world. As one trader pointed out in Karin Knorr-Cetina's research (2007, 713), '[w]hat we are really dealing in is information', irrespective of whether that information is a price or a dealing sequence.

Importantly, however, and a key point made by Knorr-Cetina (2003; 2007), is the tendency for many to continue to treat such a world of information as somehow still spatial. When we make use of terms such as 'life-world' or 'life on the screen', we continue to somehow conceptualize these as places.[4] This is problematic because it implies

> that time is something that passes in these spatial environments but is extraneous to the environment itself. We relate the existence of a lifeworld, of an environment, or of everyday reality more to the physical materiality of a spatial world than to any temporal dimension. We also express, one assumes, the durability of the physical world compared with the human lifespan through spatializing concepts. The point is that the screen reality discussed has none of this durability.
>
> (Knorr-Cetina 2003, 16)

Instead the screen reality is not better thought of *as* a process, but *is* a process. Importantly, this is not simply like a flowing river, where a body of water moves from one location to another. Certainly, information 'travels' from node to node, but the network, the infrastructure that enables the production of screen reality as a whole, is of a very different order. Instead, the screen reality '*is processual in the sense of an infinite succession of non-identical matter projecting itself forward as changing screen'* (Knorr-Cetina 2003, 16). To state this more directly, screen reality is flow, it is fluid. While related, this is neither Castells' 'space of flows' (1996; 2005), which involves movement, nor is this the same as Bauman's (2000; 2005) distinction of the fluid and the solid. As Knorr-Cetina (2003, 17) explains, 'the point about the screen reality as a flow is not that it is nomadic (without itinerary) and unmarked by the traces of social and economic structure. The point is the projection and reconstitution of this reality as one that is composite and continually emerging in a piecemeal fashion.'

Traders in that respect act in a temporal context (Knorr-Cetina 2003), not a spatial one as is the case with the worker in industrial mechanical ensemble. This is because the market as a whole continuously changes shape:

> Traders perform their activities in a moving field constituted by changing dealing prices, shifting trading interests (the indicative prices), scrolling records of the immediate past that are continually updated, incoming conversational requests, newly projected market trends, and emerging and disappearing headline news, commentaries and economic analyses. They perform their activities in a streaming, temporal world; as the information scrolls down the screens and is replaced by new information, a new market reality continually projects itself.
>
> (Knorr-Cetina and Preda 2007, 130)

It is for this reason that traders develop specific modes of affectivity that involve intensity and preparedness. As pointed out in Chapter 2, in relation to the character of the objectile and modulation, they engage in an 'informed tracing', which is more about developing 'a feel' for a situation, than about calculating (2007, 132). In short, they develop a very different sensibility without which they couldn't constitute themselves as actors. The trader focuses on the streams or flow lines of information, the actual and ongoing fluctuation, aiming to anticipate something unexpected (Cooper 2010). In short, just as the modulatory mode of power produces objectiles, so do, for example, traders.

Computer games, especially massively multiplayer online role-playing games (MMORPGs) such as *Rift*, *Eve Online*, or *World of Warcraft*, produce a similar screen reality, even if not always perhaps of the same intensity or speed as that experienced by the traders of whom Knorr-Cetina writes. In the first instance, computer games similarly produce a temporal world of ongoing streaming information, which makes the design of the interface, in terms of what appears on the screen, a key issue. However, while many games can be paused, online games can't. Indeed, with many computer games, as Galloway makes the point, you can simply walk away and they will revert to an ambient state, or what Galloway (2006) refers to as an ambient act. In these periods, things continue to change on the screen ('within' the game world so to speak), 'but nothing changes that is of any importance' (2006, 10). Galloway explains that in these moments the machine is in a state of 'pure process', because it continues to function while the operator is away, producing effects on the screen, even if they are inconsequential to the game. In effect, there is an inversion of the pause function, where it isn't the program that is paused, but the operator or participant that is paused (Galloway 2006) until they return to provide instructions (that is, a flow of code) so that they become part of and participate in the process once again.

Significantly, participants in the market (such as traders) are disembedded, or rather, are embedded differently from the worker in, for example, a factory. Knorr-Cetina (2003, 19) argues that the market participants form a 'community of time' because these participants are oriented more toward each other across time zones, than to their local environment. As she points out, even when the market, which operates on the television channel GMT, has moved out of their own time zone, they still remain engaged with it via their televisions, and whatever other media streams they are connected to, including through conversations they maintain with traders in the other time zones. This, incidentally, is very similar to MMORPG players, many of whom will remain in 'touch' with what happens in the MMORPG, which operates on a global server time, even when they are disconnected from the game, or rather, 'paused'. This they do through applications on the smart-phone, like *World of Warcraft's* armory, online discussion boards, or even through producing and sharing remixed content with other players from around the globe through media like YouTube. The MMORPG, like the market, continues to operate and produce code when the participant has left, and, just like the market, code continues to be generated about the game. The communities these players form are likewise communities of time in which players may have invested more than in many of their communities of space, and they will often structure their lives around the server time of the game, and thereby also around the actual pattern of flow that is the game in general.[5]

The screen reality's flow isn't simply composed of one flow. With traders, this is most obviously reflected in the fact that they observe multiple screens at once. Indeed, beyond that there are the conversations people have via a variety of other screens and windows, including on social media such as Twitter or Facebook, or indeed, simply e-mail. There is, therefore, a multitude of flows, each of which might produce quite different affects, often dependent on the intensity and speed of the flow, keeping in mind that flows don't move (a point I will return to in Part III). The multiple-dealing conversations that traders therefore engage in, for example, through text, are an additional flow that is maintained. They can span seconds, or days, but generally are quite complex (Knorr-Cetina 2007), and are shorter in form than text messages on a mobile phone. Indeed, in the context of the market, the term 'liquidity' refers to 'the ease of obtaining and circulating relevant information and of keeping the relevant information alive in a constantly changing market that scrolls down the screen' (Knorr-Cetina 2007), that is, the general ease of traders making a deal, which, depending on the type of market, can be at a high speed indeed. Importantly, also, these are conversations in which trust and reputation are paramount.

Similarly, in games like *Rift* or *World of Warcraft*, when players form what is called a raid group, which in some games can include up to 40 people who have to cooperate with each other, engaging in a boss-fight is often an intense experience where the speed of events, the rate of change in information displayed on the screen, requires complex information to be relayed in very short periods of time. Such raids often require specific types of character (for example, healers in a raid) to maintain at the same time their own conversations with each other, as well as with the leader of a raid and/or the raid's so-called tanks, which perform a very different role. Often, in the background, players will also be connected via voice communication software such as Ventrilo with other people in the raid as well as people not in the raid. Effectively participating in such multiple-screen realities (that is, acting within this context) requires a very specific sensibility to that environment, to the flows on the screen(s). These flows can therefore also be constituted by recognizing the emergence of a pattern on the screen (for example, a 'boss' (a non-player character)) initiating a specific sequence of spells, or additional 'mini-bosses' entering somewhere else on the screen. Those new to this specific screen reality, at least in the context of online games, are easily recognized as 'noobs', even if they illegally purchase a high-level character that might hide this fact. Just as with the screen reality of traders, trust and reputation are of paramount importance and people can find themselves put onto 'ignore' lists fairly rapidly if trust has been breached.

Of course, the examples from the screen reality of traders and gamers are some of the more obvious ones to point to. This is in part because these are instances where the interface with digital machines, and in particular with the screen, produces the most intense affects. However, this screen reality manifests itself in different intensities and speeds. It manifests itself in the conversations that people have with each other on social media like *Facebook*, for example, where conversations between individuals and groups on specific topics can last seconds, days, weeks, or months, often with long periods of inactivity, where the rate of flow is low. At the same time this screen reality is also composed of other flows, whether this be on the same screen or on other screens, including the screens of mobile phones or television screens, especially where they are digital. In that respect, there is a more general screen reality, or 'image-world' (Morse 1998) that flows, even if it is not necessarily of the same intensity and speed as that of a derivatives trader or a gamer in an online raid. Of course, that affect is also dependent on the user or participant in the flow. In short, it is a question of the overall human-machine assemblage produced by the connection. It is not solely a function of the program or the design of the interactive system, which is only a function of the components within the assemblage after all. It is the specific connection that produces specific flows.

Connection, or what some refer to as 'connectedness' is, of course, paramount in the digital ensemble. With its capacity for convergence and symbiosis, which is partly a function of the language with which digital machines operate, and partly a function of the protocols and rules people put in place, the digital ensemble as a whole can in some respects be considered to be a giant connecting machine.[6] Principally this happens because the digital ensemble constitutes the world, its world, as information, as flow. Without flow, without connections, there is no life in the digital ensemble. Money, for example (certainly when we look at the way global financial markets operate), isn't 'anchored in some fundamental, underlying value' (Cooper 2010, 178; Smith 2011). Indeed, it is the very opposite of this. It is 'a sequence of transitory values, a signifier whose value decays and must be continually supported and reproduced in order for it to retain worth' (Knorr-Cetina 2007, 711–12). More to the point, money has to flow, and it is precisely in this flow that its value is produced. As Cooper points out in relation to derivatives trading, referring to the work of Bryan and Rafferty (2006; 2007), 'what derivatives trade in...is the very contestability of fundamental value' (2010, 178).

Indeed, in the digital ensemble it isn't simply money that circulates, which it also obviously did in the industrialized mechanical ensemble, but information that circulates, or rather, flows. Information in the digital ensemble is flow. It is, as Dillon and Lobo-Guerrero state, liquefied, the prerequisite for which was precisely 'the reduction of language to communication and the differential operation of the "sign"' (2009, 11). With the further cybernetic reduction of communication to 'systems of information exchange' (11–12), information subsequently came to be reduced to code – the binary code of digital machines, and the genetic code of biological machines, which ultimately form part of the same continuum that is information. As they argue, circulating bodies 'simply' come to be 'bodies-in-formation' (Dillon and Lobo-Guerrero 2009, 12). In such a context '[f]reedom becomes the freedom simply to be in circulation' (2009, 12), or rather, freedom is the freedom to flow, as well as circulate.

It is for this reason that connectivity, which increases the chance for symbiosis, and hence new connections and increased complexity, becomes of extreme importance:

> The more things circulate the more they become associated. The more they become associated the more they become connected. In the process, the more connectivity can be understood and organized in novel ways.
>
> (Dillon and Lobo-Guerrero 2009, 13)

Facebook is nothing less than the embodiment of this. Where Foucault saw the Bentham brothers' Panopticon as 'the architectural figure of the disciplinary society' (1979, 200), perhaps we can now see Facebook as the architectural figure of Deleuze's control society.

It is at this point, at least from the perspective of operating within the industrialized mechanical ensemble, that things become very confusing. They become confusing because space, at least the perspectival space produced by the industrialized mechanical ensemble, functions by way of the difference between near and far, the difference between here and there. Such distinctions, such differences, do not make sense in the simulated spatiality of the digital ensemble. Stated in a more careful manner, such differences are placed in constant doubt, which, as Baudrillard (1994, 3) explained, is precisely the effect of any simulation.

Importantly, though, on this point we shouldn't make Baudrillard's mistake of confusing a simulation with a simulacrum – for Baudrillard these are one and the same. As Deleuze (2004) argued, however, as part of rejecting a representational approach to understanding existence more generally, unlike a simulation 'simulacra do not refer to anything behind or beyond the world – they make up the world' (Roffe 2005, 250).

Simulacra in that respect are not copies that stand in for some thing that is not present. Instead they have their own positive power, which 'can produce identities from within the world, and without reference to a model, by entering into concrete relations' (Roffe 2005, 251).

In the 'spatiality' of the digital ensemble, then, it is not so much that there is neither here nor there but, rather, that there is both here and there at the same time. It is a world, a screen reality, where 'metric distances are abolished in favor of sensitivities at a distance and collapsible horizons' (Cooper 2010, 179–80). In that respect the digital ensemble can be understood as the latest expression and product of the productive forces of capital, as it reduces the spatial moment of circulation to zero, circulation being at capitalism's core.

> The continual movement in circuits of the two antithetical metamorphoses of commodities, or the never ceasing alternation of sale and purchase, is reflected in the restless currency of money, or in the function that money performs of a perpetuum mobile of circulation. But so soon as the series of metamorphoses is interrupted, so soon as sales are not supplemented by subsequent purchases, money ceases to be mobilized; it is transformed, as Boisguillebert says, from 'meuble' into 'immeuble', from movable into immovable, from coin into money.
>
> (Marx 2007, 146)

Except that in the digital ensemble money doesn't move, even if it has high speed. In the digital ensemble it doesn't circulate, but it flows.

Within the context of the digital ensemble the site of production and circulation, then, are now one and the same (Hardt and Negri 2001, 298). We can be producers and consumers, and be so at the same time, enabling our digital 'products' – information – to be instantly on the marketplace that is the World Wide Web. However, while the spatial moment of circulation, at least as one understands this from the perspective of the spatiality of the industrialized mechanical ensemble, is not an issue in the digital ensemble, the temporal moment becomes extremely significant (Castells 1996). Indeed, it is in that sense that one can state that time and space are collapsed in the 'spatiality' produced by the digital ensemble (Cooper 2010, 179–80; Harvey 1989, 284) – though, again, a better term might be the 'temporality' of the digital ensemble. At least this seems to get away from the spatial connotations of which terms like 'cyberspace' or 'hyperspace' suffer.[7]

It is in the context of trying to get away from the spatial and visual connotations in conceptualizing – what is called 'cyberspace' or 'virtual reality' – that Deleuze's definition of the virtual is significant (Deleuze 1989). As Bogard explains, the term 'virtual reality' is something of an oxymoron from a Deleuzian point of view. According to Deleuze, the virtual and the real are not opposed to one another, as 'the virtual is what is *immediately actual*' (Bogard 1996, 14). In other words,

[v]irtual (simulated) images are not 'possible' images at all, in the sense of events that could exist 'in reality', but do not yet do so. Rather, the virtual is what is *already* actual (for example, in the same way the image on your television screen is already an actual image, not merely a possible one, that is, one that somehow could become real). This, again, is why the virtual is not part of the order of visual representation. For Deleuze, the relevant distinction involves an 'indiscernible' or imperceptible ... gap between a 'passing present' (the actual) and a 'past as preserved' (the virtual). The virtual here takes the general form of the past, as that which is always already over and fixed, and which organizes the passage of time as a kind of 'repetition in advance' ... In science fiction terms, the passing present, the actual appears as simulation, and the past as preserved (recorded, encoded, filed), the virtual, appears as immediately and fully actual.

(Bogard 1996, 14–15)

A more general perceived collapse of binary distinctions, or differences, is a general feature of the virtuality of the digital ensemble (Chesher 1997; Der Derian 2009; Dibbell 1994; Stone 2001). A wide range of authors believe that the distinctions between present/future, real/unreal, here/there, time/space, original/copy, medium/message, style/content, subject/object are considered to be in doubt in the digital ensemble (Baudrillard 1994; Der Derian 2009; Giese 1998; Harraway 1995; Mihalache 2002; Poster 1995; STG 2001; Stone 2001). One key distinction that collapses in the digital ensemble, and a central concern in much theorizing about the effects of digital technologies, is that between signifier and signified. Stated differently, digital technologies and the binary logic on which they operate are an essential component in the production of a very different understanding of knowledge (Chesher 1997; Lyotard 1984; Smith 1986), which seems to be a key factor in the perceived collapse of the binary distinctions. As Chesher explains,

[d]igital encoding frees signs from a dependence on the medium of transmission, and is another critical feature of the ontology of

digital domains. The distinction between digital and analogue representation is philosophical before it is technical. An analogue code represents what it signifies by establishing a relationship of parallel degree... The signal is analogous to what it is representing. On the other hand, a digital representation is based on a code which is originally arbitrary. Digital codes are also based on a grid, making all possible configurations finite. Where analogue involves a conversion of form, digital always involves coding and decoding.

(Chesher 1997, 86)

The effect of this is that whereas analog representation can always be traced back to what it represents, with digital encoding this can't be done, because all digital signs are made of the same stuff, everything is potentially interchangeable (Chesher 1997, 87).[8]

Knowledge, in that respect, is no longer produced with the possibility of objectivity, as it is with print (Poster 2001b; Smith 1986, 161), which is the primary unit of knowledge in the industrialized mechanical ensemble. Instead, the primary unit of knowledge in the digital ensemble is the bit, which means that '[t]here exists no longer a line of validation back to a pure text' (Smith 1986, 161). Digital photography, for example, has led to questions being asked about the verifiability of images in areas like journalism and documentary photography. For one thing, digital images can be much more easily manipulated than previously, which has produced a number of scandals around the notion of photographic truth (Newton 2007). Indeed, perhaps more importantly, digital images have also moved photography away from its 'has been' effect, enabling the images to stay 'alive' for longer because software such as GIMP or Photoshop, as well as the increased number of users, expands the creative possibilities of existing images, enabling easy manipulation of the information on the screen on an ongoing basis (Sturken and Cartwright 2009, 214). A digital image is, in that respect, more open rather than closed.

One of the effects of this, which is amplified by the easy reproduction of digital information, is that the key distinctions on which the industrialized mechanical ensemble operates, between author and text, word and deed, actor and action, and presence and absence, are no longer tenable within the context of the digital ensemble (Dibbell 1994; Hayles 1993b; Poster 1990; Smith 1986; Turkle 1995). These are differences that in some respects attain the status of a simulation, resulting in what can be understood to be a general 'smoothing over' or dissolution of difference.

This general smoothing over of difference by or within the digital ensemble is also expressed in terms of processes of production. The industrialized mechanical ensemble operates by way of a high degree of functional differentiation. This functional differentiation is expressed by each individual machine, the space it occupies, and the organization of that space. This is not the case with the machines of the digital ensemble, such as the digital computer. The digital computer is now 'the universal tool, through which all activities must pass' (Hardt and Negri 2001, 292). Negroponte makes this point even more strongly, arguing that '[c]omputing is not about computers any more. It is about living' (Negroponte 1995, 6).

Here, again, the difference between typewriting and word-processing is illustrative (Poster 2002a, 754–5). Only one specific function can be performed with the typewriter, whereas the word processor integrates a whole range of activities, a point that is further underscored when we take into account the effect of being connected to various networks. Smart-phones especially are illustrative of this. Here we have a device that is barely recognizable by its original function: phoning people. Instead, people use it to play games, including with each other, as a navigation system in their car, a diary, to surf the web, listen to music, check their e-mail, even, in the case of software such as Soundhound, to inform people what the name of a song is that they might hear being played on their analog radio. Indeed, the smart-phone is a device that functions much like the tricorder in the *Star Trek* series, especially when you can use it, for example, through Google's Goggles, to help you identify artwork, buildings, or indeed, plants (a future aim of Google's) by simply pointing the camera lens at it. The entire world, in that respect, is reduced to binary code, and whatever isn't encoded is simply non-existent until, in the case of Goggles, the user or participant uploads it to the database as part of what is a wider crowdsourcing process.

The smoothing over of difference can also be observed in terms of the ways that production, circulation, and consumption are organized in the digital ensemble. Indeed, even existing spaces such as the factories of the industrialized ensemble are reorganized. Most significantly, production and distribution have now become, and at an ever-increasing rate, deterritorialized, so that what previously were mass factories are now widely dispersed across the globe (Castells 1996; Hardt and Negri 2001). Production and distribution, in other words, are increasingly decentralized, resulting in a very different organization of the spaces that were part of the industrialized mechanical ensemble. It is in this context that the network, conceived of as horizontal, is argued to be the organizational form of the digital ensemble in terms of the organization of production, especially relations of production, and of the State (Castells 1996; Frissen 1997; Hardt and Negri 2001; Ronfeldt and Arquilla 2001). Though we need to be mindful not to confuse this network infrastructure with the screen reality, even though it is obviously instrumental to that screen reality (Knorr-Cetina and Preda 2007).

It should also be emphasized that the digital ensemble is in no way 'post-industrial' (Jameson 1991).[9] In many respects the industrialized mechanical ensemble supports the digital ensemble. Electricity still needs to be produced. Computers, mobile phones, and other material products still need to be made by the machines of the industrialized mechanical ensemble. This is not to say, as was pointed out above, that the digital ensemble has not transformed this production, as well as the spaces of that production (Castells 1996; Hardt and Negri 2001). As Hardt and Negri make clear, the transition to what they call informational production and the network structure of organization simply make efficiency of production no longer as reliant on place, proximity, and centralization as was the case in the industrialized mechanical ensemble (Hardt and Negri 2001, 295).

In many respects, then, a crucial effect of the institutionalization of the digital ensemble is that, besides transforming and reorganizing the existing spaces of the industrialized mechanical ensemble, it aims to constitute a totally smooth space. This is partly related to the 'standard of pure liquidity' that authors such as Dillon and Lobo-Guerrero write of. At the very least, that is what the digital ensemble, as a productive force of capitalism, aims toward. Whereas the space of the industrialized mechanical ensemble is a highly fragmented space, organized according to the differentiation of function, the digital ensemble is temporality, and aims for smoothness, aims for flow. This smoothness is powerfully illustrated by the differences between global financial capital (Deleuze's gaseous corporation (1992) with its high degree of fluidity) and industrial capital, which is far more connected to place (Castells 1996; Ikegami 1999, 890).

This sense of smoothness is also expressed by one of the digital ensemble's most expressive technologies – the interface. The interface, more so than the computer or the network, expresses the collapsing of boundaries. This is precisely its aim. It expresses the regulation of the relation of difference between the spatiality of the industrialized mechanical ensemble and the temporality of the digital ensemble. It also manifests the regulation of difference between the different machines of the digital ensemble, which often operate at different speeds and often use different codes. Indeed, the interface's sole function is to regulate difference. This may be difference in languages and/or difference in speed. Alternatively, it may be differences between the various assemblages of the digital ensemble and/or the various assemblages of the industrialized ensemble.

Consider, for example, the simple experience of working with a computer mouse that is dirty, a badly functioning keyboard, a faulty connection between printer and computer, or indeed, the experience of 'lag' in an online computer game. Such instances are generally experienced as moments of frustration, as moments that interrupt an otherwise smooth experience. They are moments that in a very real sense interrupt (the production and experience of) flow of information. In each of those instances the participant becomes acutely aware of the importance of the interface and its importance in smoothing over difference. Producing smoothness through the regulation of difference is therefore crucial to the interface. As Poster points out, 'interfaces are the sensitive boundary zone of negotiation between the human and the machinic as well as the pivot of an emerging new set of human/machine relations' (Poster 1995, 20–1). Our interfaces very much form our second skin in our actions in the digital ensemble, and through this skin we come to sense new differences, including lag, that is measured in milliseconds. And while this lag may seem inconsequential, in the flow of information it can make enormous differences because it directly concerns the rate of flow.[10]

The digital ensemble, then, constructs a spatial and temporal experience very different from that of the industrialized digital ensemble. It constitutes flow. This point is critical in the question concerning the constitution of self, or rather, the construction of a sense of unicity in the context of the digital ensemble. As Harvey makes clear,

> [i]f spatial and temporal experiences are primary vehicles for the coding and reproduction of social relations (as Bourdieu suggests), then a change in the way the former get represented will almost certainly generate some kind of shift in the latter.
>
> (Harvey 1989, 247)

The machines of the digital ensemble express or enable entirely different ways of doing from those of the industrialized mechanical ensemble. These new machines, indeed all machines, are who we are. One of the key differences, however, seems to be that in the digital ensemble '[t]he machine is placed under the control of subjectivity – not a reterritorialized human subjectivity, but a new kind of machinic subjectivity' (Guattari 1992, 22). This point is reiterated by, amongst others, Castells when he states that '[f]or the first time in history, the human mind is a direct productive force, not just a decisive element of the production system' (Castells 1996, 32).[11]

Where in the industrialized mechanical ensemble one is often very much subjected to the machines of which one forms a component, in the sense that many of the mechanical machines severely limit a subject's capacity for action, in the digital ensemble machines constitute the very possibility of existence and action – no digital machine, no flow. This requires an understanding of existence and action the limits of which are being reconfigured quite radically, especially when compared to that of the industrialized mechanical ensemble (Hansen 2006; Hayles 2009; Mansfield 2000, 149; Virilio 2001, 24). As Wark (2007) states, there is a new relation between the analog and the digital that is 'a change in being itself'.

Digital being

> Your appearance now is what we call 'residual self image'. It is the mental projection … of your digital self.
>
> (Wachowski and Wachowski 1999)

A key issue in interfacing with the machines of the digital ensemble is that one is dealing with machines very different from those of the industrialized mechanical ensemble. Central to this difference, as Guattari points out, is that, as machines of information and communication, they 'operate at the heart of human subjectivity, not only within its memory and intelligence, but within its sensibility, affects and unconscious fantasms' (Guattari 1995, 4). Indeed, the machines of the digital ensemble configure the information exchange in a very specific manner (Poster 1990). Connecting to such machines by way of, for example, the screen 'involves a state change from the physical, biological space of the embodied viewer to the symbolic, metaphorical "consensual hallucination of cyberspace"' (Stone 2001, 193). It is in this context that the interface's first function is to enable this connection while its second function is to allow for the construction of an assemblage that functions as one unit. This is a process that

> is often experienced as a seamless loop of input and output, inscription and invocation, where users have a tangible sense of presence

and engagement. As long as the system is working, users typing on a word processor or playing video games barely notice the detour through the digital domain.

(Bogard 1996, 84–5)

The effect of the interface, however, is not simply to eliminate the user's awareness of both the interface itself and the machine one is connected to. It also functions to eliminate the awareness of oneself as an embodied entity (Bogard 1996, 72; Stone 2001, 193). The moment one connects to the machine, one begins to recognize that 'the boundaries of self are defined less by the skin than by the feedback loops connecting the body and simulation in a techno-bio-integrated circuit' (Hayles 1993b, 72). At the moment of interface a human-machine assemblage is constituted in which the body, in some respects, ceases to function as a defining limit of one's existence (Harraway 1995, xvii).[12] The body, literally, has no place here because, quite simply, there is no 'here' in the virtuality produced through digital technologies. If anything, the body, comes to be perceived as an interruption to one's ability to act when connected to the flow/s.

That the body is perceived as an interruption to flow is well illustrated by the use of the term 'bio' in online games. Whenever human players are grouped and one member has to go to the toilet to produce a very different flow, they type or say the word 'bio'. This indicates to the group that someone is leaving their keyboard for a period, thereby interrupting the flow of the game. This is typically done in moments where the group can proceed without that person for a short term, though generally the whole group will stop. More accurately, they will effectively be paused and, like some games do (Galloway 2006, 10), be themselves turned to an ambient state and become the ambient act noted above, until the player returns and reconnects so that the flow/s of information can once again commence, and smoothness of being can once again be experienced.

As emphasized above, there is no space in the digital ensemble. So when one connects to digital machines, the body ceases to function as a marker of an inside, which is me, and an outside, which is other than me:

The absence that is at stake in virtual systems is not only that of the machine, but of the operator too (the person in this space, at this time, plugged into this machine). The technology that disappears is the whole human-machine connection, which gives way to the disembodied traveller, that astral projectionist, the 'interface, data cowboy' in cyberspace. The goal is the complete, total elimination of the gap between the real and the illusion, the grandest, highest of illusions, really, which literally eliminates illusion and transports one to a radically other (but radically same!) place and time. Here or there? Me, or someone, something else? In the imaginary of cyberspace it's a matter of complete indifference.

(Bogard 1996, 37)

The elimination of the perception of the physical body, or the 'perception of one's gravimetric mass' (Virilio 1995, 106), and with it the crucial distinction between inside and outside, me and not me, effectively means that the body is no longer a strong constitutive factor in the production of subjectivity (Poster 2001a, 17). Indeed, as noted previously, such an idea of the body has perhaps always been a fiction in any case (Cohen 2008; 2009).

The body, then, doesn't function to generate a sense of either being a space – as it did in the industrialized mechanical ensemble (Kirby 1996) – or of physically inhabiting a space. There is no sense of physical mobility that is generated by the body. You don't move from one place to another in the context of existing within the virtuality of the digital ensemble. Indeed, with the temporality of the digital ensemble you are never anywhere, yet always everywhere: 'a disembodied subjectivity messes with whereness' (Stone 1995, 399). In the context of the digital ensemble, then, it is not a question of where you are or in what space you are situated. Rather, it is a question of when and how you are (Virilio 1995, 155). One exists as immediately actual, and therefore exists as a temporal event, rather than as a spatial entity, as is the case with the industrialized mechanical ensemble. In short, in the digital one exists as code. One manifests oneself, and exists, as the flow/s of information on the screen. One exists as flow/s.

Action must therefore also take on a very specific character in such a context. Actions in the digital ensemble are not performed by actors in a space but, just like the actor, are temporal. This means that one cannot distinguish between the actor and the action. Action and actor are literally one and the same thing, or rather, one and the same moment. In that respect, in more than one sense of the word, one is pure performance, pure process. In the digital ensemble the action is the actor and the actor only exists, or rather, occurs, when the action is performed. The interface, with its elimination of the perception of the physical body, also eliminates the conceptual distinction between being and doing (Stone 1995; Virilio 1995, 106–7). Not only that, but the elimination of the perception of the body means that actions, and therefore actors, cannot necessarily be tied to a specific physical body. A specific form of existence can only be associated with, or as, a specific pattern within a stream of code in this context, but there is no specific unity of entity as such. In other words, there is no body that functions to tie or anchor the multiplicity of code to a specific subject. The subject, in other words (and 'subject', as I indicated previously, becomes a questionable concept in the context of the temporality of the digital ensemble more broadly), 'is open to, even dispersed amongst, an endlessly proliferating number of information streams' (Mansfield 2000, 155).

This mode of being is of a formless and indeterminate character. It is precisely for this reason that it needs to be conceptualized as being fluid (Shaviro 2003), that is, of the character of a flow. Indeed, the different relation that is constituted with digital machines, the different human-machine assemblage we constitute in the connection, Guattari's 'new kind of machinic subjectivity' (1992), is expressed in the production of a very different sense of time, or temporality as well. Hansen makes this point when he explains that

> [p]recisely because of its minimalness, its inscription of nothing more than the simple before-after that is common to all concrete processes of temporalization, the digital inscription of time possesses and retains a certain generality, a commonness, an *availability for divergent deployments* that, I submit, differentiates it markedly from all narrowly mediatic subsumptions of time.
>
> (Hansen 2009, 302; emphasis added)

Indeed, Hansen terms this the 'gift' of digital time. That is, it has an 'openness' with respect to temporality that other media don't have. The machines of the digital ensemble, including in their totality, produce a different 'unconscious' of time (Hansen 2009, 301). Unlike the machines of the industrial mechanical ensemble, like the television and radio, the use of digital devices 'is not predetermined in a near totalitarian fashion by the content they would channel' (Hansen 2009, 302). It is that which, for Hansen, preserves 'an openness to the alterity of time, to time as the power of alterity, to speak with Emmanuel Levinas'. More broadly, digital media enable the body 'to enframe something (digital information) that is originally formless' (Hansen 2004, 11). However, care needs to be taken here (Clough 2008), because while information might be formless (that is, a flow), this does not mean that the flows of information are somehow not human or pre-human, or that the human stands somehow separate from the machine and, more broadly, from the flow/s of information.

If we recognize the character of existence within the context of the digital ensemble to be flow/s, then it is perhaps also possible to treat Leibniz's monad as a valid description of being in the digital, as some have suggested. Monads, as Heim explains, 'have no windows, but they do have terminals. The mental life of the monad – and the monad has no other life – is a procession of internal representations' (Heim 2001, 79). Indeed, each monad mirrors the whole world to itself, though, crucially, this process is mediated by the monad's own appetites and mental activity. Each monad, as Heim (2001) explains, runs its own software. Each monad, in other words, is its own world. In addition, '[s]ince each unit represents everything, each unit contains all the other units, containing them as represented. No direct physical contact passes between the willful mental units. Monads never meet face-to-face' (Heim 2001, 80).[13]

One of the crucial characteristics of existence, as it is produced in the digital ensemble, then, is what Virilio describes as a loss of orientation – he laments, '[a] total loss of the bearings of the individual looms large' (Virilio 2001, 24). Such a loss of orientation, though, is only experienced as a loss from the perspective of industrialized mechanical being and ignores what digitization produces in a more positive sense – at the very least in the sense of how it alters the human-machine assemblage's *potentia*. In some respects, this is also expressed in the different production of multiplicity when comparing the machines of the digital ensemble with those of the industrialized mechanical ensemble.

As Turkle pointed out some years ago, one's existence in the digital ensemble is characterized by a potentially extreme degree of multiplicity (Turkle 1995). In the first instance, this can observed by the multitude of flows people are engaged in and participants of, such as the traders mentioned by Knorr-Cetina (2007). This multiplicity is not only characterized by the fact that it is very much dispersed, mainly because there is no body to directly relate or connect the identities to, but also by the fact that it is momentary. As Virilio points out, in the digital one only exists 'here and now' (2001, 24). Identity, at least as this is understood in the mechanical ensemble, becomes difficult to maintain and is not so much identified by its body, but rather, through the recognition and writing of specific patterns of code.

Of course, as argued above, multiplicity is also a characteristic of existence in the industrialized mechanical ensemble. The multiplicity characteristic of existence in the industrialized mechanical ensemble, however, is a product of existing in a number of different spaces, each with their own specific function. One's existence in the industrialized mechanical ensemble therefore takes on the character of being a fragmented whole. Further, because one cannot exist in more than one space at the same time, this fragmentation is also of a discontinuous character. That is, one can, or rather should, only exhibit any one specific subject formation or identity at any one time. Exhibiting more than one subject formation at any one time in the one space can be very problematic. In that respect, subjectivity, in the form of the individual, can be understood to reflect an ongoing attempt to unify these separately existing fragments by way of integrating them.

In the context of the digital ensemble, however, existence is not spatial but temporal. One does not physically move from space to space, each time connecting to different machinic components such as the classroom, the hospital, or the factory floor (Deleuze 1992, 5), as one does in the industrialized mechanical ensemble. Instead, one's existence is fluid, in the sense that it has no form, it is flow. Consequently, it is difficult to determine whether one is constituted of one flow or many flows, which is why so far I have at times referred to it as 'flow/s'. Existence in the digital ensemble can be a combination of many different flows at the same time, at different speeds, and therefore also different times, or different temporalities at the same moment. The temporality or intensity experienced in a 25-person raid at the end of a boss-fight, is a very different temporality or intensity experienced from having a Facebook conversation, even if you might be engaged in both at the same time. Of course, on a larger scale, as Deleuze and others have pointed out, one's education never ceases (Deleuze 1992, 5). One is also potentially always at work (Deleuze 1992, 5), regardless of the geographical location in which one is situated (Poster 2002b).[14] Another example is offered by Turkle, who argues that we can have a presence through many functionally different windows on our screens at the same time (Turkle 1995, 13).[15]

The multiplicity that characterizes existence in the digital ensemble, then, is dispersed, simultaneous, instantaneous, and continuous. It is dispersed in that it can be composed of many different flows. It is simultaneous and instantaneous because any number of flows can be accessed and constituted at any one time in any one location. It is continuous, first because none of these flows have a beginning or an end, and second, because one can swap or move with ease, with smoothness, from one flow to another, which in turn makes it difficult to clearly distinguish between the diversity of flows being accessed or participated in at any one time. In other words, whereas in the industrialized digital ensemble one always has to disconnect from one assemblage – the newspaper, the school – and go to another assemblage – the factory, the television, or the home – in the digital ensemble it is difficult to distinguish these various assemblages. This is a process in which interfaces play a crucial role. Indeed, in the digital ensemble the very thought of disconnection is a threat to one's capacity for being or action. Any technologies that enhance both the degree and scope of connection to the digital ensemble, and therefore the capacity to flow, are strongly pursued, whether they be in the form of increasing central processing unit (CPU) speed, increasing network bandwidth, increasing random access memory (RAM), adding Wireless Application Protocol (WAP) to a home or city, or extending mobile coverage.[16]

To describe the character of existence in the digital ensemble as manifesting an essence, such as that of a subjectivity composed of a different or more extreme form of multiplicity, is problematic though. To describe it as having a multiplicity suggests that it is a composition, and somehow constitutes a larger unity. To use language suggesting the existence of such a unity, essence, or the possibility thereof, is not appropriate in this context, albeit difficult to avoid. So, just as the object of the industrialized mechanical ensemble is transformed into the objectile in the digital ensemble, so one can also conceptualize a transformation of the subject to the superject (Deleuze 1993, 19–20; Jameson 1991).

The superject is comparable to the monad described earlier, as it exists temporally, is formless, and constitutes its own world. The superject, in other words, is not an essence but an event (Deleuze 1993). It operates with, or exists, by way of a very different sense of perspective, or rather, a different perception or sensibility from the subject, that is, the individual of the industrialized mechanical ensemble. Deleuze explains this in relation to Baroque perspective:

> The point of view is not what varies with the subject, at least in the first instance; it is, to the contrary, the condition in which an eventual subject apprehends a variation (metamorphosis), or: something = X (anamorphosis)... It is not a variation of truth according to the subject, but the condition in which the truth of a variation appears to the subject.
>
> (Deleuze 1993, 20)

This explanation is also useful in describing one of the key changes in the act of interfacing with the digital ensemble. This is the switch from spatial existence to temporal or digital existence, which swaps 'the system of a window and a world outside [with] one of a computer screen in a closed room' (Deleuze 1995, 157–8). In the former, one exists spatially, or visually, and in a world with depth, altering one's point of view by altering one's position in relation to the object being examined. In the latter, existence is temporal, or a projection, and altering a 'point of view', or rather its simulation, is a function of changing the world rather than one's position in it. Indeed, the superject does not have a relation to an object in the manner that the subject has. A distinction between subject and object does not exist, and to the extent that such a distinction might be simulated or even a simulacra, this is a function of the superject. This new form of existence, or being, is the product or expression of the digital ensemble, and a key assemblage in its constitution is the interface. The more complete the interface is, the more the distinction between human and machine is eliminated, and the more the superject, as the state of being of the digital ensemble, is expressed.[17]

The existence of the superject as flow/s can be illustrated, albeit limitedly, as a snapshot, where the rectangle represents not the unity of the superject or digital form of existence, but constitutes both a limiting and enabling factor in the form of the digital ensemble. In other words, it represents its corporality in the form of its material machinic components, whether these be the screen, online camera, mobile phone, or speed of connection to the assemblage (see Figure 5.1).

Unlike the individual, the superject cannot be represented in a linear and compartmentalized manner, in which, ideally, one can only exhibit one form of identity at any given time and place. Instead, existence in the context of the digital ensemble is flow/s, which gives the impression that the individual has somehow dissolved and selfhood has come to an end (Virilio 1995).

Crucially, at least for now, superjects do not flow for long periods of time. As Shaviro (2003, 140) suggests, becoming flow is a dangerous pleasure. A pleasure that has resulted in some people's deaths (Simkin 2003); there are numerous examples of this in South Korea especially, most notably through gaming addiction (Cook 2009). Further, those

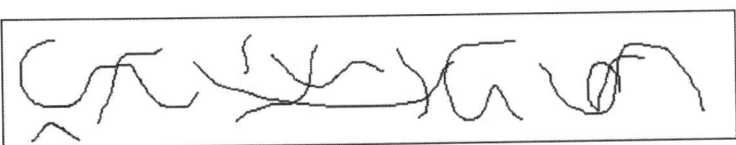

Figure 5.1   The superject

people who are intricately interfaced with various digital assemblages are not disembodied, even though they may be able to bracket their physical presence for some periods (Heim 2001). As Stone points out, '[n]o matter how virtual the subject may become, there is always a body attached' (Stone 2001, 195). From this point of view, what has occurred so far in the formation of the digital ensemble is a further splitting of the body and the subject (Stone 2001, 187; Virilio 1995). Consciousness, then, is still 'firmly rooted in the physical' (Stone 2001, 195).

From this perspective, subjectivity operates on or by way of at least two levels. On one level, the digital ensemble enables us to become superjects, or flow/s. To flow is to be 'free'. This is the very opposite of the individual whose desire, and need, for integration leads it to seek a specific and single form. However, on another level, the spatiality of the industrialized mechanical ensemble, even when transformed by the technologies of the digital ensemble, enables and requires us to constitute ourselves as individuals, with a specific capacity for mobility and action. There is, then, a twin process in operation in the constitution of subjectivity in the digital ensemble at its current state of development. A desire, and requirement, to constitute oneself as a form – the individual – is combined with and functions alongside a desire, and requirement, to constitute oneself as formless, or to dissolve oneself, to become flow/s. It is this tension, or antagonism, that is at the center of dividuality (see Figure 5.2), which was also explored in the context of the database in Part I. The notion of antagonism in this context should not necessarily be understood as reflecting a contradiction, in that the dividual cannot be two things at once, but instead reflects an inability to be any thing (Valentine 2000, 31).[18]

Finally, whereas disconnection from the machine constitutes something of a release from an otherwise limited form of existence in the

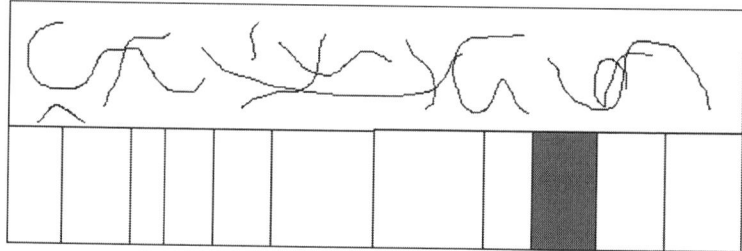

Figure 5.2   Dividuality

industrialized mechanical ensemble, in the digital ensemble disconnection is, literally, death for digital being. Being connected to the digital machinic assemblage constitutes the very possibility for digital existence. From this perspective, any form of disconnection, any possible interruption to one's connection to the machine, whether it be a power failure or a disconnection from the server, is detrimental to one's capacity for manifesting oneself, for producing flow/s and participating in flow/s. It is a reminder of one's embodied, and (at least from the perspective of digital being) one's limited, existence. From this perspective, any reminder that one is an embodied, and therefore limited entity, is a negative experience. In that respect, digital being strives for smoothness above all else. Central to the production of a smooth experience and existence is a well-functioning interface; for smoothness, of course, is only characterized by a lack of interruption.[19]

Digital politics

The politics of the industrialized mechanical ensemble, as was pointed out above, is a politics in which a unitary self or subject is very much central. This constitution of a unitary self is a starting point for the construction of the political (Cohen 2008) – a unitary self, with its clear distinction, which is established from one's sense as an embodied being, of that which is 'me', the inside, and that which is 'other than me', the outside. This primary sense of difference is the basis for the construction of a private space and a public space (Kelly 2002). In this construction, politics is often considered to be restricted to the realm of the public space, while the space of the private, the space that is the individual, is considered to be protected from interference from others, including those acting in a public capacity. The politics of the industrialized mechanical ensemble is principally about who or what constitutes a private space, a body, how such spaces are to remain free from interference, the relationship between the public and the private, what constitute reasonable degrees and forms of interference, and how such spaces constitute themselves in the first place.

A very different mode of existence is expressed in the context of the digital ensemble and in the act of interfacing with digital assemblages. This is a mode of existence that has no spatial form. Instead, existence is temporal rather than spatial. It is flow/s. The body has no function in the digital ensemble. More precisely, the body has no function because it ceases to exist in the context of the interface. From the perception of digital being, the body comes to be understood as a source of interruption to the otherwise smooth being of flow/s. This form of being, principally because it is disembodied and exists as flow/s, raises a number of issues in terms of how we understand politics and the construction of the political of the digital ensemble more generally. In many respects, this is both a being and a politics very well described by the term 'turbulence' (Parisi and Terranova 2000; Terranova 2007).

One issue concerns whether the fact that one is not embodied, that one has no spatial existence, means that one cannot produce a sense of self or, at the very least, cannot construct an initial notion of one-self as a coherent entity. In the digital, as a number of authors have pointed out, one is well and truly a machine production (Clough 2008; Dillon and Lobo-Guerrero 2009; Guattari 1992; Harraway 1991; Rose 1999, 96; Virilio 2001). One's existence, one's sense of being an actor in the world, and one's sense of action and capacity thereof, are a product of an assemblage.

The machine cannot be separated from who or what one is in the digital. In addition, and especially in the context of the network, a prob-lematic emerges in terms of what exactly constitutes the boundary of the machine or human-machine assemblage, something that is even further accentuated through the development of wireless technologies, smart fabrics (Küchler 2008), and radio-frequency identification (RFID) tag-ging (Crandall 2010; Hayles 2009). Indeed, the very aim of the interface is to eliminate such boundaries. The interface's function, both within and between assemblages, is to make one assemblage. When operating in the virtuality of the digital ensemble, therefore, the initial differenti-ation between the inside, that which is 'me', and an outside, that which is 'not me', does not derive from the differentiation of an inside and outside of the body.

The construction of the political in terms of boundaries between self/other, subject/object, and private/public ceases to make any sense, or rather, ceases to make the same sense as it does in the industrialized mechanical ensemble (Boyle 1997; Castells 1997; Giese 1998; Hardt and Negri 2001; Harraway 1995; Poster 1999; Rose 1999; Rusciano 2001; STG 2001). The conceptualization of the political expressed in the industri-alized mechanical ensemble cannot operate without a recognition, or perception, of difference between self and other, and between private and public. It is precisely the distance between citizens, and between citizens and authority of the law, as Stiegler (2009b, 36) explains, that constitutes the political. The dissolution of this difference between an inside and an outside in the context of the digital ensemble can, in that respect, be seen as the end of modern politics (Hardt and Negri

2001);[20] at least, it can be seen in that way in the context of the temporality or flow/s produced by the digital ensemble. Care needs to be taken, however, in reading this as an 'end' or 'de-actualization' of modern politics in the manner that Barlow has done (Loader 1997b, 4–5), or that Hardt and Negri do (Hardt and Negri 2001). Indeed, Stiegler (2009b) and Agamben (2005) foresee a similar end to politics.

While the construction of the political in modern politics does not appear to be suited to the digital ensemble, and there are questions as to the extent to which this ensemble affects the spatiality and being of the industrialized mechanical ensemble, this does not imply that politics in its modern mode is entirely over (Poster 2001a, 140). As Ruddick, for example, points out about Negri's work, he neglects to ask why the masses 'choose to fight for their servitude as if it was their freedom' (Deleuze and Guattari in Ruddick 2010, 34).

What occurs with the digital ensemble is a dispersal of a host of political entities. More precisely, there is a general dissolution of the boundaries that constitute such entities, whether they are subjectivities on the level of the individual or collective forms of subjectivity, such as the nation or 'the people' (Hardt and Negri 2005). This is very much a defining characteristic of the digitization of politics (Harraway 1991, 163; Robins 2000, 138). This dissolution or dispersal can be observed with institutions such as government (Bellamy and Taylor 1998; Rose 1999; Tonn and Feldman 1995), the nation state (Castells 1997; Hardt and Negri 2005; Poster 1999; Rusciano 2001), property (Hardt and Negri 2001; Poster 2001b; Scott 2001; Soderberg 2002), and the factory (Hardt and Negri 2001). As Deleuze argued in his postscript,

> in the present situation, capitalism is no longer involved in production, which it relegates to the Third World...It's a capitalism of higher-order production. It no longer buys raw materials and no longer sells the finished products: it buys the finished products or assembles parts. What it wants to sell is services and what it wants to buy is stocks. This is no longer capitalism for production but for the product, which is to say, for being sold or marketed. Thus it is essentially dispersive, and the factory has given way to the corporation.
>
> (Deleuze 1992, 6)

It is not only finance capital that, in the form of the corporation, is dispersed and has become fluid (Cooper 2010; Dillon and Lobos-Guerrero 2009; Ikegami 1999). This is also occurring with entities such as the

military (De Landa 1991; Der Derian 2009; Ronfeldt and Arquilla 2001) –
an entity that, like capital, has always contained a tension that arises
from its deterritorialized character (Deleuze and Guattari 1987). Indeed,
new forms of warfare in the form of 'netwar' operate with a very different notion of the other (Meikle 2002, 159; Ronfeldt and Arquilla 2001).
This is not an other on the outside, from whom something on the inside
must be protected, but an other that is now everywhere (Hardt and Negri
2001, 189). The War on Terror that began with 9/11 and which has been
going strong for just over a decade now illustrates this well enough.

   In other words, the boundary between state actors, and that between
state and non-state actors, has dissolved in the digital ensemble.
As Agamben points out in *The State of Exception,*

> What is new about President Bush's order is that it radically erases any
> legal status of the individual, thus producing a legally unnamable and
> unclassifiable being. Not only do the Taliban captured in Afghanistan
> not enjoy the status of POW as defined by the Geneva Convention,
> they do not even have the status of people charged with a crime
> according to American laws.
>
> (Agamben 2005, 3)

The individual, in a very real sense, has been dissolved and therefore
become formless. A point that was already established by Arquilla when
he stated that, '[t]he bottom line . . . is that the netwar concept does herald a new blurring of the line between those participating in a conflict,
and those whose motives are purely humanitarian' (Arquilla in Meikle
2002, 159). In that respect 'there is no longer an outside in a military
sense' (Hardt and Negri 2001, 189).[21]
   Such a dissolution of the distinction between the inside and the outside is a central feature of the broader digitization of politics. The character of digital being, of the superject, is one reason behind the general
evaporation of difference. It is one reason that concepts such as agency
(Stone 1995), democracy (Stiegler 2009b), private property (Hardt and
Negri 2001), citizenship (Miller and Rose 2008), and the private and
the public (Giese 1998) cease to function in a coherent manner when
applied to digital technologies. This, in turn, makes concepts such as
representation, transparency, and accountability largely useless in dealing with politics of the digital ensemble (DeLong and Froomkin 2000;
Stone 1995). As long as someone pays whatever bill needs to be paid,
all is well, as Patrick O'Malley's example of a new approach to fines
demonstrates (2010).

The fact that one's existence takes on a momentary and dispersed character and that we cannot relate any specific code back to a specific author raises a problem with respect to notions of responsibility and accountability.[22] In the mechanical ensemble, one can always relate a specific action back to the body, which is always the same body throughout one's existence. In the digital, however, one cannot establish this with certainty (Chesher 1997, 87). As Smith argues, in the digital, 'a statistical and ineluctable force takes over the command tasks; responsibility dissolves; economics gradually absorbs anthropology' (Smith 1986, 165). This isn't to say that governments don't try, of course. Money, after all, was introduced by the State precisely to enable control over commerce (Smith 2011, 47).

Such a general dissolution of difference, some commentators argue, also means that there can be no ethics in the virtuality of the digital ensemble, as it is simply a production of the world by a monad (Foster 1997; Heim 2001; Virilio 2001). Take, for example, the character Neo in *The Matrix*. At the point at which Neo becomes 'the one', that is, when Neo understands that in order to beat the matrix he actually has to become fully 'of the machine' (that is, of the digital), he has to accept the machine and its production of reality as his reality. At this moment there is only Neo, there is only himself. All else, from this point onward, becomes a production of his imagination as a machinic assemblage, from the slowing of bullets, to the changing of shape, to the jumping of great heights, which only exist if he chooses to accept their existence. Neo, in other words, becomes the matrix. In such a context, where Neo effectively becomes dictator of 'his' own world, there can be no 'other'. Others only exist as productions of Neo's will. In such a situation there can be, according to many, no ethics (Foster 1997; Heim 2001; Virilio 2001). Ethics, for these authors, requires a sense of embodiment in order to allow one to recognize one's self and constitute a relationship with others. Ethics in the virtuality of the digital ensemble, they argue, is effectively thrown out the window, or rather, does not exist on the screen, because, in the end, one's existence in the digital ensemble and the production of the 'other' are 'simply' a simulation.

Authors who adopt such positions make several errors. A first error is to treat simulacra as simulations. However, a second is to ignore the fact that embodiment is not a guarantee for the existence of ethics in any case. Indeed, 'the other' has always been a production of the imagination, a construct. Another, and more significant, error that those who put forward such positions often make is to ignore the fact that digital technologies have as their very defining characteristic 'interconnectedness'. As Poster states, '[t]he communications logic of the Internet is interconnectedness, not autochthony' (Poster 2001b, 116). It is not so much the loss of ethics that those authors seem to lament but, instead, perhaps a loss of morality. Cyberspace constitutes a shock to the reality for people such as Virilio, because it dissolves morality, and not because it dissolves ethics. Morality differs from ethics in that it is fully codified, it orders, whereas ethics is, by definition, not codified but dynamic (Deleuze 1995). It flows.

Indeed, if anything, it could just as easily be argued that in the digital ensemble there is nothing but the possibility of, and concern for, ethical relations. This is perhaps precisely because of the immediacy of existence, because one cannot be certain about the construction of self and other. But more so, I would argue, because unethical behavior, especially where a breach of trust has occurred, interrupts the process or flow/s. When a dealer in derivatives breaks this trust it has significant consequences for that person's future capacity in participating in flow/s or generation flow/s (that is, deals) (Knorr-Cetina 2007). When in an MMORPG a player 'loots' something that was either implicitly or explicitly understood to be determined by the role of a dice instead, or to go to the weakest player, they can expect to have their chances of future invites significantly reduced, especially where they establish a pattern of behavior, whether that is speaking in a derogatory manner about people, or being perceived as too selfish in some way. These are instances where the 'magic circle' of the game is instantly broken (Salen and Zimmerman 2004). Indeed, they can easily find themselves put on an 'ignore' list, the result being that the people whose list the player is on won't even see that person's flow/s of code anymore, even if, and especially, when direct contact is attempted. And obviously that 'ignore' list can have a very unethical function as well, not all that different from the use of gated communities.

The now infamous case of the 'virtual rape' should be evidence enough that people's approach to ethics isn't somehow annihilated by their connection to digital machines (Dibbell 1994). But there is also the case of the 'dog poop' woman in South Korea, who found her image and name proliferating in ways that were entirely unforeseen (Solove 2007). Examples like this make clear that our actions through our digital machines are certainly not disembodied or removed from the so-called real world, and can have a very significant impact, both on a smaller scale, if we look at the posting up on Facebook or YouTube of videos of kids bullying each other, or, on a large scale, when we look at the furor caused by Wikileaks in 2010 especially. Certainly new ethical boundaries are produced, and crossed, but this is perhaps part of a process of recognizing differences that don't exist outside of, or rather, prior to the digital ensemble. As Hayles points out, '[t]he idea that meaning and interpretation can occur across and between human and mechanical phyla contributes to an expanded sense of ethics' (2009, 68–9). This is part and parcel of how new capacities for action, new connections, produce new problems.

Guattari's (1992) argument is here much more convincing than that of Virilio in this context, for example. Guattari argues that it is precisely at moments of uncertainty as to how one ought to constitute oneself, and therefore ought to behave toward others, that the possibility exists of positioning oneself differently. It is such moments that offer both the greatest hope for the realization of the full amplitude of what Guattari refers to as the 'path/voice of self-reference' (Guattari 1992). At the same time these moments also give rise to a fear that another path/voice may reassert itself over those who feel uncertain about the future (Guattari 1992). This is something that a number of authors, and Virilio and Baudrillard are good early examples of this, fail to fully appreciate. More to the point, what seems to be lacking is a sensitivity to the possibilities, and not only those of a negative character, present in the construction or machination of a politics of the digital. To remain open to the possibilities of a politics of the digital we must avoid, as far as this is possible, approaching the construction of the political in the digital ensemble by way of the categories of the politics of the industrialized mechanical ensemble (Poster 2001a, 134; Rose 1999, 2). Rose explains this in terms of the development of a new humanism that

> would not pose its concerns in terms of what is inside and what is outside the human, of essence and supplement. It would start from the premise that humans are essentially machinated. And so is the capacity for freedom. Freedom does not arise in the absence of power: it is a mobile historical possibility arising from the lines of force within which human being is assembled, and the relations into which humans are enfolded.
>
> (Rose 1999, 96)

A new politics and construction of the political must be imagined, then, for, and by way of, a new perception, or a new sensibility. This is a politics and construction of the political that, as Derrida explained, has to 'take account of the question of prosthesis and technics' (Venn 2007, 123). Whereas being in the industrialized mechanical ensemble constructs the political in terms of difference in a spatial context, being of the digital ensemble does not constitute itself in an act of spatial separation. Indeed, it is precisely not an act of separation that enables being in the digital. Instead, it is the act of connecting, or the act of interfacing that enables the constitution of being in the digital ensemble. It is precisely this event, the coming into being of the human-machine assemblage in the digital ensemble in the interface, that produces, indeed is, the political. It is not the statement 'I think therefore I am' that is central to the construction of the political, but instead something more along the lines of 'connect and become flow/s', or as Shaviro (2003, 85) states: 'I am connected, therefore I exist' – though the use of the word 'I' might be problematic in that context. The moment of becoming flow/s, becoming fluid, which thereby enables entirely different practices of doing, is the critical moment in the constitution of being in the digital. This is precisely the moment at which a different construction of the political may be required.

One may be able to argue that there are no spaces of politics in the digital ensemble, at least not in the form familiar to modern political thought (Agamben 2005; Hardt and Negri 2001; 2005; Stiegler 2009b), but this does not signify the end of politics. The emergence of the digital ensemble changes the construct 'the political', for the emergence of a new mode of being produces an entirely new politics. In the first instance, in the context of digital technologies, politics is now both everywhere and nowhere. There is no so-called space outside of politics, outside of power, because there is no space (Stiegler 2009b). It is precisely the assemblage itself, the very act of assembling, that is political (Bergen 2010). Like being, politics in the digital is not spatial but is temporal. It is flow/s. That means that the entire temporality of the digital ensemble is politics. As Hardt and Negri state, 'it is a field of pure immanence' (Hardt and Negri 2001, 154). In that sense, politics, like being, can be understood to be fluid. Like being, politics does not occupy the entire scene, it *is* the entire scene, and in that respect politics and the scene (that is, technology) are indistinguishable.

One's being in the context of the digital ensemble, and how it is able to manifest itself, becomes a critical political issue. The extent to which one can constitute oneself, or rather constitute one's being as flow/s, which is also one's capacity to act and to exist, is crucially tied to the machines and assemblages with which one is interfaced. In other words, the pursuit of smooth connection highlights the significance of a vast range of factors that directly affect one's capacity to become flow/s. More to the point, a whole new problematic emerges in terms of the needs and interests that being in the digital generates (Arthur 2010; McLaren and Zappalà 2002). Indeed, even the manner in which the 'needs' and 'interests' of digital beings are constructed must be different.

Many of these needs and interests can be expressed in terms of access, and this is typically how politics has been approached (Reid 2009). Being of the digital does not simply require connection, though this is an important aspect of access. Other issues of concern for digital being relate to the speed of connection, the degree or amount of access to different parts of the network, and the speed of the machines to which one is connected, both in terms of processor speed and the amount of memory available. People making use of slower modem connections, for example, have very different capacities to constitute themselves compared with those who have a broadband connection. Access to the actual hardware of the machines is one issue but, a more important issue, as Lyotard pointed out very early on in the debate, concerns one's ability to speak the language (Lyotard 1984).

Another way of thinking about politics in the digital ensemble is in terms of the writing of, and being as, code (Nakamura 2001, 226). It is in this context that one can attempt to conceptualize the issue of 'difference' in another manner. The digitization of politics is not so much a dissolution of difference; it requires that we learn to recognize difference in another manner. In short, a different sensibility is required to construct and recognize difference in the digital. This means being cognizant of precisely how we are constituted, and how we constitute ourselves, as information (Clough 2008; Crandall 2010; Hansen 2009). Difference is no longer produced by way of the body or the spaces one occupies, but is instead expressed in terms of code. More precisely, difference may be recognized in terms of the recognition of patterns of code.

Code is indistinguishable, or rather, all code is the same, which is partly why it is in the nature of a fluid, but patterns of code can be distinguished from one another. After all, this is precisely how the modulatory mode of power operates. In the context of digital technologies we write ourselves as code, and specific patterns of code generate specific effects. The most obvious example of this relates to network access. A right to access is determined by a specific configuration of code, whether it be a password or an Internet Protocol (IP) address provided by an Internet service provider (ISP). In such a context different patterns of code can drastically affect one's capacity for being in the digital ensemble.[23]

Thinking of difference at the level of the writing and being as code makes it clear that difference manifests itself in another manner in the digital ensemble. In other words, when talking about the being of flow/s, and the politics of being flow/s, it is important to recognize that there is not one homogenous fluid entity, or being, produced in the digital ensemble. Being in the digital, and its politics, appears formless, indeterminate, and immediate only from the perspective of the individual of the industrialized mechanical ensemble. From the sensibility of fluid being, or the superject, however, that same sense of immediacy, of the dissolution of difference, and of somehow no longer belonging to a community, a specific space that is a dominant source in one's construction of identity, simply does not exist.

The superject, and also the dividual in its moments as superject, generates a very different sensibility from the subject and individual of the industrialized mechanical ensemble. In this context, one should not argue that community has disappeared or is threatened by digitization, but rather, that a different sense of affinity exists between superjects than that which exists between the individuals of the industrialized mechanical ensemble (Hardt and Negri 2005; Rheingold 1993; Tonn and Feldman 1995) – a sense of affinity that could increasingly be derived from shared networks, shared trajectories, and shared interruptions, rather than from geographical location (Knorr-Cetina 2003; 2007; Meikle 2002, 94–5; Sanderson and Fortin 2001). As Winner points out,

> [f]or modernism the prescribed frame for social relations was that of city and suburb. People were situated geographically and expected to find meaningful relationships close to home. But today it is increasingly obvious that for sizeable, economically important segments of our society, attachment is no longer defined geographically at all. Many activities of work and leisure take place in global, electronic settings and that is how people define their attachments.
>
> (Winner 1999, 214)

We find this in the communities of the professional elites identified by Castells (1996) and Knorr-Cetina (2003; 2007), but also in communities established through online games, as well as in the way that social media can connect people and help them to organize differently, including for political action. This isn't necessarily a 'disassociated milieu' (Stiegler 2009b), or perhaps rather, not only.

Most people connect to the Internet to participate in the flow. It is communal. It is an act of communion, an act of sharing. This is precisely what drives, for example, re-mix culture. This is precisely why people play online games. This is precisely how they engage with the world.

Crowdsourcing is precisely something communal, and often exists precisely at the boundary layer of what I refer to as fluid and solid politics, which is touched on in Part III. The aim of connecting is precisely to associate with others, in part because the so-called drudgery of day-to-day working life for so many people, the politics of the industrialized mechanical ensemble, is a 'milieu' of disassociation for so many (Stiegler 2009b). The slogan 'I logged out for this?', sold on a t-shirt by the company Jinx, makes precisely that point. Indeed, as I touch on in Part III, game developers and game distribution companies clued onto the fact that 'community' is precisely what enables them to expand the life of their product. A game like *World of Warcraft*, or *Rift*, or any MMORPG, in the end maintains itself over time precisely because it is a chatroom, even if it is a visual one. The product is not the actual game, but the opportunity of association with others that it provides.

Indeed, as Hardt and Negri make clear, cooperation, certainly in terms of what they term immaterial labor, is very much immanent to the network form of organization (Hardt and Negri 2001; 2005). Instead of thinking of the affinity that constitutes any given community as being of the nature of a relationship, therefore, one should try to think of it more in terms of an 'inclination' perhaps. It is in such a sense that new senses of community and identity can develop in the context of the network (Castells 1996; 1997). This will not be, for example, in the manner of workers adopting a national identity, but will be more in terms of people understanding their being as specific points, or rather flow/s, in a network (Poster 2002b). As Rose argues, in relation to a changing understanding of citizenship,

> [c]itizenship is not primarily realized in a relation with the state, nor does it involve participation in a uniform public sphere; citizenship, rather, entails active engagement in a diversified and dispersed variety of private, corporate and quasi-corporate practices, of which working and shopping are paradigmatic.
>
> (Rose 2000, 327)

This understanding of citizenship also seems to be reflected in what Hardt and Negri see as a new form of sovereignty, which they termed 'empire' (Hardt and Negri 2001; 2005). This form of sovereignty, they argue, is global and is 'composed of a series of national and supranational organisms united under a single logic of rule' (Hardt and Negri 2001, xii). This single logic is very much like the logic that many others have identified as that of the network form of organization (Castells

1996; Hardt and Negri 2001; Loader 1997a; Ronfeldt and Arquilla 2001). It is evident in new practices of labor (Poster 2002b), production (Hardt and Negri 2001), governance (Tonn and Feldman 1995), war (Ronfeldt and Arquilla 2001), and finance (Ikegami 1999; Knorr-Cetina 2003). A network form of organization is considered to be deterritorialized, decentered, and composed of flow/s. While the interface may be the key expression of the political in the digital ensemble, it is this network form of organization, or rather the flow/s, that can be seen as the principal expression of politics in the digital ensemble. It is in the context of flow/s that interaction or association occurs.

Returning to my example of Neo, changing who one is, both for oneself and for others, is not an easy thing to do. In many instances, it is not so much a matter of choice as it is one of necessity. Connecting oneself to digital machines by way of the interface, and operating within the digital ensemble more generally leads to a different understanding of what it means to be an actor in the world. In addition, the construction of oneself as a different actor involves, as Neo had to do, a killing of oneself. It involves a suicide of sorts. At the same time, for those less familiar with life in the mechanical ensemble, it is not about a sense of loss or nostalgia, but how life is. Either way, the digital ensemble is about the institutionalization of a very different understanding of the political, or at least, it opens up the possibility of a very different understanding and construction of the political. This has both negative aspects, and positive ones . In short, the digital machines expressive of the digital ensemble require a different constitution of self, thereby opening up a different field of action and, ultimately, the possibility for a different constitution of the political. This, in some sense, is what a digitization of politics is about. In other words, it is not only about the imposition of new and insidious forms of control or a total release from older forms of power that have inscribed themselves on the body. The digital ensemble opens up the possibility of new forms of existence, as Guattari pointed out, and this consists both of new forms of domination and of freedom.

For now, it is quite clear that most, if not all, of us are not quite as interfaced with the machines of the digital ensemble as we might be in the future. The industrialized mechanical ensemble still provides the overriding impulse in the production of self. This twofold production produces an antagonism, undermining the production of self as a unitary entity. This moment of antagonism is an opportunity for producing forms of existence that are less subject to existing forms of power. At the same time, however, this moment of antagonism also opens up the possibility that these same forms of power, these same mechanisms, or the political machines that code our behavior and conduct can reassert themselves over processes of subjectivation. It is in this context (that is, after looking at being in the context of digital technologies) that I now turn to looking at action in Part III.

Part III
The Network

6
Solid Politics

A lot of people acknowledge and theorize a shift to a politics – and a world – that is more turbulent in character (Bauman 2000; 2005; Cooper 2010; Dillon and Lobo-Guerrero 2008; 2009; Parisi and Terranova 2000). Generally this is attributed, whether implicitly or explicitly, to our use of digital machines, and the concurrent and related transformation to a world that on both the machine level and the biological level – indeed, the two become increasingly indistinguishable in the digital ensemble – is composed of information, of code – information that of necessity is in a constant state of flux. In short, it is not stable, maintains no shape, and therefore does not have form. In this respect, the world – at least as it is produced in our connection with our digital machines, the world produced through the digital ensemble – is one of fluids, and not of solids. As I previously explained, this fluid world is not quite Bauman's liquid modernity, nor is this to be only or simply thought of in the sense that a river flows through a network of pipes (Knorr-Cetina 2003; 2007), or how sand might be seen to flow in an hour-glass.

This production of, and engagement with, the flow/s of information is experienced and observable in how people are acted upon, which I examined in looking at the emergence of modulatory power in Part I. It can also be experienced and observed in how people come to constitute themselves as actors within the digital ensemble. This actor is the active and ongoing production of a sense of unicity people engage in, and while in the industrialized ensemble this takes the form of the production of individuality of an otherwise fragmented body, in the digital ensemble it manifests itself temporally as the flow/s of the superject, whose generation of flow/s of code is anticipated by the modulatory mode of power through its production of the objectile. This at least dual operation of power is at the core of the production of dividuality, both in terms of its ongoing production by differential modes of power, and in terms of the general production of a sense of unicity that enables us to maintain an existence.

Life in so-called control society is perceived, by Deleuze (1992) and most others, as less than positive. To live as a dividual is generally regarded to be living in a state of anguish. As Crandall, quoting Bataille, reflects, 'since one is always in a state of anticipation, one is always more or less in a state of anguish, for one must apprehend oneself in the future, through the projected results of one's action' (2010, 88–9). This state of anguish, irrespective of whether we accept that it is deliberately produced (Massumi 2009), is what characterizes not simply the life of the dividual, but the life of society in general. Central to the production of that anguish, at the very least indirectly, is the explosive growth in control technologies, and I mean 'control' here in the broader use of the word, not simply in terms of the negative connotations associated with surveillance technologies. Our digital machines are control technologies (Beniger 1986; Strandh 1979). As Hayles points out, however, the challenge here is to shift our focus away from how we are impacted upon and, instead, focus on how such control technologies can be used to 're-think human subjectivity in constructive and life-enhancing ways without capitulating to [their] coercive and exploitive aspects' (2009, 48), even if in the first instance that might simply be in terms of asking how people might 'bite back' (2009, 56).

As explained in Part II, these digital machines are us. They configure us differently, or more precisely they are – we are – different human-machine configurations that have a different capacity for action in the world when compared to the human-machine assemblages of the industrialized or motorized mechanical ensemble. People's sense of time is different (Hansen 2004; 2009). The affects produced in the different connections enabled by our digital machines, by our control technologies, are different. In a very real sense these digital machines constitute us, and we constitute ourselves, as code. Code that, again, of necessity, flows, albeit in different flow lines, differing speeds, and at times produces what we perceive or sense as turbulence.

Those moments or periods of turbulence are significant because they produce what in fluid dynamics at least is referred to as a flow regime that is stochastic or chaotic. Looking at it as a mathematical process, a turbulent flow regime involves a random variable and is therefore non-deterministic. It involves chance. In that respect, taking a more Deleuzean approach, turbulence isn't necessarily infused with negativity – or rather, not only with negativity. A turbulent flow regime is a moment of disjuncture, and, for many, disjuncture is generally regarded as negative in character. It interrupts smoothness. However, if we take our cue from Deleuze's work, disjuncture is precisely the possibility for life, and therefore includes not only the possibility of negative production, of negative flow lines emerging but also the possibility of positive flow lines occurring, and, indeed, the possibility of mixture, and not simply in terms of generating commercial opportunities.[1]

Binary code and Boolean logic might simply be used by us to instruct a switch to be either on or off, but in the digital ensemble this most basic difference is precisely what presents an openness and plurality that does not exist in the same way with the machines of the industrialized mechanical ensemble. Hansen's argument about the temporality of digital machines compared to that of other media demonstrates that clearly enough (2004; 2009). It is therefore perhaps a mistake to speak, as I did previously, of everything being 'reduced' to binary code. In the digital ensemble that 'reduction', that interface, is simultaneously a moment of connection, but also a moment of disconnection – the moment, the duration, that we constitute ourselves as flow/s.

This constitution of flow/s, of becoming fluid, from the perspective of the individual of the industrialized mechanical ensemble is generally treated as negative. It isn't simply the periods of turbulence that are treated negatively, but the general constitution of flow/s, of becoming fluid that is treated negatively. There are reasons for this, and Deleuze's postscript (1992), for example, is illustrative of one of these reasons. Deleuze doesn't hesitate in conceptualizing the corporation as gaseous, that is, as a fluid. The fact that something is gaseous means that it is difficult for solid entities to act upon and control. After all, punching a gas has little effect apart from a redistribution of its molecules. There can be no structural rearrangement in fluids because there is no structure in the manner that a solid has structure, and therefore a shape. In short, Deleuze's problem, and one that we need to engage with, is that we cannot act with force against a gaseous entity. This is precisely why in his postscript Deleuze is pessimistic about the possibility for political action because he conceptualizes political action as that of solid entities (that is, entities that have a definable boundary, a stable shape and, therefore, have form). Deleuze's dividual has no such form – it constantly and continuously fluctuates (that is, it is a flow), though in the postscript Deleuze only focuses on how it is acted upon, and not on how it constitutes itself as actor. This is precisely the problem he poses needs resolution.

While my own view on the production of dividuality (the focus of Chapter 2) differs somewhat from that of Deleuze, the problem Deleuze identifies is the question of how we can act in a context in which we are constituted, and act, as flow/s. This is a significant question because, from the standpoint of an individual that has form, fluids are incapable of acting with force. The answer that Deleuze (1995, 175) provides is open, stating that 'it would be nothing to do with minorities speaking out'. He recognizes that communication, the flow of code by which control operates, is the problem, especially with it having become 'thoroughly permeated by money' by its 'very nature'. The response, he suggests, might be to 'hijack speech', or to create 'vacuoles of communication, circuit breakers, so we can elude control' (1995, 175). However, what is at the root of the problem, he suggests, is that we 'most lack a belief in the world' (1995, 176); that if we believe in the world 'you precipitate events, [...] you engender new space-times, however small their surface or volume'. In that respect, it is a matter of looking into the production of subjectivity, that is, of how we exist (Guattari 1992; 1993; 1995; Hayles 2009).

However, if thinking about cyborgs and machinic subjectivity is necessary for those interested in social and political progress, then attention also needs to be paid to the actions of which such entities are capable. If the spatial and temporal reorganization brought about by the use of digital technologies has resulted in the need to reconceptualize the subject and processes of subject constitution as flow/s, as formless, then this surely must apply to the conceptualization of action as well. In the following chapters, therefore, I argue that the manner in which political action has generally been conceptualized is perhaps not always appropriate for understanding political action in the context of digital technologies, especially when these form part of a network. The focus in these chapters, therefore, is not so much on the conceptualization of the actor, which was the focus of the previous chapters, but on the conceptualization of action when considering the flow that is the larger machine, including screen, reality of the digital ensemble.

In this chapter, I briefly want to turn to how political action is generally conceptualized within modern political thought, which, as Cohen (2008; 2009) explains continues to rely on a specific fiction of the body as having a boundary. This is a fiction that was established in the first instance by Hobbes. This specific understanding of the body, the idea of the individual having a body, being a body, remains central to our legal understanding of property and copyright, to which Locke's arguments, as well as that of people such as Grotius, was important. But more importantly for my purposes, this understanding of the body, of the individual, continues to support how, at least in our more general conception, most people speak and think about political action.

This conceptualization of political action, and politics more generally, I refer to as 'solid politics', though the term 'politics of geometry' might be equally useful. Such a conceptualization, I argue, is not useful for coming to terms with political action in the context of the flow/s constituted by our use of digital machines. Instead, political action in the context of the digital ensemble might be better conceptualized as a 'politics of fluids', or a 'politics of flow/s'. It is for this reason that I describe and contrast solid forms of political action available to, what one might term, the non-networked actor, with the fluid forms of political action available to the networked actor.

The manner in which politics, but specifically political action is generally talked and written about, at least in a modern approach, is as if it concerns the actions between solid bodies acting on other solid bodies. Hobbes, in constructing a political ontology that is based on a physics in which bodies have mass and are capable of motion, radically challenged the theological view of politics at the time. In relying on physics, he established a new political imaginary and recast politics 'as a matter of human rationality and thus *for* human intervention and change' (Cohen 2008, 109). As Cohen points out, this political ontology or imaginary, continues to serve the basis for much of our thinking about politics and economics.

Our continued use of terms such as the 'body politic' and the idea that 'the State' can be structured, restructured, and even smashed, suggests that many people (at least in some capacity) continue to conceptualize politics (at least in some form) in terms of solid forms of action. Both individuals and nation states, for example, are treated as solid entities, in that they are taken to have a coherent structure. Any actions these entities perform are usually described in terms of how they affect the integrity of other solid entities. In many countries there is what can only be described as a neurotic obsession with how, for instance, boat refugees somehow threaten the integrity of the nation state; that is, threaten its capacity to maintain form. Reality television shows that focus on customs officers and border patrols only serve to reinforce this point. To be sure, this is not some groundbreaking claim. As individuals, we are solid bodies living in a material world, and, therefore, our actions can be described as being those of solids.

I have two objectives here. The first is to offer a description of the properties of solids and the characteristics that describe their actions in relation to and on one another. The second objective is to use this description to illustrate the ways in which politics and political action are often conceptualized as the action and interaction of solids. Here

I seek to show how different political concepts (such as the individual, the popular will, the nation state, rights and duties, and the State) are often imagined as either solid entities or the properties of solid entities. At no point do I suggest that such a conceptualization of politics and political action is incorrect. Nor do I want to infer that political thought has somehow not moved beyond what may come across in the following pages as a simple billiard ball model of politics. Far from it. It is simply a mechanism or starting point for beginning to think about politics, and specifically political action, indeed action in general, differently. It is, in that respect, far easier to claim or demonstrate that the reality of the digital ensemble is one of information flow, the flow of the screen reality, but it is a less easy step to then begin to think through how we might conceptualize action in a way that is less reliant on the political imaginary established by Hobbes, and on which all forms of modern political thought, in one form or another, rely.

Solid forms of action

For physicists, matter can come in one of three forms: solid, fluid, and gaseous. Geometrically, solids can be described as a closed surface in three-dimensional space. They are taken to be clearly defined entities with well-defined limits and boundaries. The existence of these limits and boundaries differentiates the solid from the non-solid (that is, the inside from the outside). More important, however, is the fact that these limits and the boundaries that define or establish a solid are relatively determinate and fixed. A solid is a physical entity or object with a stable shape, though this stability is relative. One can differentiate, for example, between soft and hard objects, though both are still considered to be solid. Solids are always structured, though not necessarily in an orderly or coherent fashion.[2] In short, they are physical or material objects that have a definite and stable shape and occupy a specific three-dimensional space.

Having these qualities means that the actions to which solids are subject, as well as those they are capable of performing take specific characteristics. The fact that a solid body has a definite and relatively stable boundary and occupies a specific space means that anything that affects the stability of this boundary affects its status as a single solid body. Solids can be subject to a number of different actions that destabilize the boundary that defines them. Generally, such actions are described and explained in terms of force, though this is not always the case.

Force, it is important to point out, is basically a measure of interaction (Sears et al. 1987, 71). It is used to describe how solid bodies affect one another. Indeed, the very concept of force implies that there is 'a mutual interaction between two bodies' (Sears et al. 1987, 81). In other words, whenever a force is exerted on a specific body, that same body exerts a force back on the other body. As Newton's third law states: 'To every action there is always opposed an equal reaction; or, the mutual actions of two bodies upon each other are always equal, and directed to contrary parts' (Newton in Sears et al. 1987, 81). The action and reaction are equal, though the action and the reaction – it is important to remember – always act on different bodies and never the same body. In short, whenever we talk about force, we talk about the way that bodies interact with one another (that is, we are talking about a relation).

One way in which force is used to explain the actions of solids is in terms of movement or motion. Solids occupy a specific three-dimensional space. They have a specific location. Solids cannot be in two places at the same time and two solids cannot have the same location at the same time. A force has to be exerted on a solid body in order for it to move from one location to another. This means that proximity, in both space and time, is important for describing some of the actions of solids.

This leads to another characteristic of solid bodies, which is that these bodies have mass. Mass refers to the quantity of matter that a body contains and is related to a number of properties of solid bodies (NSOED 1997). One of these properties is called inertia, or rather, mass is a quantitative description of the inertia that is a property of a body (Sears et al. 1987, 77). Inertia refers to a body's tendency to continue to exist in its current state, whether that be a state of rest or a state of motion. Further, when the mass of a body is large, a larger degree of force will be required to alter the current state of motion of that body than would be required if the mass of that body were small. The larger the mass of a body, the greater its inertia, as the force required to adjust its current state of motion or rest will need to be greater. Increasing the amount of force applied to a body will accelerate that body. The acceleration of a body is proportional, therefore, to the force exerted on it.

Another property of solid bodies is that their mass can be added (Sears et al. 1987, 77). Mass is a cumulative quantity and is directly correlated with quantity of matter. If two bodies are combined together, the mass of the composite body is always the equivalent to the sum of the mass of the two single bodies. Further, when several forces act on one body, whether in the same or different directions, their effects can be calculated by adding these forces. In short, while the relation between forces can be quite complex, this relation is always arithmetic.

An important point to note with respect to the cumulative property of matter relates to a difference between solids and fluids. While the mass of two solid bodies may be cumulative, the bodies will not be. Thus, when one combines two bodies of water to form one body, it is impossible to distinguish the bodies that were added together. In short, while the mass may be 2, the actual body is still 1. This is not exactly the same for solid bodies. When two different solid bodies such as two coffee cups are added together, one does not end up with one body in the same manner as when one adds two fluid bodies together. One can separate the two solid bodies with which one began.

Another way to describe the interactions of bodies is in terms of impact, which returns us to descriptions of force.[3] Matter in a solid state is subject to a range of actions to which it cannot be subject when in a fluid state. An example of this is that matter in a solid state is subject to fragmentation. Put simply, a solid body can be broken. This break-ing can take a number of different forms. It may be a simple fracture, in which a single solid body is broken into two pieces. It can also take the form of fragmentation, in which a single solid body is broken into a multitude of smaller pieces. Indeed, fragmentation can be extended even further to a single solid body being crushed or smashed.

These various ways of breaking a solid body can be the result of a num-ber of different forms of action, or rather, interactions. A solid object can be subject to a blow from another solid object. In this case, a force is exerted by one solid object on a specific point of another solid object. When a rock hits a window, the result could be that the rock simply bounces off, but the window could also be scratched, fractured, or frag-mented. Similar forms of action, such as the throwing of a rock, could also result in the penetration of a solid body. From the point of view of a solid body, any penetration results in a breaking of the boundary that constitutes the solid object in question. In short, relatively small solid objects can destroy larger objects, depending on the type and degree of force that is applied.

Solid bodies, then, can be subjected to a range of what might be called violent actions. They are violent in the sense that forms and degrees of force are applied to solid bodies that threaten the integrity of those solid bodies – that is, a range of forces can be applied that can disrupt the boundary or limit that constitutes the solid (though it should be pointed out that solids are also subject to forms of action that are not necessarily in the nature of a force). Solid bodies can be dissolved or melted, and in the process can also lose their boundary, though certainly not in the same manner as in the application of force.

While a solid body can be subjected to a range of forms of action that can threaten its status as a single solid body, it can also be subject to more productive forms of action. Unlike matter in a fluid state, matter in a solid state can be built upon, that is, solid matter can sustain loads. Solid matter, therefore, can be combined and built to produce larger assemblies of solid objects. Fluids, on the other hand, cannot sustain loads and cannot be assembled. The larger objects produced by assemblies of solid bodies require the application of a greater degree of force in order for their inertia to be overcome; at the same time, though, once they are moving, they require a greater degree of force to be applied in order for their momentum to be overcome.

Matter in a solid form is also capable of resistance. Friction is an obvious example of this capacity for resistance, as it describes an increase in the degree of force required for a solid body to be moved. This, as shown above, is demonstrated by Newton's third law – action equals reaction. Whenever one solid body acts on another solid body, a force of equal force reacts back upon it.

Matter in a solid state, then, has specific properties. Matter in solid form has a physical presence and a definite shape, that is, it occupies a three-dimensional space whose boundary is well-defined and relatively stable. Solid entities, therefore, are always structured, although such structures may be short-lived, as is the case with amorphous solids. When in solid form, matter can be subjected to a number of actions. These actions are generally explained in terms of force, the capacity of a solid body to produce a motion or stress in another body. Such entities are also capable, in varying degrees, of sustaining loads and they can be built or structured into larger solid entities, thereby increasing their mass and their inertia.

It should be pointed out, however, that even though they might form part of a larger aggregate or larger body, solid bodies can often maintain their individual characteristics, thereby allowing for them to be separated from the larger body, or at the very least identified within it.[4] Unlike the situation that occurs when fluid bodies are combined, one can count and differentiate the individual solid forms of matter that make up a larger solid body or aggregate. Finally, solid entities occupy and move in a three-dimensional space. Their existence and movement can be described geometrically. Their location and proximity in relation to one another are important for measuring the effects they and their movements have upon one another.

The dynamics of politics[5]

One of the main organizing concepts for our thinking about politics, especially in its modern form, is that of the nation state. Politics, and the study thereof, is understood in terms of an entity that occupies a specific geographical, or three-dimensional space, and has distinct and stable borders as one of its main characteristics. As Weber (1978) argued, the State has a monopoly on the legitimate use of force in a specific territory. A nation state, in other words, is conceptualized as a solid. It occupies a specific space, a territory, and it has a definite and stable boundary that differentiates it from other nation states. A nation state rarely moves from its geographical location, as it requires a great deal of force to be applied to it in order to affect its state of motion or overcome its degree of inertia. Nation states, of course, can establish embassies and can engage in or be subjected to colonization and in that manner can expand their territory or contract. Nations, of course, are separate from nation states, and these can shift location.

Nation states are defined by their boundary, or border, of which they are very protective. Any transgression of a nation state's border, any puncturing or moving of this border, is a threat to the existence and stability of the nation state. The border that defines a nation state is therefore always in need of protection. This is always a protection either from dangerous objects or projectiles, usually in the form of aggregates of smaller solid entities, such as refugees, or from other forces such as the military forces of other nation states who wish to occupy the same space, the same territory.[6] Indeed, justifications for such actions are often expressed in a solid form as well. Often the notion of 'belonging' is used to justify armed conflict, in the sense that a nation or people often argues it 'belongs' in a specific territory. Belonging reflects the nature of a solid entity more than it does a fluid entity. One reason for this is that fluid entities that do not flow become stagnant and, under the right conditions, might even become solid, as in the freezing of unmoving water. Of course, the movement of refugees is often expressed, from the point of view of a nation state, as constituting a flow, but this is more in the manner in which large aggregates of smaller objects are perceived to flow, which is a different flow than that of fluids.

Those solid entities that transgress or permeate the border of the nation state are often attributed distinctive properties. Whether the solid entities that come from another geographical location or stratum are attributed positive properties or negative properties may depend upon the location from which they come and their quantity. Small numbers of bodies from the 'right' location can be seen as capable of further solidifying the existing body of the nation, and adding to it, whereas large numbers of bodies from the 'wrong' location are seen as capable of destabilizing, fragmenting, or, more worryingly, dissolving that same solid body. The different immigration policies that nation states apply and the 'reception' of those refugees labeled 'illegal immigrants' express this aspect of the solidity of the nation state well. The larger the influx of immigrants or refugees, the greater the force they exert on the existing body of the nation or social body, so that relatively small nation states, having smaller mass, tend to feel more threatened by 'outsiders', even when those outsiders come from 'acceptable locations', compared to nation states with larger mass.

While the nation state can be thought of as a single, solid body existing in relation to other such bodies in a homogeneous space, that is, the international community, it can also be thought of as composed or constructed out of a multitude of smaller bodies. The very notion of the 'body politic', certainly as it is used by Hobbes (Cohen 2008; Gray and Mentor 1995, 455; Hardt and Negri 2001, 103), reflects this way of thinking of the solid nation state. The illustration of the original cover from Hobbes' *Leviathan* (see Figure 6.1) is a powerful example of this. Here the 'Body Politique' is composed of an aggregate of smaller solid entities, individuals, together forming, by way of 'Pacts and Covenants', a larger, single solid body (Hobbes 1968). The State, in that respect, is conceptualized as a single body, a single political power (Hardt and Negri 2001, 84–5), though this larger single body is always constructed out of, or rather, assembled from smaller bodies that, at any time, can be identified and differentiated from one another. Furthermore, this 'Body Politique', is conceived of as mechanical, having joints, mechanisms, and members, and not as organic (Gray and Mentor 1995, 454–6).[7] Other examples of nation states as solids include Rousseau's notion of the social body that has a will (Rousseau 1989); Marx's concept of the commodity as a social product (Marx 1990, 457);[8] and Locke's construct of the '*Community*' (Locke 1963, 375). The last of these is possibly the most explicitly solid and mechanical.

> For when any number of Men have, by the consent of every individual, made a *Community*, they have thereby made that *Community* one Body, with a Power to Act as one body, which is only by the will and determination of the *Majority*.
>
> (Locke 1963, 375)

One of the solid entities that makes up the larger body of the nation state, or the body politic, is the individual. The conceptualization of the

Figure 6.1   Leviathan (Hobbes 1651)

individual as a solid entity is reflected in a number of ways. First, the individual is often treated by modern political theorists as the small-est indivisible political unit (Kirby 1996). It is a solid entity because its integrity derives from its external surface. Any attempt to break this unit down further is considered a threat to the existence of this unit. Unlike larger social or political bodies, or assemblies, one cannot simply add components of one individual to an already existing one without destroying both. One can, however, build with individuals, as they are capable of sustaining a load. One cannot break them down, however, in the sense of separating the solid entities of which they consist.

Of course, as I argued in Chapter 5, individuals in themselves contain a multiplicity (Gray and Mentor 1995, 455). This is on various levels, including biologically when we consider the enormous variety of cells and organisms our own bodies are constituted of (Cohen 2008). Individuality, as I argued previously, can be seen as an attempt to hold this multiplicity together into one unit, including on a biological level (Cohen 2008; 2009). Individuals, in short, have to work at producing this sense of oneness, this sense of constituting one solid entity. It is, as I argued, the production of that sense of solidity, or the emergence of that single form of matter clearly differentiating itself from an outside, that is the crucial moment in the construction of the political in modern political thought. The key point is that, politically, the actual multiplicity of which the individual is constituted is not recognized. Indeed, those subjects exhibiting any multiplicity (such as the insane) or those who are simply not 'whole' enough, not 'one' enough (such as women and children in much of modern political thought) are not considered to belong to the category of 'the individual' and the political status (that is, the capacity for action) this affords.

As a political entity, an individual is always one and cannot be further divided. In that respect the population, which is sometimes seen as a solid body, albeit an amorphous one, is a mass of single individuals. Each individual that comprises this mass is clearly defined and, therefore, is separate and distinct from other individuals (Foucault 1979; 1991). Whenever these individuals are added or brought together, their mass is simply added. From this perspective, the larger a mass of individuals is, the larger the force that is required to move that mass in a single direction. At the same time, however, this mass can also exert a greater force on other solid entities. Both of these points are reasons, according to modern political theorists, for individuals to aggregate into a single mass. As Rousseau argued,

> since men [*sic*] cannot engender new forces, but merely unite and direct existing ones, they have no other means of self-preservation except *to form, by aggregation, a sum of forces that can prevail over the resistance*; set them to work by a single motivation; and make them act in concert. This sum of forces can arise only from the cooperation of many. But since each man's force and freedom are the primary instruments of his self-preservation, how is he to engage

them without harming himself and without neglecting the cares he owes to himself? In the context of my subject, this difficulty can be stated in these terms: 'Find a form of association that defends and protects the person and goods of each associate with all the common force, and by means of which each one, uniting with all, neverthe- less obeys only himself and remains as free as before'. This is the fundamental problem which is solved by the social contract.

(Rousseau 1989, 359; emphasis added)

Individuals are not always considered by modern political theorists to 'naturally' aggregate together. As a result, they put forward different rea- sons for why individuals should form a single, larger social and political body. There are many cases where larger political bodies, such as nation states, must hold themselves together and resist disaggregation. In such cases considerable force is often exerted on the part of the State in an attempt to maintain unity, and maybe, by way of the construction of a national identity or by way of a threat of violence, that produces a sense of affinity between individuals. Propaganda is in that respect similar to using magnetic force to line particles up in a particular direction.

Propaganda and violence are not the only techniques available to the State to integrate the population. Mechanisms are also available for coordinating the behavior of individuals in order to produce stable nation states. There are also those theorists, such as Adam Smith (1976), who argued that, in the specific assemblage that is the economy, indi- viduals acting alone and purely in their own interests actually produce a greater benefit to themselves than they would if they formed a single body with one will:

The natural effort of every individual to better his [sic] own condi- tion, when suffered to exert itself with freedom and security, is so powerful a principle, that it is alone, and without any assistance, not only capable of carrying on the society to wealth and prosperity, but of surmounting a hundred impertinent obstructions with which the folly of human laws too often encumbers its operation.

(Smith 1976, 540)

The fact that individuals are indivisible, from the point of view of mod- ern political thought at least, also makes them very weak, however. Their existence as solids means that they are subjected to a variety of different forces. Indeed, individuals themselves exert force on other individuals as solid bodies or entities. Such force can take the form of more subtle influences, but it can also be violent. Violence, as the force one body exerts on another, is very much a solid concept. Of course, individuals, acting for themselves or on behalf of other political bodies, can also exert pressure and be pressured. This appears to be a fluid term, until one recognizes that this is always a pressure applied on a surface (that is, it refers to the exertion of force on a solid object which, if great enough, threatens to crush the solid entity in question). In other words, when political entities are imagined as doing something, as acting, whether they be individuals or various forms of collections of individuals, they are always thought to exert or withstand force. It is in this context that Dahl's conceptualization of political power, as getting a person to do something they would otherwise not do, is very illustrative (Dahl 1961).[9]

Individuals, and even other political entities,[10] also have 'rights'. A right, very simply, is a mechanism or device that protects a political entity from being acted upon in a manner that threatens its status as a solid object. In short, it is a device that serves to protect a solid entity, such as an individual, from having its boundary acted upon. It may also guarantee, or perhaps rather, produce, at least some freedom of movement and action for an individual – that is, guarantee action in geometrical space. The most obvious and extreme examples of this are attempts to protect individuals from being subjected to torture, where the boundary of a solid body is transgressed or the body is dismembered or fractured. The 'state of exception' discussed by Agamben (2005), and which I touched on in Chapter 5, is significant in that respect.

A 'duty' is also conceptualized as a property of solid political entities, in that it is an expectation and prescription for how a body ought to conduct itself. In this sense, it might be thought of as one's duty to fight for the nation, or add one's mass and individual force to those produced by other bodies that comprise the nation state. Similarly, from such a perspective, the law can be understood as a form of traffic regulation for solid bodies. The law stipulates ways in which solid bodies of all sizes are to act and relate to one another. Indeed, the very notion of 'equality before the law' (isonomy) is one that guarantees that solid bodies of different mass, and therefore of different force, are all treated as equal bodies, as being isotropic. The principle of equality of the law is there to try to prevent the rule of 'might is right' (that is, to prevent bodies that have greater mass from continuously overcoming the inertia, and thereby directing the movements of bodies with smaller mass).

Just as individuals and other political entities have rights, so they are also often thought of as having 'interests'. Interests, perhaps even more so than rights and duties, are often treated as if they are a property of political entities. Interests are thought of as interior forces that compel individuals and other political entities to act in a certain manner or with a specific purpose. Interests, then, are considered to direct the mass of a specific body, which may lead it to exert force on another body. Again, these forces can come in a variety of magnitudes and forms, or rather, have different vectors. It is in such a context that one can conceptually link the notion of interests to the formation of lobbying groups.[11] Lobby groups, as aggregations of individuals and groups of individuals, form to represent a specific interest. By forming a larger political body, lobby groups are vehicles for the exertion of force on other political bodies, such as government departments or specific ministers. This is done in the hope of ensuring that departments or ministers will follow the same vector or, at the very least, in the hope that they will not disrupt the vector desired by the members of the lobby group.

Interests in that respect are said to 'collide', and Marx and Engels' notion of a 'collision' between classes is equally appropriate (Marx and Engels 1992, 12). Politics can be understood as the process in which one body exerts force on another body in an attempt to change that body's direction of motion and lead it to exert its force on a third body. Lobby groups are, again, a good example of this, but the concept of class is equally illustrative of this motion. What allows different entities to act as one is that they share the same interests, that is, their vector is, if not of the same size or velocity, at least of the same direction. By combining their mass, they also combine their force or vectors, thereby greatly increasing the influence they can exert on the mass of another moving or stationary body. As Rousseau argued, interests constitute quite literally that which forms the social bond, binding bodies with common interests into a larger social body (Rousseau 1989).

Such aggregates of political entities moving as one social or political body can at times reach dangerous proportions from the point of view of other political entities such as the State (Virilio 1986). Whether in the form of mass demonstrations, political movements, or classes, the mobilization of the masses can sometimes be perceived as a threat because, while it may be difficult to construct and get moving in a specific direction, it has a great mass and therefore a great degree of inertia that makes it difficult to affect. Indeed, here the language used in reporting the 'overthrow' of a government is illustrative of solid politics, as was the case with the rebels overthrowing Gadhafi's government in Libya in 2011, or earlier the overthrow of the Mubarak regime in Egypt. It is in that context that one also has to look more seriously at the design of cities or university campuses,[12] which play a crucial role in fostering an affinity between smaller solid bodies (such as in neighborhoods), or in directing or preventing the formation of large aggregations of individuals, which might foster people with the same interest coming together in large numbers.

The State, of course, has a number of strategies and actions at its disposal for dealing with large bodies. The State can attempt to affect a body to lead it to change its course or its vector. The State can also attempt to fracture or crush such bodies, or to decompose them into their smaller constituent elements. Both of these forms of action can be violent, but this does not have to be the case. The State can adopt a strategy of 'divide and conquer', wherein it creates a wedge between the different constituent elements of a body that threatens it. Such a strategy might take the form of promising things to some members, but not other members, of the threatening body. Indeed, the issuing of promises is in some respects akin to a form of magnetization, whereby the State (or any other authority for that matter) aligns the particles of a solid body in order for the motion of that body to be affected. Take, for example, Weber's notion of the 'charismatic leader' or 'charismatic authority' (Weber 1978), whose magnetic personality 'attracts' followers. It might be magnetic force, but it is force nonetheless that is used to describe this.

Another strategy available for attempting to avoid or eliminate the force of a specific body is for the State to disperse it, or, even worse, to dissolve it. Dispersal can take a number of forms. It can occur through the use of batons or rubber bullets. Of course, water cannons and tear gas also break down the links between bodies. Dispersal can also be achieved by preventing the emergence of ghettos through dispersing individuals of certain social classes or ethnic groups across different geographical locations in different suburbs. This might in the first instance appear as something fluid, but these are aggregate solids that are dispersed, not fluids. Examples of dissolving are also readily available. These range from the dissolution of classes (Marx and Engels 1992, 13), which indicates that classes must be conceived as at least aggregates of solid entities in the first place; the banning of specific political organizations that might be perceived as a threat (and there are numerous examples of this in the War on Terror); but also banning specific unions in some countries; to the dissolution of parliament and government, which was a great concern of Locke's (1963).

Dissolution is one of the worst things that can happen from the point of view of a solid body, as it involves a total disintegration of its stable boundary.[13] Rousseau provides a good example of this fear of dissolution when he states that by simply obeying a leader a people 'dissolves itself...it loses the status of a people' (Rousseau 1989, 366). An even more forceful expression of this fear of dissolution is found in the following passage, where he argues that

> I assume that men [*sic*] have reached the point where obstacles to their self-preservation in the state of nature prevail *by their resistance over the forces each individual can use to maintain himself in that state*. Then that primitive state can no longer subsist and the human race would perish if it did not change its way of life.
>
> (Rousseau 1989, 359; emphasis added)

Another example of the conceptualization of politics and political action as solid can be found in some discussions of power. In some versions of modern political thought, power is generally regarded as something that is held and can be passed on.[14] Power is treated as having a source and as something that can be conferred on any solid political body. This explains the strong link between the conceptualization of power and notions of sovereignty and legitimacy (Hardt and Negri 2001, 84–5; 2005). For Rousseau, sovereignty is 'not a convention between an inferior and a superior, but a convention between *the body and each of its members*' (Rousseau 1989, 369; emphasis added). Indeed, the very social contract is considered '*solid*, because it has the public force and the supreme power as guarantee' (Rousseau 1989, 369; emphasis added).

The State is one of the most significant concepts in modern political thought, and is a body that can be structured in a number of different ways to produce different forces. While it is conceptualized within various ideologies as a structure or structured body, one may not always be fully aware of its operations. This structure serves for the regulation of a multitude of moving bodies, each exerting their own force. It is in this sense that one of the aims of the State is often seen as being about the containment of flows. Flows are generally thought to threaten the State, and much of its existence can be described as an attempt to solidify various flows – to govern desire – whether it be population flows or the flows of the war machine, as described by Deleuze and Guattari (1987, 351–423). Indeed, as Berman (1983) has pointed out, this concern or fear regarding flows, which is based on the abhorrence of dissolution, is a general characteristic of modernity. In many instances, however, these flows are often like the flows of amorphous solids. In other words, they are more the spilling of sand than the flow of a fluid. A critical point here, of course, is that the flow of amorphous solids differs from the flow of the air or the sea, what Deleuze and Guattari have described as the now-conquered and re-striated 'smooth spaces' (Deleuze and Guattari 1987). It is also in that respect that such flows differ from the network, the latest smooth or nomadic space traversed by a new worldwide war machine (Deleuze and Guattari 1987, 387).[15]

7
Fluid Politics

All that is solid melts into air.

(Marx and Engels 1992, 6)

Do you think that's air you're breathing?

(Wachowski and Wachowski 1999)

Chapter 6 attempted to demonstrate how, in modern political thought, politics is generally conceptualized as being about the relations between, and the interactions of, solid bodies. Politics in this context is conceptualized as an activity involving solids. Modern politics is by and large solid politics and, for the most part, operates within the framework of a Newtonian physics. This, I realize, might open me up to the charge of constructing a gross generalization and caricature of modern politics and how we tend to talk about it, but my aim in this is to begin to get a handle on how to think positively about fluids, or rather, flow/s. Treating politics as a sphere where solid entities act in relation to other solid entities is how liberals such as Hobbes and Locke established a new political ontology – which Marxism and modern forms of feminism have continued to elaborate in various forms, albeit with different aims in mind. In that respect, it is a useful way of, very generally, conceptualizing politics and political action within a specific spatial and temporal framework. Such a conceptualization, however, is not very useful in attempting to come to terms with political action in the context of digital technologies, specifically in the context of the digital ensemble. Instead, the digital ensemble, whose infrastructure is composed of physical networks, allows some forms of action but not other forms of political action. Forms of action enabled by way of the networks that support the digital ensemble are best conceptualized as those of fluid entities, and not those of solid entities. In short, the network is part of what makes possible the expression of what I conceptualize as fluid political action.

In the first instance, I will briefly explain why the conceptualization of political action as solid is not suitable for describing political action in the context of the digital ensemble. The main argument presented here is that digital technologies, as pointed out previously, produce or constitute a specific 'spatiality' and temporality. As I indicated in Part II, in terms of our screen reality, as well as on the level of the machine, they produce information as flow/s. Any action performed is a performance of flow/s – it is a process. When acting on and by way of digital networks (and their digital machines more broadly), people are of the machine in a very different manner from the way they are with other technologies. In short, when people use the network, they become of the network. It is this form of 'being of the machine', which is the being of the networked or 'interconnected' actor, that is described by various theorists as being fluid in character. This suggests that we ought to conceptualize the action of such a being as fluid as well, which in turn affects both that being's construct of the political and the understanding of politics.

Fluid action

The forms of action available to the non-networked actor – the actor of the industrialized mechanical ensemble – are those actions that are performed in three-dimensional space. They are geometric actions. In the context of the digital ensemble, however, such a space does not exist. This means that actions, including actions that are not immediately visible in the screen reality, cannot be the actions of solid entities. Of course, such actions are often simulated, as for example is the case with the simulation of spaces in computer games in which characters move, punch, fall, or fly. But we need to recognize that in this context there are no solid entities with a clearly recognizable form, nor a clear distinction between inside and outside. If actions in the context of the network do not 'take place' in geometric or three-dimensional space, however, then we have to inquire how actions do occur. Stated differently, we have to inquire how we might recognize actions or recognize new differences that didn't exist with the machines of the industrial mechanical ensemble. As Knorr-Cetina (2007) suggests, '[p]resumably, the cognitively "created" [. . .] quality of this special lifeworld is an essential and invariable feature of global forms that leave their natural embeddedness in local settings behind and need to assemble their own symbolic basis of existence' (730–1).

If we accept the argument that 'the flow of information within systems [is] more determinative of identity than the materiality of physical structures … [then] [p]lunging into the river of information implies recognizing that you *are* the river' (Hayles 1993a, 174; emphasis added). In that respect, there is no clear boundary or indicator any more as to where the machine begins and the human ends, or rather where the resulting human-machine assemblage begins or ends (Hayles 1993b, 72; 2009; Stone 1995). It is this recognition, in the context of the network, that one is not solid but fluid, that provides an avenue for thinking about conceptualizing political action for a networked actor. If subjectivity is best conceptualized as fluid in the context of the network, then it makes sense to also conceptualize the actions of such an entity as those of a fluid. There is little point in arguing that being in the context of digital technologies is of the nature of flow/s and then maintaining a conceptualization and language of political action, indeed, of any action, that describes the actions of solid entities.

From such a perspective, then, one can view the network as both a new infrastructure and as instituting a new dimension or screen reality (Knorr-Cetina and Preda 2007). Hardt and Negri, for example, argue that the institutionalization of the network form of organization is nothing less than 'a process of the material constitution of [a] new planetary order, the consolidation of its administrative machine, and the production of new hierarchies of command over global space' (Hardt and Negri 2001, 19). They compare this to the construction of Roman roads and the railways. The main difference with the network, however, '[is] that it is embedded within and completely immanent to the new production processes … the network itself [unlike Roman roads or the railways] is the site of both production and circulation' (Hardt and Negri 2001, 298).

This is a new infrastructure and a dimension that, while expressing a certain degree of standardization of action, also expresses the possibility of new forms of action (Galloway 2006; Hansen 2004; 2009; Harraway 1991; Hayles 1993a; Lyotard 1984). For Hayles, echoing Lyotard (1984),

[t]his is the double edge of virtual reality's revolutionary potential: to expose the presuppositions underlying the social formations of late capitalism and to open new fields of play where the dynamics have not yet rigidified and new kinds of moves are possible. Understanding these moves and their significance is crucial to the technology's constructive potential.

(Hayles 1993a, 175)

The possibilities for acting in the context of the network, as already stated, are different from those available when not connected to the network. The most crucial difference between the two forms of action available to the two different forms of being – the solid and the fluid – is that whereas solid action takes place within a geometric space, fluid action occurs within a very different dimension.

> Deprived of objective boundaries, the architectonic element begins to drift and float in an electronic ether, devoid of spatial dimensions, but inscribed in the singular temporality of an instantaneous diffusion. From here on, people can't be separated by physical obstacles or by temporal distances. With the interfacing of computer terminals and video monitors, distinctions of *here* and *there* no longer mean anything.
>
> (Virilio 1991, 12–13)

Instead, action in the context of the network occurs in a dimension where space and time are collapsed into one. This means that just as simulated spatial dimensions are inseparable from their rate of transmission (Virilio 1991, 18), so too must actions be understood as inseparable from their rate of transmission. In other words (as touched on in Chapter 6), an action in the context of the network is directly related to its code's rate of flow, which is why it is perhaps more appropriate to think about this in terms of temporality (Hansen 2004; 2009; Stiegler 1998; 2009a; 2010b)[1].

In the current schema, then, there are two forms of action available to two different forms of being. There is, on the one hand, solid being and the world of the non-networked actor and, on the other hand, fluid being and the world of the networked actor. The solid actor is only capable of expressing solid forms of political action, while the fluid actor is only capable of expressing fluid forms of political action.[2] The world of the former actor – the solid actor – is the realm of solid politics, while the world of the latter actor is the realm of fluid politics. Before proceeding to discuss this fluid politics, it is best to first briefly consider fluid forms of action.

The mechanics of fluids

Standard physics text books inform us that a fluid can be a liquid or a gas, and is best described as a 'substance that can flow' (Halliday and Resnick 1988, 362; Sears et al. 1987, 306). Fluids glide, circulate, and 'move as a stream' (NSOED 1997). Fluids do so because, unlike solid entities, they have no stable, determinate, and fixed boundaries. Unlike solid entities they cannot be geometrically described as a closed surface in three-dimensional space. A fluid is not a geometric figure. A fluid has no definite, stable, or constant shape. In short, a fluid, in total contrast to a solid, is matter in a constant state of flux.[3]

The reason that fluids have no shape is because, unlike solids, they cannot exert force. To be more precise, a fluid cannot sustain a force tangential to its surface (Halliday and Resnick 1988, 363). The only manner in which a fluid can exert force is at right angles to its surface (Halliday and Resnick 1988, 363). The actions of fluids are not described in terms of mass and force, but instead, in terms of density and pressure. In explaining the state of a fluid, one's focus is not on any specific properties it may have as a determinate mass, as a lump, but on its properties 'that vary from point to point in the extended substance' (Halliday and Resnick 1988, 363). This is described in terms of density and pressure, with density being a measurement of the consistency of a fluid and pressure referring to the magnitude of force exerted on the fluid.

When two fluids of equal volume and density are added together (such as two bodies of water), one ends up with one body of water. The volume or density of the resulting body of water may have doubled but, in the end, it is still one fluid. Explained differently, when combining fluids you cannot distinguish individual bodies that make up the resulting body, unless, for example, the fluids being added have a very different viscosity. In that respect, fluids are very different from solids in the sense that they are not so much constituted through difference, but through sameness. A fluid body, unlike a solid body, is always one. By adding fluids together, one simply increases the single body's surface and volume, or its density and/or pressure. As Pascal's principle states, to apply pressure on any given part of the surface of a contained fluid is to equally increase the pressure of the fluid as a whole (Halliday and Resnick 1988, 369). With solids, pressure, or rather force, can be applied to specific areas of a body, whereas with fluids, the whole body experiences the increase in pressure equally.

To state, however, that there is no sense of difference in the context of fluids is not correct. As argued in Chapter 6, what such a statement reflects is a lack of, or undeveloped sensitivity to, the being of fluids and the different manner in which they come to be constituted as compared to solids. While fluids are always flow/s, they do exhibit sameness. This is reflected, in part, by the motion of fluids, which is described very differently from that of solids. Fluids, unlike solids, flow. It is the very definition of a fluid: a substance that flows. The path of an individual element of a flow is usually referred to as a 'flow line' (Sears et al. 1987, 318). A flow is described as 'steady' or 'stationary' if 'every element passing through a given point follows the same flow line as that of preceding elements' (Sears et al. 1987, 318). However, if at any point the fluid velocity changes, or the flow changes in its direction or magnitude (that is, if the flow line of an element changes), then the flow is described as 'unsteady' or even 'turbulent' (Halliday and Resnick 1988, 373).

When flows change their velocity or their direction, and therefore their speed at any given point, then a flow is said to consist of 'streamlines' rather than flow lines (Halliday and Resnick 1988, 373). A streamline is 'a curve whose tangent, at any point, is in the direction of the fluid velocity at that point' (Sears et al. 1987, 318). A collection of streamlines is referred to as a 'flow tube' (Sears et al. 1987, 318). The paths or streamlines that make up a flow tube can never cross because this would mean that any given fluid particle arriving at the intersection of the streamlines 'would have to assume two different velocities simultaneously, [which is] an impossibility' (Halliday and Resnick 1988, 373).

Flows that consist of streamlines can either be laminar or they can be turbulent. In a laminar flow, adjacent streamlines or layers slide smoothly past each other (Sears et al. 1987, 319). These flows, while they are curved, can still be said to have a 'steady-state pattern' (Sears et al. 1987, 319). There can be circumstances, however, in which a flow attains a 'non-steady-state pattern'. Such a flow is called a turbulent flow. In this situation, the pattern of the flow continuously changes.

Another major way in which fluids differ from solids is that they are not vulnerable to penetration. A bullet fired at a body of fluid does not affect it in the same manner as it affects a solid body, which it may even destroy. In that respect, fluids, because they have no fixed boundary, cannot be subjected to the same type of force to which solids can be subjected. Fluids, in short, are not subject to force in the same way that solids are. When different fluids interact with one another, one does not speak of fluids exerting force on one another, though they exert force on solids in some circumstances (a point I'll touch on in Chapter 8 where I discuss the boundary layer).

An important concept for dealing with the relations between fluids and their actions upon one another is that of viscosity. Viscosity refers to the tendency of a fluid, whether liquid or gas, 'to resist by internal friction the relative motion of its molecules and hence any change of shape' (NSOED 1997), with liquids being more viscous than gases. Viscosity, in other words, is to fluids what friction is to solids. In some respects, therefore, viscosity is similar to the inertia of solid bodies. The more viscous a fluid is (like a gel, for example), the slower it flows. One way to regulate the viscosity of a fluid is to increase or decrease its temperature. As temperature increases, liquids become less viscous, while gases become more viscous. Viscosity also describes the capacity of some fluids to stick to solid surfaces, like oil to a pipe.

Another important characteristic of fluids is that they can be mixed with one another. This mixing can produce different effects, depending on the different types of fluid that are mixed together. Oil, for instance, will not mix with water, and will tend to float on top of the surface of water. Another point to note is that relatively small amounts of a fluid can have a big impact when mixed with larger amounts of fluid. One drop of a specific liquid can change properties such as the color or acidity of a much larger body of a liquid.

Just as solids are vulnerable to being dissolved, so fluids are vulnerable to becoming solidified. A fluid that solidifies undergoes a progressive decrease in its rate or speed of flow. To freeze water, for example, is to stop its molecules from moving as much as they usually do. In other words, the process of solidifying a fluid basically involves stopping a substance from flowing, from existing in an unstructured manner. The process of freezing is the process of organizing molecules into an orderly long-range arrangement (Halliday and Resnick 1988, 363). Fluids, in a similar manner to solids, are also weaker, or more vulnerable the smaller their volume. In some respects, this is the equivalent of dealing with bodies of different mass. The larger a fluid body, the more difficult it is to lower its temperature enough to freeze it. At the same time, faster flow makes it more difficult to solidify a fluid.

The notion of absorption is another example of the characteristics of fluids. A small volume of fluid is more easily absorbed by a solid than a large volume. Indeed, in that respect, absorption is similar to the process of dissolving a solid. When a fluid is absorbed, it is taken up by a solid and will cease to exist as a separate entity. Of course, depending on the conditions, an absorbed fluid may evaporate, thereby providing an escape from the 'grip' of the solid. It is also worth noting in this context that there is a limit to the amount of a solid that can be dissolved. The dissolution reaches saturation point, at which time the fluid that had been doing the dissolving can be subject to absorption.

From the point of view of solid being, a fluid state of being is always unstructured being. That does not mean fluids, or rather flows, are disorganized. As pointed out earlier, a flow can be either laminar, or turbulent, or a mixture of both. In a laminar flow, the streamlines that compose the flow tube are in a steady-state pattern. In a turbulent flow, however, the streamlines continuously change, both in their velocity and direction. Turbulence usually occurs close to what is called the boundary layer, where a flow is in contact with a solid. Such turbulent flow appears as a series of vortices that sometimes become regular in their appearance.[4]

As already stated, fluids can come in both liquid and gaseous form. Their flow is what defines them as a fluid. It is this being of a flow that explains why the focus with fluids is not on their properties as specific lumps of a substance, but *on the properties that vary from point to point in an extended substance* (Halliday and Resnick 1988, 363). This is precisely the character of Deleuze's objectile (discussed Chapter 2), as well as the broader product of the modulatory mode of power. In a fluid state of being, in other words, everything is 'of the flow'. In that respect, location also has to be understood differently from the way it is understood when dealing with solids and solid forms of action.

For one thing, in the context of being of the flow, it is difficult to distinguish between here and there, and between inside and outside. A flow is not in one specific place in the same way that a solid is. A solid occupies a very specific three-dimensional space. An entity that is fluid, a substance that flows, does not occupy a given space in the same manner. A flow is always in more than one location at the same time. It is always both here and there. That is part of the character of a flow. In addition, a fluid does not have a clearly defined inside and outside. An inside and outside requires a stable and solid boundary. The moment fluids have such a boundary, the moment they attain form, is the moment they cease to be a fluid. Gas provides the simplest example of this. It is difficult to say that a gas has an inside and an outside in the same way that a solid has. A gas, for instance, is simply dispersed within a given area and the larger the area, the more dispersed it becomes, continuously flowing, but never existing in one specific location, or one place, as such. As explained in Chapter 5, it is the entire scene.

This point is illustrated by Deleuze and Guattari, who conceptualized the nomad as being of the nature of a flow:

> It is thus necessary to make a distinction between *speed* and *movement*: a movement may be very fast, but that does not give it speed; a speed may be very slow, or even immobile, yet it is still speed. Movement is extensive; speed is intensive. Movement designates the relative character of a body considered as 'one', and which goes from point to point; *speed, on the contrary, constitutes the absolute character of*

a body whose irreducible parts (atoms) occupy or fill a smooth space in the manner of a vortex, with the possibility of springing up at any point.

(Deleuze and Guattari 1987, 381)

This also points to another characteristic, which is that flows do not move, whereas solids do. Fluids, unlike solids, do not move from one location to another location. Fluids flow and therefore one does not speak of the movement of a fluid, as one does with a solid. Instead one speaks of the speed of the flow, of its rate of flow (again, this is not the movement of a body of water, like a river).

To sum up, fluids are defined by virtue of their flow. This means that they have no stable shape. Indeed, any shape would suggest the existence of a stable boundary defining an inside and outside, and therefore the cessation of flow. It is this being of the flow that makes fluids so different from solids. It also means that the relations that exist between fluids are very different from the relations that exist between solids. More importantly, it means that fluids and solids act in a different manner, or rather, their behavior has to be described and conceptualized differently. The main difference in terms of the description of this behavior is that fluids do not exercise force on one another. Also, fluids do not move in the sense that solids do. Fluids, because they flow, do not move. Instead, they have speed, or rate of flow. It is the rate of flow that provides a starting point for a discussion of fluid forms of political action in the context of the network, the rate of flow being a key determinant of what I call 'machine-power' in the digital ensemble.

The politics of fluids

One of the first things that needs to be emphasized is that, when thinking about political action in the context of the network, one is not in the first instance dealing with entities that act with force, moving or throwing their weight around in an attempt to affect the state of relations of the bodies around them. One is not dealing with bodies that are trying to overcome the inertia, momentum, or direction of movement of other bodies by way of establishing social contracts. Such bodies do not, indeed, cannot exist in the context of the network. This means that political action in the context of the network, which is the political action of the networked actor or of digital being and, ultimately, of the interfaced dividual, cannot be appropriately conceptualized or imagined through the concepts and images associated with solid political action. This point should also be kept in mind in coming to terms with the emergence of modulation as a mode power and other new forms of control. As indicated in Part I, the modulatory mode of power operates through its production of objectiles. The objectile *is* the actual anticipation of the emergence of patterns of code, of information flow. The objectile, I stressed, is flow. The modulatory mode of power produces and recognizes only flow/s.

However, while much work similarly recognizes the emergence of a mode of power that produces, or operates in, a fluid environment where process dominates, and that is turbulent and geared to anticipation (Cooper 2010; Massumi 2009; Terranova 2007), it is quite difficult to think of political action in more positive ways in such a context. This is perhaps partly due to new forms of control that appear quite ominous (Deleuze 1992), but it might also be due partly because we think of ourselves as solid bodies inhabiting a spatial world. In short, thinking of politics and political action as not being the action of solids is a challenging thing to do. Much of the language and vocabulary available for talking about politics and political action relies on concepts of political actors, and therefore their actions, as being solid and spatial. Kirby, for instance, has questioned whether any other language (that is, a language that does not rely on spatial forms) is even possible (Kirby 1996, 3). Indeed, Deleuze and Guattari are perhaps the only people who, as Daniel Smith (2011, 37) points out, have made a case 'that the notion of a *flow* should be the fundamental concept of political philosophy'. However, here I'm trying to be more strictly focused on coming to terms with actions in the context of the code that constitutes the digital ensemble, whether as our screen reality, or as the code that we don't see translated on our screens, though obviously the interface functions to code and uncode the sorts of flows that Deleuze and Guattari put as central.

An important point to emphasize here is that the notion of fluidity is considered to be extremely problematic within modern thought more generally (Berman 1983). This is a feature of modern thinking that a number of feminist theorists have also identified (Irigaray 1985; Kirby 1996; Moi 1986). Fluids, these theorists argue, are considered problematic within much of modern thought, including its science, precisely because they have no form (Kirby 1996, 139). From a solid perspective, fluid entities cannot have identity (Irigaray 1985, 109). Indeed, physicists acknowledge their lack of understanding of 'real' fluids and argue that this is because they are simply too 'complicated' (Halliday and Resnick 1988, 372).

In some respects, this can be seen as an obvious response from the point of view of solid entities. In the language of solid politics, the terms 'fluid' and 'volatile' are used to describe scenes that are difficult to predict and analyze. Fluid terminology is present in descriptions of situations that are explosive, and, therefore, destructive to solid entities; it is also present in descriptions of situations as being those on which one cannot get a grasp. That is, a fluid situation describes a scene that is turbulent, where no stable entities can be detected and no movements can be determined. In such a situation, solid actors cannot adequately evaluate their position vis-à-vis others. This also means solid actors cannot clearly establish their interests and aims beyond maintaining shape and coherence, which, as Massumi (2009) points out, is perhaps a deliberate aim of power.

Rather than perceiving the fluid nature of the network as a problem, thinking about politics has to be approached in a more positive manner. In short, most attempts to describe political action in the context of the network, using the language of solid politics, result in a fairly negative description of this political action. As Meikle has observed of media activism and the Internet, not only has the use of the unique properties of the Internet not yet been fully developed, but when genuinely new forms of political issues, action, or organization do emerge they tend to be made to fit the narrative pattern of 'protesters clash with police' (Meikle 2002, 94). In addition, as Reid (2009) points out, there is a need to move beyond couching questions in terms of access, and to instead, taking Deleuze and Guattari's lead, couch questions more in terms of asking what our connections to our digital machines do. We need to move beyond generally imagining fluids or flows as capable of acting in anything other than a destructive manner in that regard, which from the point of view of solid politics is difficult to imagine because fluids are generally associated with dissolution.[5]

One of the first aspects of fluid politics, then, is that networked actors are not in any specific location in the same sense that non-networked or solid actors are. On a certain level the actors, or more precisely the actions they perform, are deterritorialized (Castells 1996, 93; Stratton 2000, 723).[6] Fluid forms of action (as I stated earlier) do not 'take place', but are 'performed'. The very definition of a flow, as pointed out in the Section 'The mechanics of fluids', is that it does not occupy a specific space in the sense that a solid entity does. A political action in the context of the network is therefore always performed over the entire flow that forms part of a network, and not simply in one location within a space, though such flows can always be 'contained'.[7] In short, the distinction between local and global does not make sense in the context of the network (Castells 1996), as any action effectively occurs over the entirety of the network.

To explain this point further, a political action in the context of the network occurs in terms of the specific flow/s of code it constitutes and generates, and in terms of the specific flow/s it affects. Such actions can affect the entire flow that is the network, or they can affect specific flow lines and streamlines of which such a flow consists. Many forms of fluid action, for instance, occur in the context of a specific flow, or flow tube. The Microsoft Corporation and the flow/s of which it is constituted and that it generates, for example, are frequently affected by the generation and constitution of flow lines and streamlines that affect not the entire flow that is the corporation, but may only affect a specific streamline of which that flow consists. Some viruses, for example, have only affected the Windows XP operating system, but not Microsoft's other operating systems. The flow generated by way of the earlier 'Code Red' and the 'Nimda' viruses, for example, only affected Microsoft Windows NT and Windows 2000 operating systems. Other viruses may only affect Internet Explorer. The crucial point is that, in the context of the network, such actions affect the entire flow, or screen reality, that is Internet Explorer or, more precisely, a specific version of it. It does not distinguish, in other words, between Internet Explorer installed on a machine located in Sydney and Internet Explorer installed on a machine in New York. In that respect, at least some aspects, some flow lines, of Internet Explorer are all of the same flow, whether it is understood as gaseous or fluid.

From such a perspective, any string of code could be understood as a moment of either a flow line or a streamline that may flow as part of a larger flow or flow tube; though, it could be equally productive to think of a string of code as a flow line or streamline in itself. Whenever a flow line changes velocity,[8] thereby becoming a streamline, it affects the streamlines that flow next to it. It can thereby increase the rate of flow of some flows, and decrease the rate of flow of other flows. Nor does it necessarily have to affect the flow of the flow tube as a whole, which may remain in a steady pattern.

One example to illustrate this is how a person might be producing or participating in a specific flow. This could be you writing something on a word processor, having a conversation on Facebook, playing a game, watching a YouTube video, or, indeed, listening to music. You might be connected to, and participating in, various flows that operate at different speeds, some of which might simply be a gel in an ambient state, at a speed of near zero. You might have e-mail open in the background, be logged into Skype, as well as logged into Facebook. One of these flows increases its rate of flow for a brief moment. A sound or flashing icon in the bottom right-hand side of the screen indicates the momentary increase of that rate of flow, literally. It both affects and effects your participation in, and constitution of, your main flow line, or even an entire flow tube. There is, at the very least, the briefest vortex that distracts you, that makes you think whether you should check it.

If you do check it, you open a new window or screen (it might be your mobile phone screen). You effectively participate in, and constitute, a new flow line. Or rather, you've increased the rate of flow of one flow line, however briefly. This itself, depending on the rate of flow (that is, what you might experience as intensity), might well result in your previous main flow line not simply reducing its rate of flow, but perhaps producing a turbulent flow tube. The distraction might be so much (for example, an e-mail from your work requiring some other activity on your part) that you have to disconnect and return to your solid state altogether, and cease your existence as superject.

Similarly, the slow speed of one of the other flow lines might well be the cursor flashing on the screen, waiting for you to become part of the process again and to undo your 'Pause' state in that particular flow line, or in that process, as Galloway might phrase it (2006, 10). The machine, after all, doesn't pause. It continues to flow, and produce code, even if you give it no input. It 'keeps' time, it keeps producing your screen reality even if you give it no input. Even if the screen on your mobile phone goes blank to save energy, the machine keeps processing code until you switch it off (though even then it might never really be switched off). It doesn't become solid, or rather, the code produced by the machine, and ultimately by us, never stops. Only people do when they disconnect. Indeed, depending on how 'connected' a person is, even when they are not connected to their machines, they might still think about the flow/s being produced that they are not participating in – 'I wonder how the market will react to the President's speech', 'I wonder if my guild buddies are online', 'I wonder if I got a response to that e-mail'.

Switching off, as in the case of the traders Knorr-Cetina (2003; 2007) studied, is never really possible. They always have to stay 'in touch' with the screen reality that is the market. Indeed, their own constitution as flow/s when connected to their multiple screens is at a very rapid speed, which I compared to the experience of online gaming in Chapter 5. Furthermore, for traders the 'constitutive components of financial markets' are what they call orders and flows (Knorr-Cetina 2003, 16). Orders in the financial markets are 'requests for trades once the price of a financial instrument reaches a certain level; when an order is executed, it becomes a flow' (Knorr-Cetina 2003, 16). The overall effect of these flows, the execution of orders, is that

> markets have characteristic 'speeds' indicated by the price movements which are at the center a changing market process. In currency spot trading, which is the direct exchange of currencies, prices tend to change within split seconds during periods of average activity. As a consequence, the currency trading timeworld moves forward at a breath-taking pace.[9]
>
> (Knorr-Cetina 2003, 18)

Of course, it isn't only traders and gamers that experience this flow, but anybody who is connected to digital machines, even if at a very different level of intensity. More and more people have to produce labor through digital machines, or entertain themselves, or communicate with each other through digital machines, and as they do so participate in, and constitute themselves as, a variety of flow lines, streamlines, and flow tubes.

Indeed, the construction of the political in the context of digital technologies (as I argued in Chapter 5) occurs at the moment of connection, at the moment of the constitution of flow. It is that connection, and the resultant assemblage (Bergen 2010), that in effect constitutes a new body, which makes asking Spinoza's question, and also Deleuze's, of what a body can do first and foremost a question of politics. It means that a political action is anything that affects the constitution of flow, whether that be in the ability to participate in a flow, the ability to constitute a flow in the first instance, or any change in an already constituted flow. This is partly why so many political issues surrounding digital media are couched in terms of access: no connection, no flow, and poor connection, poor flow.

Once connection is enabled, action is best understood in terms of the constitution and effects of flows (that is, in terms of how it may affect an existing flow tube) or in terms of how it may constitute a new flow tube or part thereof. In short, access is such a focus of attention in much scholarship precisely because connection – the construction of the digital human assemblage – is what enables all subsequent actions in the digital ensemble to occur, whether they be economic, social, or cultural. As explained in Part II, this is also how digital machines differ from the machines of the industrialized mechanical ensemble. They simply enable an entirely new world of action and thought: they make new connections possible, always recognizing that this can be both positive and negative, and is in a very real sense the product of people's desire. This makes connection, access, the ability and capacity to constitute yourself as flow within the digital ensemble, whether individual or collective, a primary political issue.

Farmers, especially those in remote areas, provide a useful example here. Most obviously, connection to the network enables a farmer to access markets around the world (that is, it enables the connection to other people, whether they be distributors or consumers). But access can also come in the form of farmers knowing how to respond to consumer groups. For example, in the case of one US farmer, Troy Hadrick, he recognized that the screen reality produced both through social and traditional media could have a dramatic impact on his life. After one negative article came out in the *New York Times*, he noticed how, 'on Monday morning, calf prices dropped, future prices dropped and every single consumer that read that article that weekend had their perception of the beef industry shifted further away from reality one more time' (Courtney 2011). Following this incident, he began to produce, and participate in a variety of flows, including through a blog and sites like Twitter, Facebook, and YouTube, thereby bypassing traditional media:

> This spring, you know, I used it actually to give people an opportunity to watch us as we were going through calving season. And I tagged all of my posts on Twitter with the term 'calving'. And I think it was an interesting experiment for us because we picked up a lot of people who started following that, you know, and started asking us questions about what they were seeing on those pictures I was posting. And so, you know, it's an amazing tool for having conversations, for giving real-time updates, and the real beauty thing about it is a lot of it you can do on your phone. So it's always with you and it's handy and whenever you got a couple of seconds, you can do some of that kind of thing.
>
> (Courtney 2011)

Hadrick also began to insert his own code in existing flow lines of organizations and businesses. When he discovered that an Australian company, the winery Yellowtail, offered monetary support, a flow of money, to an animal rights group he saw as anti-farmer, he left a comment on the company's Facebook page. In addition to that, he asked his own Facebook and Twitter followers to do the same. A first effect of this was that it altered the flow of information that was Yellowtail's

Facebook screen reality, in effect coloring Yellowtail's Facebook flow differently through adding his own flow to theirs. A second effect, which was enhanced by the upload of a YouTube video 'Yellow Tail is Now Yellow Fail', is that it significantly increased the rate and volume of flow of code. As Hadrick states, 'holy smokes, it was like releasing the hounds' (Courtney 2011). This change to one of Yellowtail's flow lines, producing a streamline in the process, produced other streamlines in Yellowtail's flow tube, to the point that the flow line of money in that tube no longer involved the animal rights group. This demonstrates the relatively low viscosity (a fluid's internal resistance) of social media like Facebook, Google+, and Twitter when compared to the higher viscosity of more traditional media like radio and television, and the even higher viscosity of print media.[10]

Indeed, it isn't simply that social media have a different viscosity, but that the flow lines produced through social media are now also part of the more established flow tubes of more traditional media. This is both, worryingly, in terms of the ownership of media, but also comes in the examples of television presenters reading out live Twitter messages during the airing of a program, or in the form of journalists reading Twitter messages to give a 'live' update of events. In any case, the point is that the flow lines, streamlines, and vortices can affect one another, and together constitute a larger fluid. Of course, this also applies to the groups of people who connect, as Hadrick's partner comments:

> What we've seen are many different factions within our agricultural industries come together and start using social media and different tools to get out there and tell their story that consumers definitely are listening, they're connecting, they're following them on Twitter, they're following them on Facebook, the blogs that are going out. That's the way that you can sit in a large town like New York City or Chicago and really connect with somebody even 100 miles outside of Chicago and make that connection with where your food's coming from.
>
> (Courtney 2011)

Wikileaks and campaigns such as Kony 2012 provide more obvious examples of how flow/s can operate, as does the earlier McSpotlight, which is a precursor on a smaller scale. The latter, as Meikle showed, was one of the first ways in which the unique properties of the Internet were used to counter McDonald's communication strategies (2002, 75–87). Prior to the emergence of McSpotlight, McDonald's had been very effective in preventing the spread of any critical news concerning McDonald's. In other words, they had always been very good at preventing the emergence of news that could damage the flow that is McDonald's. The makers of the McSpotlight website put up critical information about McDonald's and, because of the deterritorialized nature of the network, were able to avoid being subjected to UK libel laws (Meikle 2002). Not only that, but as a flow it is deliberately constituted to affect the larger flow tube constituted by McDonald's, not in quite as direct a manner as the example of the farmer's use of Facebook, but the point is similar, and an important one when considering that according to McSpotlight 'McDonald's spends over $2 billion a year broadcasting their glossy image to the world. This is a small space for alternatives to be heard' (McSpotlight 2011). McDonald's, in short, cares greatly about its screen reality because it recognizes that these flows affect the flow of money like no other.

The McSpotlight website, unlike print media but like McDonald's, is a fluid entity and McDonald's was unable to prevent its flow from affecting it. The same was the case with Wikileaks. These are useful examples of how different flow/s come to affect one another, or, as a solid might say, a good example of fluid-on-fluid action. Such a constitution of flow/s and the emergence of fluid and gaseous entities was also seen in the early use of the Internet by subcommander Marcos of the Zapatista National Liberation Army (EZLN) (Knudson 1998). Another example of fluid-on-fluid action can also be found in cyberwar or netwar (Meikle 2002; Ronfeldt and Arquilla 2001), and not simply between so-called state actors, as the alleged cases of cyberwarfare between China and the USA illustrate. This also involves some hacker groups such as Anonymous shutting down government websites in Egypt and Libya during the Arab Spring, thereby stopping their flow. Indeed, Anonymous also came to the defense of Wikileaks when MasterCard and Visa cut off their service (Isikoff 2011).

Focusing on flow enables the recognition of a host of actions, of problems, that might not necessarily be recognized as 'political' when using the framework of solid politics, or certainly would not be treated as seriously as the actions of solids. Any constitution of flow, anything that affects flow, is a political event in its own right within the context of the network. Increasing the rate or volume of flow can also be used in more negative ways than the example of the farmer Hadrick above. Many of the actions performed by the Electronic Disturbance Theater (EDT), with their development of 'FloodNet' (Meikle 2002, 140; Ronfeldt and Arquilla 2001), are good examples of this. Well over a decade before

Haddick increased the rate of flow on Yellowtail's Facebook page, for example, EDT called for a 'digital storm' on the Mexican government.

> This call for a 'digital storm' was an alert for a *virtual sit-in* – it's not a call to action in the real world, such as a blockade of a physical space. It's an event which happens wholly within the networked virtual space between the participants and their target. In a virtual sit-in, supporters swarm a targeted website and deluge it with bogus requests to reload the page. The idea is that the server will be unable to cope with the volume of traffic and that this will block out other visitors.
> (Meikle 2002, 142)

Such FloodNet action, if large enough, could affect the bandwidth of network, thereby slowing down, if not wholly ceasing, other flow/s within the network (Meikle 2002, 144). To state that differently, in increasing the rate and/or volume of a flow line or flow tube, you can produce a turbulent flow that ceases to flow in any organized sense, preventing any action from occurring.

While the EDT in this example employed a solid concept, that of the sit-in, the Critical Art Ensemble (CAE), established in 1987 (CAE 2009), tried to totally dispense with solid forms of political action. They 'argued that gathering in the street was a dead tactic. If power was now nomadic and decentralized, then physical protest at a physical site was like picketing a monument to dead capital' (Meikle 2002, 147). Their proposal was a form of 'electronic civil disobedience' through an alliance of hackers and activists whose aim should be 'to combat decentralized power . . . [proposing] decentralized, cell-based organization' (Meikle 2002, 147). Indeed, they were very critical of the notion of the virtual sit-in, arguing that in the end it is 'just symbolic', and, instead, pushed for strategies that would destroy 'the system' (Meikle 2002, 149).[11]

These forms of action, which usually take the form of denial-of-service attacks, tend to have a very negative character. This negativity reflects the fact that they always aim to disrupt streamlines and, ultimately, the flow/s these constitute. The greater the volume of flow they generate, the greater the effect will be on the existing steady-state pattern of the network. Stated differently, their joining and redirection or streamlining of a flow aims to create a general non-steady pattern of flow (that is, turbulence). In short, many of the political actions that occur in the context of the network operate by way of the logic that '[i]f corporate power is everywhere and nowhere, nomadic and dispersed, then opposition to that power needs to be likewise' (Meikle 2002, 91).

This, however, is a very negative approach toward conceptualizing fluid and political action in the context of the network. Indeed, the very concept of 'opposition' is one that belongs to the realm of solid politics. The concept operates by way of the assumption of two opposing forces. This negative conceptualization of political action and politics in the context of the network more generally was presented by Hardt and Negri in their *Empire* as 'the essential key to every active political position in the world, every desire that is effective – perhaps of democracy itself' (Hardt and Negri 2001, 211). Conceptualizing politics and the political as a 'being-against' (Hardt and Negri 2001, 211), and here I take Guattari's cue (1992), is a major impediment to coming to grips with politics in the context of digital technologies. It is a major impediment because it effectively denies any capacity on the part of fluid being for positive political action, and being. Hardt and Negri's problem, in short, is that they are still strongly rooted in the politics of solids, so much so that the only entity they can think of as having any capacity for political action is an entity that is entirely impervious and incapable of adaptation. In short, they are thinking of a solid body with such a high degree of inertia that it cannot be moved. As they state it in their earlier *Empire*,

> [t]he will to be against really needs a body that is completely incapable of submitting to command. It needs a body that is incapable of adapting to family life, to factory discipline, to the regulations of a traditional sex life, and so forth.
>
> (Hardt and Negri 2001, 216)[12]

Our capacity for freedom, as I pointed to earlier by way of Rose (1999), is a machination. It is not the product of an absence of power but is, in fact, a product of power (Rose 1999, 96). It is an ongoing process of production in which we ourselves are constantly engaged. In effect, one becomes inert if one takes the position of refusing to engage or, more precisely, of limiting engagement to a refusal to move (that is, to flow or adapt). This effectively leaves much of the production of 'freedom' to the flow/s of fluid entities that do reflect a positive understanding of fluid action. The dominant flow/s that are capable of fluid action are, at this point in time, the military and the corporation, including those in the computer game industry. They constitute what Der Derian describes as the 'military-industrial-media-entertainment-network' (Der Derian 2009). Taking the form and stance of a solid within the fluidity of that network means that one becomes incapable of acting as a fluid, thereby realizing Deleuze's fear of existence in the control society (1992).

The key problem at this point, then, is to try and begin to conceptualize both the being and doing of fluidity, of flow/s, positively. Turbulence, for example, has often been considered, certainly from the point of view of solids, as a very negative experience and situation. Central to that perception is the unpredictability of its onset and consequences (Cooper 2010; Massumi; 2009; Parisi and Terranova 2000). However, some fluid entities, most notably financial corporations (Bailey 1996; Parisi and Terranova 2000), the US military (De Landa 1991; Der Derian 2009), but also corporations with an interest in genetic engineering and molecular biology (Parisi and Terranova 2000), have put a lot of effort into coming to terms with turbulence. Some of this research has focused on predicting the onset of turbulence by way of the Reynolds number (De Landa 1991). Such scientific research, of which chaos theory is a prime example (Prigogine and Stengers 1985), increasingly views turbulence as productive rather than destructive (Cooper 2010; De Landa 1991; Massumi 2009).

Indeed, it is in such a context that pattern recognition, the production of an objectile, must be seen as a fluid action. Financial corporations invest large amounts of money into machines and software that can anticipate very small temporal 'gaps' in the market – a fluid entity – where profits can be made (Bailey 1996). As Parisi and Terranova have argued, by comparing the fluidity of the network to that of the female mode of indefinite reproduction, such research into turbulence and the mechanics of fluids is considered essential for providing an 'inexhaustible source of surplus' (Parisi and Terranova 2000; Terranova 2007). It is in such a context that fluids are productive, not destructive.

It is on this point that Hayles (2009) suggests we can begin to think in more positive ways, in the first instance by utilizing the forms of visibility utilized in the machine that is the modulatory mode of power. Crowdsourcing, through open-source software such as that provided by Ushahidi (a not-for-profit company) is one example here (Crandall 2010). Their platform, they advertise, can be used to crowdsource information using multiple channels, whether this be e-mail, SMS, Twitter, or the Web. Indeed, their Swift River platform is aimed at democratizing access to a set of tools that can be used to 'filter and make sense of real-time information' (Ushahidi 2011), whether this be acts of violence, corruption, or disasters. Indeed, it was formed in response to a media blackout in Kenya following the 2007 elections there. Of course, it could perhaps be similarly used to help people map restoration efforts, or help to identify causes of accidents. In short, it exists to enable people, in a participatory way, to deal with an overwhelming flow of information in real time. As the founder, David Kobia, states in an interview, 'something that is happening thousands of miles away is actually happening in your digital backyard' (2011). In that respect, Ushahidi is very much about association and collaboration, and has a very low viscosity because of its participatory character. In fact, it is all about enabling an increase in the rate of flow, as well as an increase in who can institute and constitute specific flow lines, and obviously could be used to identify patterns in order to pre-empt. Indeed, its popularity has caused a range of similar platforms to be produced, including by companies such as Google, which would obviously want any increase in flow to occur by way of Google's flow tubes.

The constitution of flow is central to all fluid-on-fluid action. The moments in which a rate of flow is affected are instances of fluid action. This can be achieved by way of increasing or decreasing the viscosity of a flow, as in the case of a large domain name system (DNS) attack, or can be accomplished by affecting the stream lines of a flow, as in the case of Hadrick, or McSpotlight and Wikileaks. Whenever any given stream line increases its rate of flow, it affects the stream lines flowing around it. Such increases can often produce turbulence, a situation that should not necessarily be seen as negative. Indeed, to some extent, turbulence may be normal for the network, rather than exceptional (De Landa 1991; Parisi and Terranova 2000). In this context, one can also distinguish between laminar flows and turbulent flows. Of course, yet another form of fluid action could be an alteration of the direction of a stream line and therefore, possibly, the direction of the flow, which is what Hadrick achieved so successfully. In some respects, the act of altering web-sites could be treated as an example of this, but with the use of social media the alteration can simply come in the form of positive or negative comment. There is, then, a range of possibilities for fluid political action in the politics of fluids.

It is in such a context that one can speak of a politics of fluids, as many actions in the context of the network can be understood in terms of the constitution of flow/s. Anything that affects the constitution of flow must be considered to be political. A platform such as Ushahidi, irrespective of the uses to which it is put, is political simply because of its capacity to produce specific types of flow line. Anything that affects the smoothness of flow/s in that respect is also political. Altering the speed or rate of flow is a critical political action because it directly affects flow. The rate of flow is a major concern for financial corporations and for the military. The faster or more sensitive one's machine is, the faster one can anticipate an event, and therefore the greater the chance that one anticipates it before anyone else does. In this respect, the production of a flow by way of a 9600-baud rate modem is totally disproportionate to the production of a flow by way of a direct network connection. Different speeds of flow, then, are a critical political issue in the context of digital technologies – and it may be necessary in the first instance to conceptualize political equality in the context of the network in terms of an equality of speed. Stated differently, it is not simply access to the network that should be a determinant of equality. The quality of access must also be an issue, especially when considering or attempting to overcome the 'digital divide'.

Political action in the context of the network is flow/s. Anything that affects the smoothness of flow is, in effect, political action, whether that be its rate of flow, its flow lines, or streamlines. From this perspective, what constitutes political power in the context of the network is not only knowledge and access to it (Lyotard 1984; McLaren and Zappalà 2002; Reid 2009), but, more importantly perhaps, also what I call machine power. The speed and the capacity of the machines by which the flows are conducted are key determinants in an actor's capacity for action. To return to Deleuze and Guattari's question, it is a matter of asking what an assemblage can do. For a fluid, the inability to flow or circulate is death.

Machine power, in other words, is a vital component in the constitution of the human-machine assemblage in the context of digital technologies, and I don't mean that simply in terms of CPU speed. The moment that one's being becomes of machines, or expressive of the digital ensemble, is the moment that one's doing becomes of those machines. In other words, one's capacity to exist, or to constitute oneself in the context of the network, is directly tied to the machines by way of which one connects (that is, by way of which one becomes of the machine). In that respect, the interface is not only the key moment in the construction of the political, but, therefore, is a very political issue in itself. It is in that context that the much older debate concerning the differences between the Macintosh and DOS operating systems were quite important, and which are repeated today in debates about open-source software.

This was the serious point behind Umberto Eco's playful claim that the differences between the Macintosh and DOS computer operating systems were analogous to a religious schism. The Mac interface, Eco suggested, was Catholic, with its ease of use making it possible for all to enter the kingdom of spreadsheet heaven; the difficulty of DOS, by contrast was a more demanding faith, which assumed that some would make it all the way.

(Meikle 2002, 103–4)

In other words, the interface has a role to play in the extent to which fluid being can flow. The Mac interface restricted the manner in which fluids can flow, while the DOS interface at the time, though initially making it more difficult to constitute fluid being in the first place, provided a greater range in terms of the direction of flows.

The importance of machine power in enabling fluid forms of action (of which the creation of the interface is only one important element) points to some of the different ways in which flow/s can be governed or regulated in the context of digital technologies. The regulation of flow/s, including preventing access to the code of the operating system, and creating an infrastructure that is capable of a very limited rate of flow, is often also a way in which solid political entities (such as the State, or corporations) attempt to deal with the flow/s of the network (such as financial flows). Indeed, much of the political action that occurs in the context of the network takes the form of fluids trying to circumvent solid political entities, and the latter attempting to direct and stop what are considered to be dangerous or risky flow/s, including WikiLeaks. This interaction between the politics of solids and the politics of fluids is the focus of Chapter 8.

8
The Boundary Layer

So far part of my aim has been to establish a distinction between how we generally conceptualize the political actions of what we might call a non-networked or solid actor and how we might generally conceptualize political actions available to a networked or fluid actor. I attempted to delineate these two general approaches in conceptualizing political action in terms of a solid politics and a fluid politics, treating them as completely separate from one another. Such a clear binary distinction in examining the effects of digital media is problematic, of course (Gunkel 2007). The example of the use of Ushahidi, in Chapter 7, should make that clear. Indeed, especially issues surrounding copyright and censorship, for instance, involve a mixture of solid and fluid politics, with solid entities such as the State acting in response to various flows that are considered a threat to the cohesion of solid political entities. It is this contact at the surface of the fluid and the solid – what in the study of fluids is referred to as the boundary layer – that I now want to turn to briefly.

Flow can be seen as central to Deleuze and Guattari's theory of politics and the social. In Deleuze and Guattari's approach, flow is treated as something more broad than what I have delineated so far. Relying on the work of Marx, Freud, and, significantly, Keynes (among others), for Deleuze and Guattari the political economy and the libidinal economy are only differentiated from one another by the fact that they have differing regimes (Smith 2011). Apart from this, they are effectively the same, encompassing flows of people, flows of money, flows of thought, flows of blood and milk, flows of traffic, flows of stupidity, flows of advertising, and so on (Smith 2011, 37–8). So while in previous chapters I drew a deliberate and strict distinction between discipline and modulation, the individual and the superject, and the solid and the fluid, in actuality, from Deleuze and Guattari's perspective, flow is found everywhere.

That doesn't mean we shouldn't distinguish between different flows. Indeed, the critical political question for Deleuze and Guattari is how the variety of flows are coded and controlled, whether this be the flow of genetic code, the flow of people, or the flow of money. In some respects what I am suggesting is that these various flows are also channeled through the digital ensemble, in the process perhaps translated and modified by it. Stated differently, I don't deny that fluids as a body can move, and can be channeled, but in the digital ensemble we also need to consider a different aspect of fluids – their capacity to flow rather than to move as a fluid body in toto. As Daniel Smith, for example, explains in relation to stocks, stocks and flow are the same thing but refer to different units of that thing.[1]

The flow of code that I considered as partly constituting our screen reality deals with this aspect of flow. Indeed, Deleuze and Guattari's approach to flow stresses aspects of movement, which is partly why I wanted to isolate the flow that is our screen reality. This is precisely the aspect of flow that people such as Knorr-Cetina (2003; 2007) point to. Castells' 'space of flows' (2005) is an important aspect of the digital ensemble, as is the movement of flows such as the various markets that move around the globe in a 24-hour period (Knorr-Cetina 2007), but instead I've tried to stress a different aspect of fluids, that is, the actual flow – a substance that continuously changes.

This aspect of flow cannot be understood in terms of movement, certainly not in terms of movement alone. As I stressed in previous chapters, this aspect of flow is not the flow of a river, nor the flow of an aggregate solid, such as a flow of sand, or a flow of people on the street. Instead, we need to consider what is specific to fluids if we want to begin to think in more positive terms about flows within the context of the digital ensemble. So that, instead of thinking that a fluid, a gas, can't move, can't act with force, or can't be organized, we need to consider fluid characteristics. As I attempted in Chapter 7, we need to begin to consider the viscosity of a fluid. Its flow lines and streamlines, as well as its rate of flow or speed, and how changes in speed and velocity affect a flow line or produce a streamline. In addition to that, we need to consider how flows can compose a multiplicity as a single flow tube, in turn making us consider the relation of flow tubes to each other, recognizing that flow lines and streamlines can never cross. We need to recognize better the composition and constitution of laminar flow as well as turbulent flow.

In Part I, laminar and turbulent flows were examined with respect to how a new modulatory mode of power aims to anticipate events, both in terms of how modulatory power produces the anticipation of the emergence of laminar flows, as well as turbulent flows. This anticipation of patterns of code, and hence anticipation of flow/s, is what I suggested constitutes the main product of modulation: the objectile. Indeed, turbulent flow is precisely what so many people have focused on in examining the operation of new forms of power (Cooper 2010; Massumi 2009; Parisi and Terranova 2000; Terranova 2007).

Significantly, turbulence is precisely something that is produced more at the moment of contact between fluids and solids than it is produced at moments of fluid-to-fluid contact. Turbulence is mostly produced at the surface, the boundary layer, where fluid and solid encounter each other. It is with this encounter, the moment where the flow of code that constitutes the digital ensemble (irrespective of whether it is projected as the flow of information on the screen reality or exists solely as the flow of binary code on the machine level that we don't immediately see), that a different problematic has emerged over the past few decades.

In what follows I want to first summarize the main differences between solid and fluid forms of political action. As part of this I will here utilize Deleuze and Guattari's distinction (1987, 380) to argue that the politics of solids is that of the *polis*, while the politics of fluids is that of the *nomos*. I then focus on the moment of interaction – the encounter – between solid and fluid politics, which takes place at the boundary layer. Here I want to argue that solid politics aims to produce useful forces out of the flows that constitute the digital ensemble – to, if you like, increase the pressure on various fluids to extract more surplus. In short, what perhaps results from the encounter is a hydraulic machine that is constantly in danger of springing leaks and breaking apart due to the pressures created by the various flows within it. To state this more in Deleuze and Guattari's terms, the connection of the digital ensemble to the industrialized mechanical ensemble produces a hydraulic machine – a new engine of capitalism – for the purposes of producing, and attempting to contain, new lines of flight.

Solid and fluid politics

A first obvious difference between solid and fluid politics is that solid politics deals with structured bodies. In other words, solid politics deals with bodies of stable shape and mass. Fluid politics, on the other hand, has no entities of stable composition and size. Indeed, while in solid politics various bodies can be added together and easily distinguished from one another within the larger body, in fluid politics such a distinction is much more problematic. For instance, one can assemble a group of individuals, forming them into one solid political or social body, perhaps by way of a contract, to which one attributes a general will (Hobbes 1968; Rousseau 1989), but in fluid politics the whole notion of individuality makes no sense, as whenever flows are added together they are always both one and many (Colwell 1996; Deleuze 1992). Indeed, the very act of adding fluids together is likely to create a moment of turbulence.

One major point of difference, therefore, between solid and fluid politics is that the former has the smallest indivisible political unit, the individual, while fluid politics has no such unit. In fluid politics there is simply no entity comparable to the individual of solid politics. There is no entity that can be attributed a specific mass, which has a direction in the form of a vector or force, guided by rights or interests, and which can act on another body. Fluid politics only deals with fluid entities, which by definition have no stable, specific shape. Indeed, to be made into such a shape would lead to the destruction of the fluid entity in question.

Another crucial difference between solid and fluid politics is that they each consist of two very different forms of action. All political action in the context of solid politics is reducible to force. Forces, regardless of their mass or size, can be opposed to one another; they can also be added to one another or fragmented. In fluid politics, however, all political action can be reduced to the constitution or being of flow/s. Flow/s may be added, in the sense that their volume or density and, therefore their pressure, increases. One cannot bring them back to their original flow/s. One cannot have single, determinate units of gas making up a larger gaseous substance. Further, while solids can exert pressure on one another, it is precisely through pressure that fluids can determine their liquid or gaseous state, the rate of flow or speed, and their size or volume.[2] Increasing pressure, for fluid being, is tantamount to increasing the constitution of flow. It is, in some respects, an addition to being; whereas for solids, it is always a description of one's relation to, and interaction with, other solids.

The difference between movement and flow in solid and fluid politics is also very important. In solid politics political actors occupy a very specific space, that is, they have a place or a location and exist in relation to political entities occupying the same space in a similar manner.[3] Solid politics is conceptualized as operating in a geometrical space. In this space, political action tends to revolve around the ways that actors relate to one another, both in terms of how they can hold on to the space they occupy (that is, their place), but also in terms of how they can move themselves into a better location vis-à-vis others. These others could be individuals with whom they are in competition, including those in a structurally advantaged position that enables them to exert more force upon other individuals.

In fluid politics, on the other hand, actors do not move. There are in that respect no structurally advantageous positions. Fluid or networked actors are always in the nature of a flow. In that respect, what matters is not their movement, for they have none, but the speed at which they flow, or rather, their rate of flow and their viscosity. From this perspective, fluid politics is not conceptualized in terms of an actor's place or location and how it situates that actor in relation to other actors. Instead, action has to be thought of in terms of the rate of flow or speed. What matters from the point of view of fluid politics is machine power and the rate of transmission of code.

This difference in terms of the different conceptualization of space and movement is also reflected in a different conceptualization of the political (Hardt and Negri 2001; 2005; 2009; Stiegler 2009b). Virilio frames this distinction and its political consequences very well, albeit negatively:

> This sudden reversion of boundaries and oppositions introduces into everyday, common space an element which until now was reserved for the world of microscopes. There is *plenum*; space is not filled with matter. Instead, an unbounded expanse appears in the false perspective of the machines' luminous emissions. From here on, constructed space occurs within an electronic topology where the framing of perspective and the gridwork weft of numerical images renovate the division of urban property. The ancient private/public occultation and the distinction between housing and traffic are replaced by an overexposure in which the difference between 'near' and 'far' simply ceases to exist, just as the difference between 'micro' and 'macro' vanished in the scanning of the electron microscope.
>
> (Virilio 1991, 13)

To some extent, this distancing is what Stiegler engages with (2009b) when he explains the difference between the dissociated milieus and the need for associated milieus.

In short, the division between public and private spaces, which is one of the key divisions within solid politics, and one of the critical boundaries in its construction of the political, cannot operate within fluid politics. This is because everything is conceptualized in terms of a flow rather than in terms of the occupation of a specific space. In some respects, then, the very notion of 'belonging' does not make sense in fluid politics, or rather (as discussed previously), there is a different sense of belonging. This 'belonging' can be explored in different ways, so that, for example, in the context of the digital ensemble, the notion that something is one's private property – some thing that is yours or mine – does not make much sense either, although it certainly does outside of that context.[4] To state this in more fluid terms, in the context of the digital ensemble everything is in effect constituted as part of the same flow, the same screen reality, or more accurately 'screen realities', we all experience in different degrees of intensity. To distinguish any specific aspect of that flow to be the property of someone can seem an odd idea.

This is not to say that there is no attempt to take ownership of flow/s or, as Deleuze and Guattari would argue, that there is no attempt to further territorialize or code a flow. Facebook is one example of this, when they state in their terms that while a user might own all of the content they post up, that

> For content that is covered by intellectual property rights, like photos and videos (IP content), you specifically give us the following permission, subject to your privacy and application settings: you grant us a non-exclusive, transferable, sub-licensable, royalty-free, worldwide license to use any IP content that you post on or in connection with Facebook (IP License).[5]

> (Facebook 2011)

Especially, for example, with Facebook's introduction of Timeline (the aim of which is to produce a map of everything a user has posted, as well as features aimed at marketing companies that enable people to instantly observe the code that others are producing), the issue of ownership of these flows is contentious. In effect what Facebook aims to do is to extract value – code in Deleuze and Guattari's sense – from the flow tube that is Facebook's members and their relations with each other and other things. Facebook, in other words, is a data mine, with the ultimate aim of being able to code the flow that its members are, but to do so in much more specific ways.

Not, of course, that its members are uncoded flow in the first place – uncoded flow from Deleuze and Guattari's perspective is a spare existence at best (Smith 2011). Instead, the aim is to anticipate and code its members' flow in more direct ways, in part through the mechanisms of the modulatory mode of power. Facebook functions to sell more opportunities to others for increasing their own rate of flow of money. It functions as modulatory power to anticipate its users' flow lines, indeed, ideally its users' flow tube. Rather than have its users pay a fee for a service, its users (or rather, its users' flow lines) become the actual product that Facebook aims to sell. This is a pattern repeated in various ways across a variety of 'media platforms' – that is, a variety of flow tubes.

If distinctions of public and private, of near and far (Stiegler 2009b), no longer operate the same as they perhaps once did, then the difference between what I term solid and fluid politics needs to be approached differently. For Deleuze and Guattari such a difference in both the conceptualization of space and its occupation is one that in *A Thousand Plateaus* they frame as the difference between the *polis* and the *nomos* (Deleuze and Guattari 1987, 380). The *polis* is the space of the State, a sedentary space that is the space of what I term solid politics; whereas the *nomos* is the 'space' of the nomad, a smooth space, the realm of fluid politics. As they explain it (and it is worth quoting Deleuze and Guattari at length here),

> [t]he *nomos* came to designate the law, but that was originally because it was distribution, a mode of distribution. It is a very special kind of distribution, one without division into shares, in a space without borders or enclosure. The *nomos* is the consistency of a fuzzy aggregate: it is in this sense that it stands in opposition to the law or the *polis*, as the backcountry, a mountainside, or the vague expanse around the city ('either nomos or polis').
>
> (Deleuze and Guattari 1987, 380)[6]

From this perspective, the sedentary space of the *polis* is a striated space, divided by walls and enclosures. The nomad space, on the other hand,

> is smooth marked only by 'traits' that are effaced and displaced with the trajectory...The nomad distributes himself [*sic*] in a smooth space; he occupies, inhabits, holds that space; that is his territorial principle. It is therefore false to define the nomad by movement. Toynbee is profoundly right to suggest that the nomad is on the

contrary *he who does not move*. Whereas the migrant leaves behind a milieu that has become amorphous or hostile, the nomad is one who does not depart.

(Deleuze and Guattari 1987, 381)

They further indicate that

It is in this sense that nomads have no points, paths, or land, even though they do by all appearances. If the nomad can be called the Deterritorialized par excellence, it is precisely because there is deterritorialization *afterward* as with the migrant, or upon *something else* as with the sedentary (the sedentary's relation with the earth is mediatized by something else, a property regime, a State apparatus). With the nomad, on the contrary, it is deterritorialization that constitutes the relation to the earth, to such a degree that the nomad deterritorialized on deterritorialization itself.

(Deleuze and Guattari 1987, 381)

Of course, the nomad coexists with the *polis*, or rather, they have a relation. They define one another (Agamben 2005; Stiegler 2009b). This relationship between the *polis* and the nomad, between striated and smooth spaces, is in some respects a trajectory that can be carried on in the distinction between solid and fluid politics. Indeed, the Internet is nothing if not a product of the State and its war machine. Until the 1990s most of the Internet was in public ownership – that is, owned by the US government. It is therefore very much a reconstituted smooth space that represents a new nomadism (Deleuze and Guattari 1987, 387). This is one reason that the relation and distinction between solid and fluid politics is never clear cut. The new nomadism constantly threatens the State, and vice versa, while at the same time allowing for a continuous displacement of the limits of capitalism (Deleuze and Guattari 1977; Stratton 2000, 722). In short, the relationship between solid and fluid politics is constituted out of forms of political action that are both positive and negative. In some respects, it could be argued that this tension or antagonism is similar to that explored with respect to dividuality. In short, it could be argued that there is a productive antagonism between solid and fluid politics.

Fluidics and the dissolution of the body politic

In the first instance, it is difficult to imagine how fluids can do more than react to solid forms of action being exerted upon them. Further, when it comes to solids acting upon fluids, it is difficult not to attribute an active and productive role to solids, while attributing a more passive and negative role to fluids. After all, as a product of the US Defense department, the Internet was designed to facilitate solid forms of political, or rather, military action. The flows that constitute the network can be conceived of as being produced and guided through a system of pipes and gateways. Fluids, in the context of the network, appear to be controlled much in the manner of a hydraulic, or rather, a fluidic system. In other words, the fluids that constitute the network are used, through the regulation of pressure in the production of force, to produce solid forms of political action. More precisely, the network can be understood as an array of two-state devices functioning very much like flip-flop circuits to produce specific flows or outcomes, including turbulent flows.

Yet a number of different events have emerged that suggest that fluid politics is not totally subject to solid politics. Fluid politics itself acts upon solid politics in such a way as to constitute a threat to that politics (Castells 1997; Henderson 2000; Meikle 2002). Some flows have been produced that threaten to dissolve aspects of solid politics, in turn encouraging the production of solid forms of action that attempt to redirect or block these threatening flows. In short, while the network may be conceived of as a hydraulic or fluidic system, the various pressures that build up within it are both potentially productive and destructive. Of course, whether they can be viewed as productive or destructive depends on whether one looks at the pressures from the point of view of solid politics or with the sensibility of fluid politics.

One of the principal effects of the fluidity of the network, for example, is to threaten to dissolve the construction of democracy as solid politics (Hardt and Negri 2001; Ikegami 1999, 889; Poster 2001a, 112; Stiegler 2009b). Central to the construction of democracy as solid politics is the idea that each individual has a right to one vote, regardless of whether it is actually enacted or not. Each individual, at least in most voting systems, has the numeric value 'one'. In the context of solid politics, then (at least as this is set up in representative democracies), the more votes that a government has (that is, the more force they gather behind them), the greater their legitimacy and authority. As Rose points out,

> [d]emocratic power is calculated power, and numbers are intrinsic to the forms of justification that give legitimacy to political power in democracies. Democratic power is calculating power, and numbers are integral to the technologies that seek to give effect to democracy

as a particular set of mechanisms of rule. Democratic power requires citizens who calculate about power, and numeracy and a numerized space of public discourse are essential for making up self-controlling democratic citizens.

(Rose 1999, 200)

In the context of the fluidity of the network, however, these forms of authority and legitimacy are destabilized. One of the reasons they are destabilized and threatened with dissolution is that the concept of democracy has always been directly linked to a geographical location and a concrete spatiality that is the nation state (Ikegami 1999, 889), in which individuals exist as solid entities. As Ikegami argues,

the ideology of cyber-financial globalization, predicated as it is on the desirability and inevitability of unrestricted international capital flows, appears to challenge the territorial-spatial foundations of democracy. Furthermore, the temporal pace of the collective decision-making that characterizes the democratic process appears glacially slow in comparison to the speed of cyberspace transaction, in which investors can move huge capital sums in a matter of seconds.

(Ikegami 1999, 889)

The 2009 global financial crisis (GFC), and perhaps more so the crisis affecting the European Union in 2011 with respect to Greece, for example, amply illustrate this.

In short, the current construct of democracy in solid politics only works within a specific spatiality and temporality. As Poster points out, any concept of cyberdemocracy will need to be very different:

[i]f the term *democracy* refers to the sovereignty of embodied individuals and the system of determining officeholders by these individuals, a new term will be required to indicate a relation of leaders and followers that is mediated by cyberspace and constituted in relation to the mobile identities found therein.

(Poster 2001a, 112)

This latter point returns us briefly to the matter of a different sense of belonging mentioned earlier. One example is provided in the form of the 'professional' elite who inhabit world cities such as New York, London, Singapore, and Hong Kong. These are people who in many respects operate the networks (Castells 2005), and live in what Castells refers to as 'secluded spaces of consumption' (2005, 364). As they shift from node to node in the network, they are secluded, and seclude themselves, from the world through protected 'gateway' communities, business lounges and separate cues. To return to the example of online gamers, their sense of belonging can be more with the online communities they form, rather than the locality in which they live. Their reality is very much the screen reality they produce and maintain, and it is these flows, and the maintenance of them, that principally concern them.

The destabilization of authority in solid politics does have other aspects, of course. One of these is the manner in which the properties of the network enable the circumvention of solid entities such as the State. Wikileaks is the obvious example here. However, it can occur by way of several different flows. Financial flows, for example, are extremely difficult to regulate, even when they can be made visible to the State (Castells 1997; Salisbury and Barnett 1999). Government responses to the GFC noted above are obviously illustrative of this, but so are attempts at imposing taxation on the financial flows of the network. The circumvention of censorship laws are other flows that nation states find hard to regulate (Chen 2000; Meikle 2002; Rajagopal and Bojin 2002), although some authoritarian states (such as Singapore, Cuba, and China) seem to have had some degree of success in doing so. China, for example, has had some success with its construction of an Intranet, while Singapore amplified its disciplinary mechanisms significantly some time ago (Rodan 1998), especially in the form of enhancing the panoptic principle within its citizens (Birch and Lee 2000).

Copyright is also one of the main solid institutions affected by the flow/s of the digital ensemble. A principal effect is in terms of networks enabling the rapid flow or distribution of information. Many products in the context of the network are almost instantly available, regardless of the geographical location in which one produces, purchases, or consumes them. At the same time, as Poster has pointed out, '[p]roperty rights are put in doubt when information is set free of its material instrument to move and to multiply in cyberspace with few constraints' (Poster 1995, 29). The digital ensemble, in other words, has enabled the production of a flow that threatens to dissolve the very concept of property rights. One of the main reasons for this is that they dissolve the distinction between original and copy (Poster 1995). The other principal reason, of course, is that any copying – and in the context of digital technologies there is only copying (Poster 2001b, 48) – is costless and effortless.

The current, solid, construction of property rights is partly based on Locke's conceptualization of private property (Cohen 2008, 2009; Kelly 2002). As touched on previously, Locke argued that one's body is one's own property and that, therefore, any labor one performs with one's body is one's property as well (Locke 1963). As Locke put it,

> [t]hough the Water running in the Fountain be every ones [*sic*], yet who can doubt, but that in the Pitcher is his only who drew it out? His *labor* hath taken it out of the hands of Nature, where it was common, and belong'd equally to all her Children, and *hath* thereby *appropriated* it to himself.
>
> (Locke 1963, 331)[7]

According to Locke, this is such an important principle – and even a 'Law of Nature' – that '[t]he great and *chief end* therefore, of Mens [*sic*] uniting into Commonwealths, and putting themselves under government, *is the Preservation of their Property*' (Locke 1963, 395). Facebook or, indeed, any social networking site (including crowdsourcing platforms) might in that respect argue that they've made the effort of taking information out of the flow of code. They've put the effort into 'making sense', producing information, out of what is otherwise simply a stream of non-descript data.

The key link that governments aim to guarantee, however, is the link between body, labor, value added, and property. That link dissolves in the context of producing things by way of the network because, as argued in Chapter 5, there is no embodied existence in the context of being and doing by way of digital technologies. Stated differently, once something is produced in the context of the network, there is little that allows for a distinct connection between the product and the producer of that product, as the difference between the analogue and digital author testifies (Poster 2001b).

Of course, to some extent this general decoding of flows – this deterritorialization – and how the digital ensemble and its fluid politics dissolves key aspects of solid politics is, according to Deleuze and Guattari, the general feature of capitalism. The introduction of money, the constitution of a pure and abstracted flow (Brown and Fleming 2011, 45–6), is in that respect simply a first step in what is a general history of a progressive decoding of flows. In that respect the introduction of digital technology has made this much more immediately obvious. Perhaps, over time, things will become sufficiently recoded or reterritorialized so that this may be less obvious, and obviously the use of the law in maintaining key rights of solid politics can be treated as an example of this.

So far, a number of strategies have been adopted by solid entities seeking to cope with the threat of dissolution posed by the fluidity of the network. The first and most obvious from the point of view of solid political action is to prevent dissolution by this flow. This is the strategy taken by major recording companies, which have tried to solidify both the product and the rights to the product by insisting on their sole right to (re)produce solid objects. The earlier court cases that involved Napster, for instance, are in that respect prime examples of a solid form of political action being taken upon a fluid, with the State trying to enforce property rights, that is, maintain their form. In short, the flows of the digital ensemble can produce significant turbulence at the boundary layer, in addition to threatening to erode (if not dissolve) that boundary layer, and hence the boundary that constitutes the solid body (that is, a body of form). Essentially, some of these court cases have resulted in the State blocking flows at their point of origin, although new versions of these flows continuously spring up, as is the case with the variety of file-sharing sites.

At the same time, many game developers and distributors recognize that to maintain a flow of money they have to enable people to invest themselves into their products differently when it comes to negotiating the boundary layer. In part they recognize that, in enabling players to rewrite the code of the game in the form of, for example, modding, players will understand themselves as participating in the game. When game developers enable the code of their games to be altered, and allow these alterations (the mods) to be freely distributed, they effectively make their product less viscous, much in the same way that social media are a less viscous flow. It enables users to participate in a flow to the point that they can produce different streamlines, which in turn enables the flow of money to the developer to continue for much longer.

Equally important, as noted before, it enables the formation of a community of players – that is, a new flow tube. Once such a flow tube forms, participants are reluctant to cease the flow because ceasing the flow ceases the sense of community, of belonging, that forms. This is a key lesson learned from a range of MMORPGs, including Blizzard's *World of Warcraft*. While a single player game will have a more limited flow life, depending on its capacity to be modded, an MMORPG, even if no new content is added for significant periods, will sustain its flow through the flow tube that is the community of players. To state this more simply, MMORPGs like *World of Warcraft* or *Rift*, which in terms of game design simply employ a rock-paper-scissor model, can be seen as nothing other than glorified chatrooms, where the playing of the game is simply an excuse for logging on– a privilege that, in the case of some MMORPGs, costs around US $14 a month. So if you then consider that in the case of a game like *World of Warcraft* there are millions of subscribers, then that coded desire, at least from Deleuze and Guattari's perspective, translates into a lot of uncoded money. In short, there are different ways in which the fluid and the solid can encounter each other on the surface that is the boundary layer. Notably Blizzard, the owner of *World of Warcraft* takes a very strict and solid politics approach to the ownership of the code in the game, including the code produced by the players – both of the flow tube of the game, as well as the flow tubes that involve the game's code outside of the game. The game's boundaries are in that respect quite broad.

A different encounter of the fluid and the solid, perhaps rather, a different boundary layer, is maintained with Felicia Day's web-based show *The Guild*, which made its first appearance in 2007. The show, which avoids copyright issues by taking a fairly generic approach, is about a group of MMORPG players who are part of the same guild, and is composed of short episodes. Initially only a couple of short episodes were filmed and posted on YouTube, after which Day indicated that if fans wanted the show to continue they could donate money via PayPal. The response was such that the show now spans several seasons over several years, generating other merchandise around the show. The show remains free to view even if the viewer chooses not to make a donation. Indeed, even when Microsoft purchased it, the producers of the show insisted that it remain free to view for all.

Other approaches taken to maintain flows, while maintaining a boundary layer, come in the form of, for example, digital rights management (DRM). Basically what this usually means is that in order to constitute a flow, you have to verify yourself first. So that, as with an MMORPG, for example, you first log in to a site, and only then are able to play or participate. In some cases this has drawn a very angry response from the wider gaming community. The release of the game *Spore* in 2008 is one example that initially drew an angry response, as did, for example the release of the 2010 *Asssassin's Creed II*. The latter required players to log in and verify themselves every time they wanted to play. More significantly, it required players to be constantly connected, even for a single player and stand-alone game. The response often offered by companies is that this means players can play their game on any machine (that is, on the cloud). In effect, they argue, the game can exist on any machine that the player uses, provided they verify themselves.

Other strategies adopted by companies that attempt to maintain control over such flow/s has been to bind software to hardware devices. Essentially this means that machines are designed with one specific purpose, such as playing games, playing music, or reading books. In short, such an approach links a material (solid) component to the immaterial (fluid) component (Soderberg 2002). Sony's OpenMG software, which was anything but open, is a good example of this. Sony was trying to prevent the unregulated copying of music by developing hardware that would only read code in a specific format. This code could only be read by its own software and hardware devices. Further, any music that was recorded by these hardware devices (such as the MiniDisc recorders, at the time) could only be read by the OpenMG software and couldn't be converted to a different format.[8] However, because such devices impose serious restrictions on the capacity for flow by going against the digital ensemble's capacity for convergence, they have been very unpopular, even when technically superior in quality.[9]

Another form of political action that has emerged to cope with the threat of the dissolution of copyright has been a fluid form of action – or, perhaps more precisely, a plastic form. This is the strategy taken by the major movie production companies. Instead of attempting to prevent dissolution, they have attempted to pre-empt the success of dangerous flows by producing their own flows. This strategy is based on the view that consumers do not need to get hold of solid objects, but can simply tap a stream or flow tube for a small charge, with the guarantee that buyers get the 'genuine' article. In short, they aim to produce such a great volume of flows that any pirating will have little impact.

What many of the strategies aimed toward regulating flows are concerned with is digital technology's capacity for convergence (that is, its capacity to constitute a network of smooth flow/s). In short, they try to eliminate the very characteristic of this technology that is essential for its functioning. These strategies aim to develop interfaces that only enable the production of very specific flow/s, thereby preventing their gas-like expansion in the form of pirating. In short, what these strategies aim for is a containment of flow/s. To achieve this, however, would be to eliminate one of the key productive elements of the network (Soderberg 2002). While total, disciplined control may prevent both unregulated expansion of flow/s and the emergence of any turbulence within the network, it also eliminates one of the key productive capacities of the network, which is to produce new flow/s and new velocities of flow/s.

It is in such a context that modulatory forms of regulation that anticipate flow/s may be far less damaging to the smoothness of flow, in that they do not aim to discipline flow/s, which is perhaps a price that people are more than willing to pay (Abe 2009).

Such a state of affairs, in which a general slowing of the rate of flow occurs, is problematic both for fluid politics and for solid politics. Solid political actors, while on the one hand antagonistic to the various flows that threaten to dissolve them, also rely greatly on the productive capacity of some of these flows. Most obvious here is the circulation of capital. The role of financial flows is generally used as an indicator of the health of an economic system. In this regard, it is difficult for solid actors, such as states, to do away with fluid politics. They depend on them. These very flows and the tension between solidity and fluidity they produce are essential to the health of both solid and fluid politics.

Indeed, as the example of crowdsourcing in Chapter 7 indicated, flows can also be generated to make solid politics function in more appropriate ways. They can be used precisely to map corruption and violence, establishing a less viscous flow tube that bypasses more viscous media such as television or radio. Of course, crowdsourcing could also be used to generate flows about people's consumption activities. In this respect the use of, for example, weight-tracking and dieting applications on smart-phones collects what are also commercially valuable flows.

This constant state of tension between solidity and fluidity is a determining feature of the relations between solid and fluid politics on all levels. On the one hand, solid political actors aim to maintain their integrity, thereby placing themselves in constant tension with the various flows that impact upon them. On the other hand, unless solid actors are capable of fluid forms of action, they cannot act politically in the context of the networked world. This is a troubling issue for solid political actors of all sizes from the individual to the nation state. If one is incapable of constituting oneself as a fluid, then one cannot act politically in the context of the network, but can only be acted upon.

In order to come to terms with political action in the context of the network, one has to differentiate between solid and fluid forms of political action. In short, a distinction needs to be made between forms of political action available to the non-networked actor and the forms of political action available to the networked actor. I have argued that the former are the actions of solid entities acting on other solid entities, while the latter are the actions of fluid entities acting in relation to other fluid entities. In other words, the politics of the non-networked actor is that of solid politics, while that of the networked actor is that of fluid politics. Neither of these exists in isolation from the other. Indeed, they are more or less mixed, and increasingly so, producing a constant state of productive tension.

In order to come to terms with political action in the context of digital technologies, then, it might be necessary to adopt two conceptual frameworks of political action – that of solid politics and that of fluid politics. While there are instances where each exists in isolation from the other, in general one has to assume that they are in contact at the boundary layer. In other words, in order to be able to deal with politics in the context of digital technologies, one has to conceptualize political action both in terms of solid and fluid politics, and in terms of the relation between them. This means that, just as one has to constitute oneself as a solid in order to be capable of solid political action, so one has to constitute oneself as fluid in order to be capable of fluid political action. In order to act politically on a liquid or a gas, one has to be capable of fluid forms of action. In short, one has to constitute oneself as a fluid entity. From the point of view of solid entities, however, such a reconstitution is dangerous and ultimately destructive of self, and of the State.

Conclusion

One of the aims of this book is to provide a basis for conceptualizing politics in the context of digital technologies. Central to this investigation is the view that different technologies express different social forms and a different politics. In order to begin an investigation into this politics and the forms it might take, I focused on what I saw as three key assemblages of what I call the digital ensemble: examining the operation of power, the constitution of subjectivity, and the forms political action might take. In order to come to terms with the construction of the political and in order to come to terms with politics in the context of digital technologies more generally, I propose that a very different sensibility is required. In short, what is needed is a different understanding or conceptualization of difference in the digital ensemble.

The need for a reconceptualization of many of the institutions and entities that are central to modern politics and modern political thought is widely expressed in the literature dealing with politics in the context of digital technologies. The dissolution of the individual in the context of databases, the sense of disembodiment expressed in the context of the interface, and the impotence or destructive character of institutions and entities such as property and the State in the context of the network all suggest a need to move away from a conceptualization of politics that is expressed in modern thought. However, what I want to suggest as part of this is that digital technologies should not be seen as an end of politics. Instead, politics in the context of digital technologies is a very different politics requiring a very different sensibility.

At the same time, I am not of the view that a digitization or fluidization of politics can be comprehended or explained through some general theory that somehow manages to bring all the different elements or flows together. In that respect, this book points to only a selection of the multitude of issues raised by a digitization of politics. For one thing, this book only momentarily touches on the issue of our understanding of knowledge in the context of digital technologies. When that is extended to the operation of power, or how this fully relates to the mode of power called modulation, a host of new questions emerges, not least of which is whether any notion of fluidity (at least in the manner that I explored it), can be of use in explaining this. Another major issue that is not addressed in this book is governance. In particular, the question of how governmentality and biopower relates to modulation is, in my view, an extremely rich area of research. This is precisely because it concerns the construction of populations and the governance of those populations. Similarly, while I mainly address the constitution of subjectivity in terms of singular entities, little attention is paid to that of collective entities, especially in terms of their constitution as flow/s.

A key concept that can bring different elements together (as I stated earlier) is that of fluidity. For it is through the concept of fluidity that many of the different elements of the chapters can be discussed and related to one another. The relation between modulation and its construction of the objectile, the constitution of dividuality, the being of the superject as the being of flow/s, and, of course, fluid forms of action, are all elements of a digitization of politics whose relations require further exploration. This requires a subtle appreciation and sensibility of the fluid, and, given that fluids are poorly understood in any case, this is not the easiest task. Indeed, fluids have a far greater degree of complexity than is suggested in this book. In that respect, this book is very much a starting point in coming to terms with any digitization of politics.

It is at this point that care needs to be taken with respect to approaching politics in the context of digital technologies. As I argued previously, those who need to posit an 'enemy' will find such a politics extremely problematic. The delineation of an enemy is reflective of a much older approach to conceptualizing politics. There is a danger, in other words, that politics in the context of digital technologies is approached with too great a sense of nostalgia. Such nostalgia prevents recognition of the productive capacities, especially those of a positive character, of digital technologies. In other words, 'being-against' an enemy that is 'everywhere' simply does not makes sense. Those who adopt these views require, indeed almost desire, a construct of 'the enemy' and have far too negative a view of politics, though it is an attitude that is difficult to rid oneself of.

At the same time, care needs to be taken with positions that herald the digital as an end of modern politics, indeed, of all politics. Getting rid of the politics of the Enlightenment can be seen as a good thing, as it has extremely negative productions. To take up such a position, however, is also to ignore its more positive productions. To agree to dispense with, or support, a dissolution of the notion of the individual in the context of digital technologies is not only an opening up of possibilities. It is also a closing off of possibilities. Any dissipation or dissolution of the individual, and consequently dissolution of a body politic and State, means not simply a dissolution of structures of control and exploitation, but also of structures such as 'rights' (Cohen 2008). As Agamben (2005) points out, in a different albeit not unrelated context, an erasure of the individual, as part of a general 'liquidation' of democracy, leads to the creation of legally unnamable and unclassifiable beings, creating not, for example, people charged with a crime, but simply 'detainees'. Rights are strongly tied to the construct of the individual and in that respect the State is not simply a structure that is destructive of a potential for being, but also enables possibilities for being.

Whether or not a general dissolution of the concepts and categories of modern politics and modern political thought is something that can be prevented, or even should be prevented, is therefore questionable. What this involves is a questioning (and this is an aspect of the digitization of politics the book did not focus on) of processes of digitization as currently driven by different interests, that is, desire. These interests – Deleuze and Guattari's flows (Smith 2011) – whether they be business interests, military interests, consumer interests, shareholder interests, or government interests, result in an institutionalization of digital technologies and new practices with very specific aims in mind.[1]

It is in that respect that both the positive and negative aspects of politics in the context of digital technologies need to be recognized. Such recognition requires a very different sensibility. As I tried to show in this book, many of the concepts and structures of politics that are so familiar (and in many respects so taken for granted) are not always holding up very well in the process of digitization. There are, then, several questions that need to be asked. One of these arises from the fact that current concepts do not describe politics in the context of digital technologies very well, and leads to a concern with the sort of a politics that is operating. Another question concerns whether specific concepts that seem so familiar and normal should be abandoned, or whether it makes sense to hold on to them.

In many respects, then, this book creates far more questions than it answered. That is, hopefully, a measure of success, for it indicates the complexity of any understanding of a digitization of politics. The digitization of politics, then, is not a unitary process. It is certainly not something that I want to be read into my claim that the digitization of politics is a fluidization of politics. The digitization of politics is more than one thing. That is one of the main reasons why (as explained above) I chose to focus on three broader themes by way of three assemblages of the digital.

The database, as I argued, is an assemblage that, when looked at in isolation, expresses the operations and productions of at least two very different modes of power. One of these produces us as objects that have form, while the other anticipates us as patterns of code, as objectiles that are constantly varying. The interface, when looked at in isolation, expresses an entirely different form of being, and consequently an entirely new construction of the political. To state that this is a being of flow/s is not to suggest that this being and its construction of the political are easily contained and easily explained through the notion of fluidity. Just as there are difficulties with the notion of solidity in explaining political actions outside of the network, so there are difficulties with the notion of fluidity in explaining or describing political action within the context of the network. Indeed, to refer to the notions of solidity or fluidity as having 'difficulties' in terms of explaining or describing political action is somewhat problematic for it suggests that there is some unitary process or totality that one day can be 'properly' explained.

As I showed, the notion of fluidity is very much a starting point for coming to terms with the digitization of politics. More specifically, it is a useful way of helping us think about politics and what might constitute politics in the context of digital technologies. The fluid, therefore, is not one unitary thing through which all the different elements and facets of a digitization of politics and a digitization of being can be explained. The fluid is more than one thing. It makes more sense, therefore, to think of 'fluidities' rather than 'fluidity' in thinking about politics in the context of digital technologies. This, I hope, is one avenue through which to develop a sensibility and language for coming to terms with politics in an increasingly digital world.

Finally, what is especially critical, is that issues often couched in terms of access need to be 'unpacked'. This is more difficult than it appears – in principle (as I argued) because access, interface with the digital machine, constitutes the very possibility for being and doing. That connection, the constitution of the human-machine assemblage, is precisely what is political. The task, in that respect, is to recognize how different flows of desire are coded, which at least on the digital machine's level are literally coded as packets of binary code. The task, in short, is to consider how new connections through the digital ensemble give expression to desire, and to consider, importantly, how desire is coded and uncoded within the digital.

Notes

1 The Emergence of Modulation

1. The observation is very much constant in a digital world. If a person who normally resides in Australia travels to the USA and purchases something using their credit card, without having first notified the bank of this, they shouldn't be surprised to get a phone call from the bank within minutes of making the purchase to verify it.
2. A point that perhaps resonates with Agamben, when, in looking at gesture and cinema, he compares mime with porn (Levitt 2008, 202–4).
3. In Japan NEC trialled the use of billboards that make use of facial recognition software and which, while still using broad-based data, already aim to distinguish gender, identity and age. In some cases vending machines are similarly equipped cameras that in addition to making use of facial recognition also take into account weather conditions (*The Guardian* 2010).
4. However, such a view cannot account for a 'surprise', as all 'surprises', all unforeseen events, should already have been prepared for in advance – a problem that is increasingly plaguing the US military (Der Derian 2009), which possibly explains the increased use of scenario planning (Cooper 2010).
5. Brian Massumi (2009) terms it pre-emptive power. My point, however, as I will develop further on, is that it does more than pre-empt as part of its general functioning, and has quite a complex relationship with other modes of power, though here I principally look at its connections with the disciplinary mode of power.
6. Again, while the production of that code might have disciplinary consequences, and, indeed, governmental ones, for the moment I am principally interested in the non-disciplinary or modulatory consequences.
7. If, for example, Microsoft Word, through its automated language detection, establishes from a number of French words in a sentence that a document should be spell-checked in French from that point on, rather than English, it can produce a very interrupted experience on the part of the user.
8. As Manuel De Landa shows, however, 'the more one tries to achieve total certainty, the greater the increase in the information flow needed to run the operation, and therefore the more uncertain the final result' (De Landa 1991, 79). In short, the more precise information that is gathered about which flows might eventuate and manifest themselves in what is treated as an otherwise turbulent world, the more turbulent and unstable that world becomes.
9. This should not be confused with disindividuation, which, as Stiegler (2010a, 146) points out, is precisely a product of the disciplinary mode of power.
10. Claritas, before it became part of Nielsen, advertised on one of its earlier websites that they have 24 profiles for specific areas of consumption, so that as a consumer you are in one of those 24 categories (Claritas 1999). You aren't

required to become one of these norms; you already, and always, are one of them, even if you have no interest of any kind in the specific product in question. You still fit a profile, but not a profile that a company would have any value spending its advertising dollar on.

2 Dividuality

1. While this point relating to time, effect, and digital machines is addressed in Part II, a more detailed consideration is given by Hansen (2004; 2009). Note, though, that Hansen's approach, including his use of Deleuze's work, has drawn some criticism (Brown and Fleming 2011; Clough 2007; 2008).
2. Alternatively it might be useful to refer to it as a virtuality, but care needs to be taken with this term in this context, as Derrida pointed out (on this point, see Venn 2007).
3. While Deleuze (1993) made much of this argument in relation to the Leibniz and Baroque perspective, it should be kept in mind that Leibniz played a role in developing the binary code by which digital technologies operate.
4. For a more in-depth examination of care, see Stiegler (2009b; 2010a).
5. Notably, prior to the use of digital microcomputers, Habermas pointed to a prediction made by Herman Kahn that there would be a large increase in the number of techniques for controlling behavioral and personality change (Habermas 1971, 117). Habermas lists several of these techniques, all of which are currently in prominent use.
6. As noted in the latter half of this chapter, another way to characterize this is in terms of the algorithm. See especially Bogard (1996), but also, to a lesser extent, Manovich, who uses a distinction between what he calls 'the database' and the algorithm (Manovich 2001). A good example of this form of anticipation can be found in financial investment applications, where firms use existing financial data to have their systems find patterns that inform them of opportunities, sometimes lasting only a few minutes, for profitable trades (Bailey 1996, 148).
7. The help wizards in software applications such as Microsoft Word or Microsoft Excel are one example of this, as they often attempt to anticipate the help you require, or rather, will need. For a more sophisticated explanation of such 'customization' than that provided by Negroponte (1995), see Manovich (2001), especially the section of his first chapter discussing 'modularity'.

3 The Human-Machine Assemblage

1. This does not mean that technology by itself is expressive of human being, nor of human being alone. See, for example, Mumford (1995c).
2. Arthur (2010, 170) sees the collective of technology, following Maturana and Varela, as autopoietic or self-producing. What is generally termed insight is for Arthur the removal of a blockage: 'The insight comes as a removal of blockage, often stumbled upon, either as an overall principle with a workable combination of subprinciples, or as a subprinciple that clears the way for the main principle to be used. It comes as a connection, always a connection, because it connects a problem with a principle that can handle it' (2010,

116). This means that when it comes to invention there is no such thing as 'first' (Williams in Arthur 2010, 126).

3. As Castells states 'the dilemma of technological determinism is probably a false problem, since technology *is* society, and society cannot be understood or represented without its technological tools' (Castells 1996, 5).

4. Marx points to this as well, though instead of using the term 'assemblage', he refers to very much the same concept when using the term 'epochs of production': 'However, all epochs of production have certain common traits, common characteristics. Production in general is an abstraction, but a rational abstraction in so far as it really brings out and fixes the common element and thus saves us repetition. Still, this general category, this common element sifted out by comparison, is itself segmented many times over and splits into different determinations. Some determinations belong to all epochs, others only to a few. Some determinations will be shared by the most modern epoch and the most ancient. No production will be thinkable without them; however, even though the most developed languages have laws and characteristics in common with the least developed, nevertheless, just those things which determine their development, that is, the elements which are not general and common, must be separated out from the determinations valid for production as such, so that in their unity – which arises already from the identity of the subject, humanity, and of the object, nature – their essential difference is not forgotten' (Marx 1973, 85).

5. See also *Anti-Oedipus* (Deleuze and Guattari 1977, 32). 'That is why technical machines are not an economic category, and always refer back to a socius or a social machine that is quite distinct from these machines, and that conditions this reproduction. A technical machine is therefore not a cause but merely an index of a general form of social production: thus there are manual machines and primitive societies, hydraulic machines and "Asiatic" forms of society, industrial machines and capitalism.' For a different characterization of technological ensembles and the relation between technology and society see, for instance, Castells (1996, 16–18), who uses the term 'modes of development' rather than 'technological ensembles' in expressing a very similar point.

6. See also Kern (1983) on this, and more recently Stiegler (1998; 2009a; 2010b).

7. Also note Mumford's point here that '[e]ven in describing only the material components of technics, this practice overlooks the equally vital role of containers: first hearths, pits, traps, cordage; later baskets, bins, byres, houses, to say nothing of still later collective containers like reservoirs, canals, cities. These static components play an important part in every technology, not least in our own day, with its high-tension transformers, its giant chemical retorts, its atomic reactors' (Mumford 1995c, 306).

8. Kirby argues that in theorizing subjectivity, people have tended to pay a disproportionate amount of attention to the importance of the concept of time, which with Stiegler (1998; 2009a; 2010b) and Hansen (2009) forms a central focus in their more recent work, than to that of space (Kirby 1996). Her's is an excellent text explaining the importance of the conceptualization of space in the work of theorists conceptualizing subjectivity.

9. Harvey also makes this point, arguing that '[e]ach distinctive mode of production or social formation will…embody a distinctive bundle of time and space practices and concepts' (Harvey 1989, 204).
10. See also Guattari's *Chaosmosis* (1995).
11. At no point should it be forgotten that the choice of which technology to adopt or why some technologies are given precedence over others involves very real political decisions. Even, or perhaps especially, those that may appear to us as fairly mundane technologies, from the development of the fridge to the dominance of the car, involved very political processes. Langdon Winner's (1977; 1986) work is very useful on this. For examples of this aspect of politics and technology as it relates to the Internet, see Meikle (2002), especially pages 101–11.

4 Mechanical Being

1. Carlyle did not totally reject mechanism with its sole focus on means and ends, but argued that it had become too dominant in all aspects of life. Carlyle's solution to this problem of the dominance of 'Mechanism' was to relegate it to its 'proper' place and to allow the other science of 'Dynamism' to operate hand in hand with mechanism. In that respect Carlyle's argument could be viewed as a precursor to that of Habermas' paper on Marcuse's *One Dimensional Man*, where Habermas argued that one could not be against technology and instrumental reason, as these were necessary to human existence, but that they should not be allowed to dominate over what he calls 'communicative reason' (Habermas 1971; Marcuse 1964). See also Stiegler (1998) for a more detailed discussion of Habermas' view on technics, including how it relates to Heidegger's views.
2. The standardization of time is a process that had begun much earlier, most notably with the introduction of the monastery clocks, but it is rail travel on a national scale and the need for timetables that well and truly standardized time and made it uniform on a national scale like never before (Beniger 1986; Schivelbusch 1986, 43).
3. Adam Smith's work points to the more positive aspects of the division of labor (Smith 1976), a view of which Marx was very critical (Marx 1990).
4. Of course, the production of the new spatiality so central to the industrialized mechanical ensemble, and so familiar to us because it is our spatiality, started much earlier with the production of linear perspective. Romanyshyn's *Technology as Symptom and Dream* (1989) is an excellent work on the invention of linear perspective and its ramifications. As Virilio has pointed out, even today '[i]t has still not been emphasized enough how profoundly the city, the politics, the war, the economy of the medieval world were revolutionized by the invention of perspective' (Virilio 2001, 23–4).
5. Hence the close association of discipline and the factory and the concurrent emergence of governmentality as a mode of power. The mechanical ensemble and its efficient operation requires an entirely different organization and distribution of people, both as a collective entity (governmentality) and in terms of their individual constitution (discipline). It requires enormous programs of (re-) education.

6. Heller (1990) is correct in associating the manifestation of ourselves as subjects with modernity; and if there are any machines that express this best, they are the invention of linear perspective (Romanyshyn 1989), an abstract machine, and the steam engine, a material machine, and the different use of energy it expresses.

7. See, for example, the various time and motion studies and the enormous effort exerted on the body by various sciences (Crary and Kwinter 1992).

8. Note, for instance, Heidegger's understanding of modern technology as being about constructing people and things as resources stored and arranged in such a manner as to be ready for use (Chesher 1997; Heidegger 1993a).

9. Linear perspective was an invention of the fifteenth century (Romanyshyn 1989), but only with the industrialization of space and time in the industrialized mechanical ensemble does it become a key organizing principle on a mass scale (Schivelbusch 1986).

10. Though always an object in the form of an autonomous individual.

11. Rose points out that statistics, and the census, break the polity into a range of different groups and classes (Rose 1999, 219). In short, statistics reflect, but also further increase, existing processes of fragmentation.

12. Of course, accountability in this industrialized technological ensemble relies on the ultimate connection between bodies and the actions performed by way of those bodies. Agency in this industrialized mechanical ensemble, as Stone points out, is still traced to its 'original human's physical presence, where the buck stops' (Stone 1995, 400). Another important point here is the concern with numbers and its relation to democracy and notions of equality (Porter 1986; 1996; Rose 1996). Numbers and quantification are critical for standardization, which, as Rose points out, 'is a condition for interaction in diversified societies with an expanding division of labour' (Rose 1999, 206–7).

5 Digital Being

1. At the same time, I do not want to suggest that the space-time of the industrialized mechanical ensemble has disappeared, which is exactly what the use of the term 'annihilation' would imply.

2. Following Virilio's arguments, this annihilation of 'real' space by speed is not necessarily purely a product of the digital ensemble. In some respects it is foreshadowed by ballistic technology. It is simply that with digital technologies this 'erasure' of space reaches its completion (De Landa 1991; Der Derian 2009; Mansfield 2000; Virilio 1986).

3. For the machines, the screens are of no consequence, of course.

4. The use of the word 'space', and spatial metaphors more generally (such as 'cyberspace' and 'virtual space') in explaining digital technologies reflects how deeply people's sense of existence is still a product of them functioning mostly as a component in the industrialized mechanical ensemble. However, as Kirby points out, we may not be able to make use of a language without spatial overtones (Kirby 1996).

5. In *World of Warcraft*, for example, players who are on a US server, but live in the Oceania region, will more likely go raiding when it is evening in the

USA, even though it might only be 7 a.m. in the morning for them. So that the population of the game fluctuates as the planet revolves around the sun. On its initial release, only game time, or the central server time, was visible. Only later was a function introduced that also displayed local time, thereby reminding participants of their 'non-screen reality'.

6. Note that this does not necessarily mean it is a rhizome in Deleuze and Guattari's use of the word (1987). On this point, see Buchanan (2009).

7. On the temporality of digital machines, see, for example, Stiegler (1998; 2009a; 2010b). For a view that is critical of Stiegler's argument, and takes a more positive approach to digital machines and temporality, see Hansen (2009).

8. Chesher has argued that he no longer feels the digital/analog distinction to be useful in describing the devices of what in this book is referred to as the digital ensemble. He argues that instead the term 'invocational media' is far more useful in characterizing these machines (Chesher 2002), as they ascribe a sense of magic quality to them because we cannot see inside them. A similar point was also suggested by Dibbell (1994, 256), and, in a different context, by Arthur C. Clarke (Chesher 1997). Note also Lev Manovich's *The Language of New Media*, in which an argument is presented as to why the term 'digital' is not very useful (Manovich 2001, 52–4).

9. A term, for that matter, which was already in use in the 1920s. See, for example, Penty's *Post-Industrialism* (1922).

10. One example is provided by online games, where users experience lag as a major issue, because it means one person cannot act at the same speed as another person, which in some of these games is the difference between winning and losing, even if it is only measured in milliseconds. Something that in the industrial mechanical ensemble might seem inconsequential.

11. Which is not to say that this force is not exploited (Castells 1996), whether that be in the Marxist use of the word or any other sense.

12. Stone, for instance, points to the communication prosthesis Stephen Hawking makes use of and how it differs from the microphone as it raises questions about where exactly Stephen Hawking stops (that is, where his edges are) (Stone 1995, 395).

13. From this perspective, Neo in the movie *The Matrix* makes his crucial transformation in constitution of self when he realizes that he *is* the matrix and everything else is a product of his imagination – the moment where in the first movie he becomes the all-powerful being. Of course, what happens when 'others' make that realization as well is another, and more important, question, to which Heim gives an unsatisfactory answer (Heim 2001). As I pointed out earlier in the chapter, trust and reputation are of primary concern, because breaches of trust interrupt the flow – they are, in the case of the traders described by Knorr-Cetina (2007), deal-breakers, as they are in the case of player behavior in MMORPGs.

14. Take, for example, mobile phones and Wireless Application Protocol (WAP), which turns people into resources that can be available on a 24-hour basis regardless of their location. Digital technologies, then, can very much fall in line with Heidegger's argument concerning modern technology's character (Chesher 1997; Heidegger 1993a), though care must be taken in attempting

to characterize all digital technologies as having that effect (Poster 2001b, 32)

15. One simple example here is how some gamers in online role-playing games, like *World of Warcraft*, do not just have multiple avatars, but might also play different avatars on multiple screens at the same time. Indeed, many people carry multiple screens with them at any one moment by way of their mobile phone, especially if they have a smart-phone.

16. Mobile and wireless technologies are especially interesting here, and there are fewer and fewer moments where many people living within the digital ensemble are not in some way permanently connected to a network of some kind, whether this be in the form of simply carrying a mobile phone, having automated notifications of updates on their phone or on a Facebook page, or being plugged in with a laptop while sitting in a lecture or on the bus.

17. The interface was from early on in the development of digital technology much neglected (De Landa 1991). However, especially with the further development of biotechnologies, nanotechnologies, and bioinformatics, machines will become an increasingly fundamental part of human being (Küchler 2008). Research to enable fighter pilots to enact a change in direction or speed simply by thinking it, or the attempt to restore people's sight using digital technologies come to mind here.

18. Valentine has argued, in the process of explaining Laclau's and Mouffe's position, that it is this notion of antagonism that is actually the basis of the political as heterogeneity and is the very condition of identity. This is a point that the constitution of subjects, functioning as ideology, conceals.

19. Here distraction is something that takes on interesting qualities, because distraction might well be constructed as a space or moment to breathe (Bogard 2008; Shaviro 2003, 5).

20. Hardt and Negri, making use of Guy Debord's *Society of the Spectacle* (Debord 1995), argue that the end of the outside is the end of liberal politics, but they seem to ignore the fact that all forms of modern political thought rely on a similar notion of the outside. Also, there is a strong argument to be made that liberal political thought, because it is the only form of modern political thought that principally concerns itself with governance, unlike Marxist or much feminist thought, is more capable of adjusting itself to any newly emerging politics (Burchell et al. 1991). See also Massumi (2009) on this last point.

21. It is no coincidence in that respect that the boundary between the military-industrial complex and the media-entertainment network was being dissolved as part of that process (Der Derian 2009).

22. Here the actual response of political leaders to the global financial crisis (GFC) of 2009 is instructive, despite some demand for accountability continuing to be exercised.

23. This is already a critical issue, but when operating at the genetic level the effects of this will become even more drastic, as movies like *Gattaca* suggest. A related issue here concerns the ownership of specific patterns of code, both on the genetic level and within the digital ensemble more generally. On this, see Cooper (2010) and Thacker (2004).

6   Solid Politics

1. Having made that point, the commercialization of the Internet since the 1990s is what has generated a lot more positive productions. The key problem, and a problem that is not changed in digitization, is that these productions are primarily driven with the aim of producing more flow in the form of money. In that regard, what some identify as 'gamification' (the reduction of games to the status of a commidity) and the commodification of play more broadly, to 'entertainment' is a significant issue. On this, see Bogost (2011).
2. Note that one can differentiate between 'crystalline solids' and 'amorphous solids'; the latter sometimes behave more like a liquid.
3. On this point, it is important to note that there are different types of force, such as sheer force, gravitational force, and electro-magnetic force.
4. Unless you melt them into one genuine solid body of course.
5. The term 'dynamics' has a number of different uses. One is as a branch of science or mechanics that treats of the motion of bodies under the influence of forces. Another is as 'the motive forces, physical or moral, in any sphere' (NSOED 1997). For an example of the latter, see Carlyle (1984).
6. Note also that nation states are also subjected to internal threats that can threaten their stability.
7. Conservative political thought, which emerged as a response to modern, specifically liberal political thought, is an example of more organic theories.
8. As Marx argues, '[t]he commodity, from being the individual product of an independent craftsman [*sic*], becomes the social product of a union of crafts-men, each of whom performs one, and only one, of the constituent partial operations' (Marx 1990, 457).
9. See also Lukes (1974) and Clegg (1989).
10. Though often such other political entities, such as women, people with disabilities, children, or aboriginal populations, never quite have the same political and legal status as that of individuals. Indeed, this may be why the US administration, for example, resisted the recognition of Palestine as a state by the United Nations. Giving it that status means it is recognized as a solid and (even if gel-like, depending on the level of recognition) capable of reacting as an entity or force again. In short, our language for talking about politics continues to make use of terms that describe a relationship between solid entities.
11. Note that Deleuze and Guattari see a lobby group as a 'group with fluid con-tours', which suggests they see it either as partially melting or as an aggregate solid (Deleuze and Guattari 1987, 366). 'Influence' in that respect could be seen as adding a color to an otherwise fluid entity, but, in solid politics, prob-ably better as an attempt to change the vector by 'bending' an existing solid body's 'will' in some way (that is, overcoming their inertia and altering the direction and/or velocity).
12. See Virilio's (1986) discussion of the streets of Paris, for example.
13. In this context, think also of the notion of things 'heating up in parliament'. This not only indicates an increase in the velocity at which particles move but also implies that if things heat up enough solids will melt or simply burn, thereby losing their solid structure and existence. At the same time,

there is also the opposite example of freezing things to such an extent that they attain an inertia that they cannot be overcome. Here the use of the term 'Cold War' suggested a freezing of relations and a high degree of immobility or inertia in the relations between two entities.

14. For a more in-depth and considerate discussion of power and its analysis in political thought see, for example, Clegg's *Frameworks of Power* (1989).

15. On this, see Harper (2009).

7 Fluid Politics

1. In relation to explaining the bandwidth of networks, Negroponte has argued that while the notion of fluids is constructive, it can also be misleading (Negroponte 1995, 35). His argument is that while you may be able to regulate a flow, by closing a tap, that this is not like increasing or decreasing bandwidth, because it is still the same amount of water molecules that move as a group. Negroponte, however, makes the mistake of thinking of flows as the flows of amorphous solids, or the flow of water as one body across the landscape or in a pipe. See Knorr-Cetina (2003) for a more detailed explanation of this point.

2. This is illustrated in the movie *The Matrix* (Wachowski and Wachowski 1999) and specifically the point where Neo, the hero, is first made to realize, with his uploading of a Kung Fu program, the difference between acting within the matrix and acting outside of the matrix. When acting within the matrix, not only does Neo's subjectivity become fluid, in that he can simply 'become' a kung fu master, but also his actions, as they are now tied directly to both his capacity for writing himself as code, and to the rate of transmission of the code. This is also an idea that was explored in the earlier movie *Tron* (Lisberger and MacBird 1982), which predates Gibson's novel *Neuromancer* (Gibson 1984).

3. The only sense in which a fluid can have a shape is by way of being determined by a container. This, however, like all molding, is a solid-fluid form of interaction, addressed in the Section 'The politics of fluids' of this chapter.

4. The onset of turbulence can be predicted by way of the Reynolds number. For an interesting and useful explanation of turbulence and the Reynolds number, see De Landa (1991).

5. Note also how 'hacking' has taken on entirely negative connotations when in its initial usage it had a very positive connotation (Vegh 2002). Another word that portrays a very negative image in the use of computers is 'virus' (Best and Lewis 2000; Lupton 1995). Indeed, difficult as it is, and as David Gunkel (2007) has argued, we need to be more careful in using binaries to discuss digital media more generally. In that respect, Deleuze and Guattari's understanding of flows avoids this, though here my aim is primarily to come to terms with how we can think about action in the context of networks.

6. I say 'on a certain level' because, as shown in Chapter 5, subjectivity, in the form of the dividual, is still on some level embodied for much of the time. The superject is not a dominant form of existence, at least not yet. Actors, in other words, are still territorialized in terms of the locality and space they live in. This often provides the impetus for political action in the context

of the network in the first place. On the other hand, as Castells points out: 'Although major corporate centers provide the human resources and facilities necessary to manage an increasingly complex financial network, it is in the information networks connecting such centers that the actual operations of capital take place. Capital flows become at the same time global and increasingly autonomous *vis-à-vis* the actual performance of economies' (Castells 1996, 93).

7. They can be contained in that they do not go beyond a local area network (LAN), or they can be contained in the manner that most anti-virus programs contain specific lines of code that are suspected of being capable of affecting the production or constitution of flow/s of code.

8. As noted earlier, a change in velocity can be a change in direction and/or a change in the rate of flow.

9. Recognizing that the currency market doesn't 'move' forward, but rather proceeds, flows. It does, of course, move in the sense that a market moves around the planet from time zone to time zone, and obviously the flow that is the market is not independent of the time zone and related geographical area it is in, as this affects the flow. The Australian markets, for example, always wait to see how the US or European markets might respond or behave to try and anticipate what might happen.

10. This shouldn't be compared to McLuhan's idea of hot and cold media. These categories refer instead to a different form of participation, so that for McLuhan hot media refer to involving less participation (watching a movie), while cool media refer to more participation being required by the audience (a lecture). Nor is viscosity the same as interactivity. Many computer games, for example, such as *Rift* and *World of* Warcraft, are very interactive, but are highly viscous, while others, such as *Minecraft*, are very interactive, but have a low viscosity.

11. Steve Kurz, one of the CAE's founders, was arrested on charges of bioterrorism in 2004. On this, see the appendix to CAE's *Marching Plague* (2006). The charges were dropped in 2008.

12. See also Katsiaficas (2006) who is critical of Hardt and Negri's approach.

8 The Boundary Layer

1. 'Once again, we must note that stocks and flows are one and the same thing, but that they relate to fundamentally different units: stock is the attribution of value at a given point in time, whereas flow is what changes the value of stock over time...flow is the rate of a change in a stock...In mathematical terms, the stock is the integral of the flow, while the derivative is the flow of changes in the stock' (Smith 2011, 51). 'The water in a bathtub could be considered a stock if a gallon of water drains out of the tub every minute, while at the same time a gallon of water is added from the faucet, the stock will remain the same, even though there is a constant flow' (2011, 52).

2. In the language of solid politics one often speaks of pressuring somebody to do something, but in such cases this pressure is always reducible to the force that is applied over a given area. In short, pressure in the context of solid politics is still about the specific application of force.

3. Some forms of solid politics (here various liberal theories come to mind) tend to operate with the notion of singular bodies existing in the same space, for instance. Other forms of solid politics think more geophysically of individuals being defined by the layers they occupy in relation to one another (here Marxist thought is the best example).

4. In other words, the ownership of specific networks, cables, or databases is solid politics, but once one is acting on the network (that is, in the realm of fluid politics) such a notion of ownership is problematic.

5. In addition to this, they state that: 'This IP License ends when you delete your IP content or your account unless your content has been shared with others, and they have not deleted it... When you delete IP content, it is deleted in a manner similar to emptying the recycle bin on a computer. However, you understand that removed content may persist in backup copies for a reasonable period of time (but will not be available to others)' (Facebook 2011).

6. It is worthwhile reading the footnote inserted at this point of Deleuze and Guattari's text regarding the original uses of these two terms. The *polis* was the city, while the *nomos*, unlike its current use, was the area outside of the city walls, that is, the desert or wilderness (Deleuze and Guattari 1987, 557). For a different approach to this, see Agamben's *Homo Sacer* (1998)

7. It should be noted that Locke emphasized that limits ought to be put on the amount of property a person could own. Locke's argument was that one could own '[a]s much as any one can make use of to any advantage of life before it spoils; so much he [sic] may by his labour fix a Property in. Whatever is beyond this, is more than his share, and belongs to others' (Locke 1963, 332).

8. Of course, the digital signal can always be converted to an analogue signal and then back again to a digital signal, which can then be read by other software and hardware devices.

9. Similarly, companies have performed fluid-on-fluid actions in that they have not enabled specific flow tubes to be constituted through their machines. Apple's refusal to adopt Adobe's Flash media on its iPad is one example of such overt action.

Conclusion

1. To be sure, much interesting work is done on this, and Cooper's *Life as Surplus* (2008), placing political economy more centrally, is a key text here.

Bibliography

Abe, K. 2009. 'The Myth of Media Interactivity Technology, Communications and Surveillance in Japan.' *Theory, Culture & Society* 26(2–3): 73–88.

Agamben, G. 1998. *Homo Sacer: Sovereign Power and Bare Life*, Trans. D. Heller-Roazen. Stanford, CA: Stanford University Press.

Agamben, G. 2005. *State of Exception*, Trans. K Attell. Chicago: Chicago University Press.

Agre, P.E. 1994. 'Surveillance and Capture: Two Models of Privacy.' *The Information Society* 10(2): 101–27.

Arthur, B.W. 2010. *The Nature of Technology: What It Is and How It Evolves*. London: Penguin Books.

Bailey, J. 1996. *Afterthought: The Computer Challenge to Human Intelligence*. New York: Basic Books.

Baudrillard, J. 1994. *Simulacra & Simulation*, Trans. S.F. Glaser. Ann Arbor: The University of Michigan Press.

Bauman, Z. 2000. *Liquid Modernity*. Cambridge: Polity Press.

Bauman, Z. 2003. *Liquid Love*. Cambridge: Polity Press.

Bauman, Z. 2005. *Liquid Life*. Cambridge: Polity Press.

Beck, U. 1992. *Risk Society: Towards a New Modernity*. London: Sage.

Bell, D. 1976. *The Coming of Post-Industrial Society: A Venture in Social Forecasting*. New York: Basic Books.

Bellamy, C. and J.A. Taylor. 1998. *Governing in the Information Age*. Buckingham: Open University Press.

Beniger, J.R. 1986. *The Control Revolution: Technological and Economic Origins of the Information Society*. Cambridge: Harvard University Press.

Benjamin, W. 1969. *Illuminations*. New York: Schocken.

Bergen, V. 2010. 'Politics as the Orientation of Every Assemblage.' Trans. J. Gilbert. *New Formations* 68: 34–41.

Berman, M. 1983. *All That Is Solid Melts into Air: The Experience of Modernity*. London: Verso.

Best, K. and J. Lewis. 2000. 'Hacking the Democratic Mainframe: The Melissa Virus and Transgressive Computing.' *Media International Australia, Incorporating Culture & Policy* 95: 207–26.

Birch, D. and T. Lee. 2000. 'Internet Regulation in Singapore: A Policy/Ing Discourse.' *Media International Australia, Incorporating Culture & Policy* 95: 147–69.

Bogard, W. 1996. *The Simulation of Surveillance: Hypercontrol in Telematic Societies*. Cambridge: Cambridge University Press.

Bogard, W. 2008. 'Distraction and Digital Culture.' *Critical Digital Studies: A Reader*, ed. A. Kroker and M. Kroker. Toronto: Toronto University Press.

Bogost, I. 2011. 'Persuasive Games: Exploitationware.' *Gamasutra*. 3 May <http://www.gamasutra.com/view/feature/6366/persuasive_games_exploitationware.php> Accessed 25 September 2011.

Boyle, J. 1997. 'Foucault in Cyberspace: Surveillance, Sovereignty, and Hard-Wired Censors.' <http://www.law.duke.edu/boylesite/foucault.htm> Accessed 25 September 2011.

Boyne, R. 2000. 'Post-Panopticism.' *Economy and Society* 29(2): 285–307.

Braithwaite, J. 2000. 'The New Regulatory State and the Transformation of Criminology.' *British Journal of Criminology* 40(2): 222–38.

Brown, B. and D.H. Fleming. 2011. 'Deterritorialization and Schizoanalysis in David Fincher's Fight Club.' *Deleuze Studies* 5(2): 275–99.

Bryan, D. and M. Rafferty. 2006. *Capitalism with Derivatives: A Political Economy of Financial Derivatives, Capital and Class*. New York: Palgrave Macmillan.

Bryan, D. and M. Rafferty. 2007. 'Financial Derivatives and the Theory of Money.' *Economy and Society* 36(1): 134–58.

Buchanan, I. 2009. 'Deleuze and the Internet.' *Deleuze and New Technology*, ed. M. Poster and D. Savat. Edinburgh: Edinburgh University Press.

Burchell, G., C. Gordon, and P. Miller, eds. 1991. *The Foucault Effect: Studies in Governmentality*. London: Harvester Wheatsheaf.

Critical Art Ensemble. 2006. *Marching Plague: Germ Warfare and Global Public Health*. Brooklyn: Autonomedia.

Critical Art Ensemble. 2009. 'Critical Art Ensemble.' <http://www.critical-art.net/> Accessed 25 September 2011.

Carlyle, T. [1829] 1984. 'Signs of the Times.' *A Carlyle Reader: Selections From the Writings of Thomas Carlyle*, ed. G.B. Tennyson. Cambridge: Cambridge University Press.

Castel, R. 1991. 'From Dangerousness to Risk.' *The Foucault Effect: Studies in Governmentality*, ed. G. Burchell, C. Gordon and P. Miller. London: Harvester Wheatsheaf.

Castells, M. 1996. *The Rise of the Network Society*. Oxford: Blackwell Publishers.

Castells, M. 1997. *The Power of Identity*. Oxford: Blackwell Publishers.

Castells, M. 2005. 'Grassrooting the Space of Flows.' *The Global Resistance Reader*, ed. L. Amoore. London: Routledge.

Chen, J. 2006. 'Discover RFID-Enabled Solutions in the Retail Industry.' *DeveloperWorks*. IBM <http://www.ibm.com/developerworks/library/wi-rfidretail/index.html?ca=drs-tp3606> Accessed 25 September 2011.

Chen, P. 2000. 'Pornography, Protection, Prevarication: The Politics of Internet Censorship.' *University of New South Wales Law Journal* 23(1): 221–6.

Chesher, C. 1997. 'The Ontology of Digital Domains.' *Virtual Politics: Identity and Community in Cyberspace*, ed. D. Holmes. London: Sage.

Chesher, C. 2002. 'Why the Digital Computer Is Dead.' *CTheory*. <http://www.ctheory.net/text_file.asp?pick=334> Accessed 25 September 2010.

Chun, W.H.K. 2006. *Control and Freedom: Power and Paranoia in the Age of Fiber Optics*. Cambridge: The MIT Press.

Chung, W.H.K 2006 'Introduction: Did Somebody Say New Media?' *New Media, Old Media: A History and Theory Reader*, ed. Chung, W.H.K and Keenan, Thomas new York: Routledge.

Claritas. 1999. *Claritas*. <http://www.claritas.com> Accessed 10 December 1999.

Clark, N. 1985. *The Political Economy of Science and Technology*. Oxford: Blackwell Publishers.

Clegg, S.T. 1989. *Frameworks of Power*. London: Sage.

Clough, P.T. 2007. 'Biotechnology and Digital Information.' *Theory, Culture & Society* 24(7–8): 312–314.

Clough, P.T. 2008. 'The Affective Turn: Political Economy, Biomedia and Bodies.' *Theory, Culture & Society* 25(1): 1–22.

Clough, P.T., S. Han, and R. Schiff. 2007. 'Book Review.' *Theory, Culture & Society* 24(7–8): 387–93.

Cohen, E. 2008. 'A Body Worth Having? Or, a System of Natural Governance.' *Theory, Culture & Society* 25(3): 103–29.

Cohen, E. 2009. *A Body Worth Defending: Immunity, Biopolitics, and the Apotheosis of the Modern Body.* Durham: Duke University Press.

Cook, I. 2009. 'The Body Without Organs and Internet Gaming Addiction.' *Deleuze and New Technology*, ed. M. Poster and D. Savat. Edinburgh: Edinburgh University Press.

Colwell, C. 1996. 'Discipline and Control: Butler and Deleuze on Individuality and Dividuality.' *Philosophy Today* 40(1): 211–16.

Cooper, M. 2008. *Life as Surplus: Biotechnology & Capitalism in the Neoliberal Era.* Seattle: University of Washington Press.

Cooper, M. 2010. 'Turbulent Worlds Financial Markets and Environmental Crisis.' *Theory, Culture & Society* 27(2–3): 167–90.

Coyne, R. 1998. 'Cyberspace and Heidegger's Pragmatics.' *Information Technology & People* 11(4): 338.

Courtney, P. 2011. 'The Medium Is the Message.' *Landline.* Canberra: ABC <http://www.abc.net.au/landline/content/2010/s3293020.htm> Accessed 25 September 2011.

Crandall, J. 2010. 'The Geospatialization of Calculative Operations Tracking, Sensing and Megacities.' *Theory, Culture & Society* 27(6): 68–90.

Crary, J. and S. Kwinter, eds. 1992. *Incorporations.* New York: Zone Books.

Cresswell, A. 2011. 'Patients See Pitfalls in Paperless Records.' *The Weekend Australian* 10–11 September.

Dahl, R. 1961. *Who Governs? Democracy and Power in an American City.* New York: Yale University Press.

Dandeker, C. 1990. *Surveillance, Power and Modernity: Bureaucracy and Discipline from 1700 to the Present Day.* Cambridge: Polity Press.

Davis, D. 2010. *Disconnect.* Melbourne: Scribe.

De Landa, M. 1991. *War in the Age of Intelligent Machines.* New York: Zone Books.

Debord, G. 1995. *The Society of the Spectacle*, Trans. D. Nicholson-Smith. New York: Zone Books.

Deleuze, G. 1989. *Cinema 2: The Time Image*, Trans. H. Tomlinson and R. Galeta. Minneapolis: University of Minnesota Press.

Deleuze, G. 1992. 'Postscript on the Societies of Control.' *October* 59: 3–7.

Deleuze, G. 1993. *The Fold: Leibniz and the Baroque*, Trans. T. Conley. Minneapolis: University of Minnesota Press.

Deleuze, G. 1995. *Negotiations*, Trans. M. Joughin. New York: Columbia University Press.

Deleuze, G. 2004. *The Logic of Sense*, ed. C.V. Boundas, Trans. M. Lester with C. Stivale. London: Continuum.

Deleuze, G. and F. Guattari. 1977. *Anti-Oedipus*, Trans. R. Hurley, M. Seem, and H. Lane. Minneapolis: University of Minnesota Press.

Deleuze, G. and F. Guattari. 1987. *A Thousand Plateaus*, Trans. B. Massumi. Minneapolis: University of Minnesota Press.

DeLong, B.J. and M.A. Froomkin. 2000. 'Speculative Microeconomics for Tomorrow's Economy.' *First Monday* 5(2) <http://firstmonday.org/htbin/cgiwrap/bin/ojs/index.php/fm/article/view/726/635> Accessed 25 September 2011.

Der Derian, J. 2009. *Virtuous War: Mapping the Military-Industrial-Media-Entertainment Network.* London: Routledge.

Derrida, J. and B. Stiegler. 2002. *Echographies of Television,* Trans. J. Bajorek. London: Polity.

Dibbell, J. 1994. 'A Rape in Cyberspace; or, How an Evil Clown, a Haitian Trickster Spirit, Two Wizards, and a Cast of Dozens Turned a Database into a Society.' *Flame Wars: The Discourse of Cyberculture,* ed. M. Dery. Durham: Duke University Press.

Dillon, M. and L. Lobo-Guerrero. 2008. 'Biopolitics of Security in the 21st Century: An Introduction.' *Review of International Studies* 34(2): 265–92.

Dillon, M. and L. Lobo-Guerrero. 2009. 'The Biopolitical Imaginary of Species-Being.' *Theory, Culture & Society* 26(1): 1–23.

Ellul, J. 1964. *The Technological Society,* Trans. J. Wilkinson. New York: Vintage Books.

Facebook. 2011. *Facebook.* <http://www.facebook.com/terms.php?ref= pf> Accessed 25 September 2011.

Featherstone, M. 2009. 'Ubiquitous Media: An Introduction.' *Theory, Culture & Society* 26(2–3): 1–22.

Feeley, M. and J. Simon. 1992. 'The New Penology: Notes on the Emerging Strategy of Corrections and Its Implications.' *Criminology* 30(4): 449–74.

Feenberg, A. 1999. *Questioning Technology.* London: Routledge.

Finneman, N.O. 1999. 'Modernity Modernised – the Cultural Impact of Computerisation.' *Computer Media and Communication: A Reader,* ed. P.A. Mayer. Oxford: Oxford University Press.

Forbes, R.J. 1958. 'Power to 1850.' *A History of Technology,* ed. C. Singer. Oxford: Clarendon Press.

Foster, D. 1997. 'Community and Identity in the Electronic Village.' *Internet Culture,* ed. D. Porter. New York: Routledge.

Foucault, M. 1970. *The Order of Things: An Archaeology of the Human Sciences,* Trans. Tavistock Publications. London: Tavistock Publications.

Foucault, M. 1979. *Discipline and Punish: The Birth of the Prison,* Trans. A. Sheridan. Harmondsworth: Penguin Books.

Foucault, M. 1991. 'Governmentality.' *The Foucault Effect: Studies in Governmentality,* ed. G. Burchell, C. Gordon and P. Miller. London: Harvester Wheatsheaf.

Foucault, M. 2003. *Society Must Be Defended: Lectures at the Collège de France, 1975–1976,* Trans. D. Macey. London: Penguin Books.

Foucault, M. 2007. *Security, Territory, Population: Lectures at the Collège de France 1977–1978,* ed. M. Senellart, Trans. G. Burchell. New York: Picador.

Foucault, M. 2008. *The Birth of Biopolitics: Lectures at the Collège de France, 1978–1979,* ed. M. Senellart, Trans. G. Burchell. New York: Palgrave Macmillan.

Frissen, P. 1997. 'The Virtual State: Postmodernisation, Informatisation and Public Administration.' *The Governance of Cyberspace: Politics, Technology and Global Restructuring,* ed. B.D. Loader. London: Routledge.

Galloway, A.R. 2004. *Protocol: How Control Exists after Decentrilization.* Cambridge: The MIT Press.

Galloway, A.R. 2006. *Gaming: Essays on Algorithmic Culture.* Minneapolis: University of Minnesota Press.

Gandy, O.H., Jr. 1993. *The Panoptic Sort: A Political Economy of Personal Information.* Boulder: Westview Press.

Gendron, B. and N. Holmstrom 1979. 'Marx, Machinery, and Alienation.' *Research in Philosophy and Technology* 2: 119–35.

Gibson, W. 1984. *Neuromancer.* New York: Ace Books.

Giese, M. 1998. 'Self without Body: Textual Self-Representation in an Electronic Community.' *First Monday* 3(4) <http://firstmonday.org/htbin/cgiwrap/bin/ojs/index.php/fm/article/view/587/508 > Accessed 25 September 2011.

Gordon, C. 1991. 'Governmental Rationality: An Introduction.' *The Foucault Effect: Studies in Governmentality*, ed. G. Burchell, C. Gordon, and P. Miller. London: Harvester Wheatsheaf.

Gowan, P. 1999. *The Global Gamble: Washington's Faustian Bid for World Dominance.* New York: Verso.

Gray, C.H. and S. Mentor. 1995. 'The Cyborg Body Politic: Version 1.2.' *The Cyborg Handbook*, ed. C.H. Gray. New York: Routledge.

Guattari, F. 1992. 'Regimes, Pathways, Subjects.' *Incorporations*, ed. J. Crary and S. Kwinter. New York: Zone Books.

Guattari, F. 1993. 'Machinic Heterogenesis.' *Rethinking Technologies*, ed. V.A. Conley, Trans. J. Creech. Minneapolis: University of Minnesota Press.

Guattari, F. 1995. *Chaosmosis: An Ethico-Aesthetic Paradigm*, Trans. P. Bains and J. Pefanis. Sydney: Power Publications.

Gunkel, D.J. 2007. *Thinking Otherwise: Philosophy, Communication, Technology.* West Lafayette: Purdue University Press.

Habermas, J. 1971. *Toward a Rational Society: Student Protest, Science, and Politics*, Trans. J.J. Shapiro. London: Heinemann Educational.

Habermas, J. 1992. *The Structural Transformation of the Public Sphere: An Inquiry Into a Category of Bourgeois Society*, Trans. T. Burger and F. Lawrence. Cambridge: Polity Press.

Hacking, I. 1991. 'How Should We Do the History of Statistics?' *The Foucault Effect: Studies in Governmentality*, ed. G. Burchell, C. Gordon, and P. Miller. London: Harvester Wheatsheaf.

Halliday, D. and R. Resnick. 1988. *Fundamentals of Physics.* New York: John Wiley & Sons.

Hansen, M.B.N. 2004. *New Philosophy for New Media.* Cambridge: MIT Press.

Hansen, M.B.N. 2006. *Bodies in Code: Interfaces with Digital Media.* Hoboken: CRC Press.

Hansen, M.B.N. 2009. 'Living (with) Technical Time: From Media Surrogacy to Distributed Cognition.' *Theory, Culture & Society* 26(2–3): 294–315.

Hardt, M. and A. Negri. 2001. *Empire.* London: Harvard University Press.

Hardt, M. and A. Negri. 2005. *Multitude.* London: Penguin Books.

Hardt, M. and A. Negri. 2009. *Commonwealth.* Cambridge: Harvard University Press.

Harper, T. 2009. 'Smash the Strata! A Program for Techno-Political Evolution.' *Deleuze and New Technology*, ed. M. Posters and D. Savat. Edinburgh: Edinburgh University Press.

Harraway, D.J. 1991. *Simians, Cyborgs, and Women: The Reinvention of Nature.* London: Free Association Books.

Harraway, D.J. 1995. 'Cyborgs and Symbionts: Living Together in the New World Order.' *The Cyborg Handbook,* ed. C.H. Gray. New York: Routledge.

Harvey, D. 1989. *The Condition of Postmodernity: An Enquiry into the Origins of Cultural Change.* Oxford: Basil Blackwell.

Hayles, K.N. 1993a. 'The Seductions of Cyberspace.' *Rethinking Technologies,* ed. V.A. Conley. Minneapolis: University of Minnesota Press.

Hayles, K.N. 1993b. 'Virtual Bodies and Flickering Signifiers.' October 66: 69–91.

Hayles, K.N. 2009. 'RFID: Human Agency and Meaning in Information-Intensive Environments.' *Theory, Culture & Society* 26(2–3): 47–72.

Hegel, G.W.F. [1830] 1971. *Hegel's Philosophy of Mind: Being Part Three of the 'Encyclopaedia of the Philosophical Sciences' (1830),* Trans. W. Wallace. Oxford: Clarendon Press.

Heidegger, M. 1977. *The Question Concerning Technology and Other Essays.* New York: Garland Publishing.

Heidegger, M. 1993a. *Martin Heidegger: Basic Writings,* ed. D.F. Krell, Trans. D. Lovitt. New York: HarperCollins Publishers.

Heim, M. 2001. 'The Erotic Ontology of Cyberspace.' *Reading Digital Culture,* ed. D. Trend. Oxford: Blackwell Publishers.

Heller, A. 1990. 'Death of the Subject.' *Thesis Eleven* 25: 22–38.

Henderson, D.R. 2000. 'Information Technology as a Universal Solvent for Removing State Stains.' *The Independent Review* IV(4): 517–23.

Henman, P. 1997. 'Computer Technology – a Political Player in Social Policy Processes.' *Journal of Social Policy* 26(3): 323–40.

Hobbes, T. [1651] 1968. *Leviathan,* ed. C.B. Macpherson. Harmondsworth: Penguin Books.

Holmes, D. 1997b. 'Virtual Identity: Communities of Broadcast, Communities of Interactivity.' *Virtual Politics: Identity and Community in Cyberspace,* ed. D. Holmes. London: Sage.

Horkheimer, M. and T.W. Adorno. 1982. *Dialectic of Enlightenment,* Trans. J. Cumming. New York: Continuum.

Hunsinger, J., L. Klastrup, and M. Allen. 2010. *The International Handbook of Internet Research:* New York: Springer.

Hutton, W. 2011. 'China Will Implode if It Stifles Freedom.' *The Guardian Weekly* 85(8): 19.

Ikegami, E. 1999. 'Democracy in an Age of Cyber-Financial Globalization: Time, Space, and Embeddedness From an Asian Perspective.' *Social Research* 66(3): 887–914.

Irigaray, L. 1985. *This Sex Which Is Not One,* Trans. C. Porter and C. Burke. Ithaca: Cornell University Press.

Isikoff, M. 2011. 'Hacker Group Vows "Cyberwar" on US Government, Business.' *MSNBC.COM.* MSNBC <http://www.msnbc.msn.com/id/41972190/ns/technology_and_science-security/t/hacker-group-vows-cyberwar-us-government-business/> Accessed 25 September 2011.

Jameson, F. 1991. *Postmodernism, or, the Cultural Logic of Late Capitalism.* London: Verso.

Jay, M. 2010. 'Liquidity Crisis: Zygmunt Bauman and the Incredible Lightness of Modernity.' *Theory, Culture & Society* 27(6): 95–106.

Katsiaficas, G. 2006. *The Subversion of Politics: European Autonomous Movements and the Decolonization of Everyday Life.* Oakland: AK Press.

Kelly, K.A. 2002. 'Private Family, Private Individual: John Locke's Distinction Between Paternal and Political Power.' *Social Theory and Practice* 28(3): 361–80.

Kern, S. 1983. *The Culture of Time and Space: 1880–1918.* Cambridge: Harvard University Press.

Kirby, K.M. 1996. *Indifferent Boundaries: Spatial Concepts of Human Subjectivity.* New York: The Guildford Press.

Kittler, F. 2006. 'Science as Open Process.' *New Media, Old Media: A History and Theory Reader*, ed. W.H.K. Chun and T. Keenan. New York: Routledge.

Kittler, F. 2009. 'Towards an Ontology of Media.' *Theory, Culture & Society* 26(2–3): 23–31.

Knorr-Cetina, K. 2003. 'From Pipes to Scopes: The Flow Architecture of Financial Markets.' *Distinktion: Scandinavian Journal of Social Theory* 4(2): 7–23.

Knorr-Cetina, K. 2007. 'Global Markets as Global Conversations.' *Text & Talk* 27(5–6): 705–34.

Knorr-Cetina, K. and A. Preda. 2007. 'The Temporalization of Financial Markets: From Network to Flow.' *Theory, Culture & Society* 24(7–8): 116–38.

Knudson, J.W. 1998. 'Rebellion in Chiapas: Insurrection by Internet and Public Relations.' *Media, Culture & Society* 20(3): 507–18.

Küchler, S. 2008. 'Technological Materiality: Beyond the Dualist Paradigm.' *Theory, Culture & Society* 25(1): 101–20.

Lefebvre, H. 1991. *The Production of Space*, Trans. D. Nicholson-Smith. Oxford: Basil Blackwell.

Levitt, D. 2008. 'Notes on Media and Biopolitics: "Notes on Gesture".' *The Work of Giorgio Agamben: Law, Literature, Life*, ed. J. Clemens, N. Heron, and A. Murray. Edinburgh: Edinburgh University Press.

LiPuma, E. and B. Lee. 2004. *Financial Derivatives and the Globalization of Risk.* Durham: Duke University Press.

Lisberger, S. and B. MacBird. 1982. *Tron* dir. S. Lisberger. USA: Disney Studios.

Loader, B.D., ed. 1997a. *The Governance of Cyberspace: Politics, Technology and Global Restructuring.* London: Routledge.

Loader, B.D. 1997b. 'The Governance of Cyberspace: Politics, Technology and Global Restructuring.' *The Governance of Cyberspace: Politics, Technology and Global Restructuring*, ed. B.D. Loader. London: Routledge.

Locke, J. [1690] 1963. *Two Treatises of Government*, ed. P. Laslett. Cambridge: Cambridge University Press.

Lukes, S. 1974. *Power: A Radical View.* London: Macmillan.

Lupton, D. 1995. 'The Embodied Computer/User.' *Cyberspace, Cyberbodies, Cyberpunk: Cultures of Technological Embodiment*, ed. M. Featherstone and R. Burrows. London: Sage.

Lyon, D. 2001. *Surveillance Society: Monitoring Everyday Life.* Buckingham: Open University Press.

Lyon, D. ed., 2006. *Theorizing Surveillance: The Panopticon and Beyond.* Devon: Willan Publishing.

Lyon, D. 2009. *Identifying Citizens: ID Cards as Surveillance.* Cambridge: Polity Press.

Lyotard, J.F. 1984. *The Postmodern Condition: A Report on Knowledge*, Trans. G. Bennington and B. Massumi. Minneapolis: University of Minnesota Press.

Mandel, E. 1978. *Late Capitalism*, Trans. J. de Bres. London, Verso.

Manovich, L. 2001. *The Language of New Media*. Cambridge: MIT Press.

Mansfield, N. 2000. *Subjectivity: Theories of the Self From Freud to Harraway*. St Leonards: Allen & Unwin.

Marcuse, H. 1964. *One Dimensional Man: Studies in the Ideology of Advanced Industrial Society*. Boston: Beacon Press.

Marx, K. [1857] 1973. *Grundrisse: Foundations of the Critique of Political Economy (Rough Draft)*. London: Penguin Books.

Marx, K. [1867] 1990. *Capital*. London: Penguin Books.

Marx, K. and F. Engels [1848] 1992. 'The Communist Manifesto.' *The Communist Manifesto*, ed. D. McLellan. Oxford: Oxford University Press.

Massumi, B. 2009. 'National Enterprise Emergency: Steps toward an Ecology of Powers.' *Theory, Culture & Society* 26(6): 153–85.

McLaren, J. and G. Zappalà. 2002. 'The 'Digital Divide' among Financially Disadvantaged Families in Australia.' *First Monday* 7(11) <http://firstmonday.org/htbin/cgiwrap/bin/ojs/index.php/fm/article/view/1003/924 > Accessed 25 September 2011.

McLuhan, M. 1964. *Understanding Media: The Extensions of Man*. New York: McGraw-Hill.

McSpotlight. 2011. *McSpotlight* <http://www.mcspotlight.org/index.shtml> Accessed 25 September 2011.

Mehta, M.D. and E. Darrier. 1998. 'Virtual Control and Disciplining on the Internet: Electronic Governmentality in the New Wired World.' *Information Society* 14(2): 107–16.

Meikle, G. 2002. *Future Active: Media Activism and the Internet*. Annandale: Pluto Press Australia.

Mihalache, A. 2002. 'The Cyber Space-Time Continuum: Meaning and Metaphor.' *The Information Society* 18: 293–301.

Miller, P. and N. Rose, eds. 2008. *Governing the Present: Administering Economic, Social and Personal Life*. Cambridge: Polity Press.

Moi, T., ed. 1986. *The Kristeva Reader*. Oxford: Basil Blackwell.

Moran, D. 2000. *Introduction to Phenomenology*. London: Routledge.

Morse, M. 1998. *Virtualities: Television, Media Art and Cyberculture*. Bloomington: Indiana University Press.

Mumford, L. 1947. *Technics and Civilization*. London: George Routledge & Sons.

Mumford, L. 1995a. 'The First Megamachine.' *The Lewis Mumford Reader*, ed. D.L. Miller. Athens: The University of Georgia Press.

Mumford, L. 1995b. 'The Monastery and the Clock.' *The Lewis Mumford Reader*, ed. D.L. Miller. Athens: The University of Georgia Press.

Mumford, L. 1995c. 'Technics and Human Development.' *The Lewis Mumford Reader*, ed. D.L. Miller. Athens: The University of Georgia Press.

Munster, A. 2006. *Materializing New Media: Embodiment in Information Aesthetics*. Lebanon: University Press of New England.

Nakamura, L. 2001. 'Race in/for Cyberspace: Identity Tourism and Racial Passing on the Internet.' *Reading Digital Culture*, ed. D. Trend. Oxford: Blackwell Publishers.

Naone, E. 2011. 'Internet Activists Mobilize for Japan.' *Technology Review*. 14 March. Video <http://www.technologyreview.com/communications/35097/?p1=A1> Accessed 25 September 2011.

Nef, J.U. 1960. *Cultural Foundations of Industrial Civilization*. New York: Harper & Brothers.

Negroponte, N. 1995. *Being Digital*. Rydalmere: Hodder &Stoughton.

Newton, J.H. 2007. 'Influences of Digital Imaging on the Concept of Photographic Truth.' *Digital Media: Transformations in Human Communications*, ed. M. Messaris and L. Humphreys. New York: Peter Lang Publishing.

Niccol, A. 1997. *Gattaca*, dir. A. Niccol. USA: Columbia Pictures.

Nielsen. 2011. *About Us*. <http://www.nielsen.com/us/en/about-us.html> Accessed 25 September 2011.

NSOED. 1997. *New Shorter Oxford English Dictionary*. Oxford: Oxford University Press.

Nunes, M. 1997. 'What Space Is Cyberspace? The Internet and Virtuality.' *Virtual Politics: Identity and Community in Cyberspace*, ed. D. Holmes. London: Sage.

O'Malley, P. 2010. 'Fines, Risks and Damages: Money Sanctions and Justice in Control Societies.' *Current Issues in Criminal Justice* 21(3): 365–82.

Parisi, L. and T. Terranova 2000. 'Heat-Death.' *CTheory* <http://www.ctheory.net/text_file.asp?pick=127> Accessed 10 May 2011.

Penty, A. 1922. *Post-Industrialism*. London: George Allen and Unwin Ltd.

Pollock, G. 2007. 'Liquid Modernity and Cultural Analysis: An Introduction to a Transdisciplinary Encounter.' *Theory, Culture & Society* 24(1): 111–16.

Poovey, M. 1995. *Making a Social Body: British Cultural Formation, 1830–1864*. Chicago: University of Chicago Press.

Porter, T. 1986. *The Rise of Statistical Thinking, 1820–1900*. Princeton: Princeton University Press.

Porter, T. 1996. *Trust in Numbers: The Invention of Objectivity*. Princeton: Princeton University Press.

Poster, M. 1990. *The Mode of Information: Poststructuralism and Social Context*. Cambridge: Polity Press.

Poster, M. 1995. *The Second Media Age*. Cambridge: Polity Press.

Poster, M. 1999. 'National Identities and Communications Technologies.' *The Information Society* 15(4): 235–40.

Poster, M. 2001a. *The Information Subject*. Amsteldijk: G + B Arts International.

Poster, M. 2001b. *What's the Matter with the Internet*. Minneapolis: University of Minnesota Press.

Poster, M. 2002a. 'Everyday (Virtual) Life.' *New Literary History* 33(4): 743–60.

Poster, M. 2002b. 'Workers as Cyborgs: Labor and Networked Computers.' *Journal of Labor Research* 23(3): 339–53.

Poster, M. 2009. 'Afterword.' *Deleuze and New Technology*, ed. M. Poster and D. Savat. Edinburgh: Edinburgh University Press.

Prigogine, I. and I. Stengers. 1985. *Order Out Of Chaos: Man's New Dialogue with Nature*. London: Fontana Paperbacks.

Quividi. 2011. *Automated Audience Measurement* <http://www.quividi.com/audience_measurement.html> Accessed 25 September 2011.

Rajagopal, I. and N. Bojin. 2002. 'Digital Representation: Racism on the World Wide Web.' *First Monday* 7(10). URL: <http://firstmonday.org/htbin/cgiwrap/bin/ojs/index.php/fm/article/view/995/916 > Accessed 25 September 2011.

Reid, J. 2009. 'Politicizing Connectivity: Beyond the Biopolitics of Information Technology in International Relations.' *Cambridge Review of International Affairs* 22(4): 607–23.

Rheingold, H. 1993. *The Virtual Community: Homesteading on the Electronic Frontier.* New York: Addison-Wesley Publishing Company.

Robins, K. 2000. 'Cyberspace and the World We Live In.' *The Cybercultures Reader,* ed. D. Bell and B.M. Kennedy. London: Routledge.

Rodan, G. 1998. 'The Internet and Political Control in Singapore.' *Political Science Quarterly* 113(1): 63–89.

Roffe, J. 2005. 'Simulacrum.' *The Deleuze Dictionary,* ed. A. Parr. Edinburgh: Edinburgh University Press.

Romanyshyn, R.D. 1989. *Technology as Symptom and Dream.* New York: Routledge.

Ronfeldt, D. and J. Arquilla. 2001. 'Networks, Netwars, and the Fight for the Future.' *First Monday* 6(10) <http://firstmonday.org/htbin/cgiwrap/bin/ojs/index.php/fm/article/view/889/798> Accessed 25 September 2011.

Rose, N. 1996. 'Psychiatry as a Political Science: Advanced Liberalism and the Administration of Risk.' *History of the Human Sciences* 9(2): 1–23.

Rose, N. 1999. *Powers of Freedom: Reframing Political Thought.* Cambridge: Cambridge University Press.

Rose, N. 2000. 'Government and Control.' *British Journal of Criminology* 40(2): 321–39.

Rousseau, J.J. [1762] 1989. 'On the Social Contract.' *Classics in Political Philosophy,* ed. J.M. Porter. Ontario: Prentice Hall.

Ruddick, S. 2010. 'The Politics of Affect: Spinoza in the Work of Negri and Deleuze.' *Theory, Culture & Society* 27(4): 21–45.

Rusciano, F.L. 2001. 'The Three Faces of Cyberimperialism.' *Cyberimperialism? Global Relations in the New Electronic Frontier,* ed. B.L. Ebo. Westport: Praeger.

Salen, K. and E. Zimmerman. 2004. *Rules of Play: Game Design Fundamentals.* Cambridge: The MIT Press.

Salisbury, J.G.T. and G.A. Barnett. 1999. 'The World System of International Monetary Flows: A Network Analysis.' *The Information Society* 15(1): 31–49.

Sanderson, D. and A. Fortin. 2001. 'The Projection of Geographical Communities Into Cyberspace.' *Technospaces: Inside the New Media,* ed. S.R. Munt. London: Continuum: 189–204.

Schivelbusch, W. 1986. *The Railway Journey: The Industrialization of Time and Space in the 19th Century.* Leamington Spa: Berg.

Scott, B. 2001. 'Copyright in a Frictionless World: Toward a Rhetoric of Responsibility.' *First Monday* 6(9) <http://firstmonday.org/htbin/cgiwrap/bin/ojs/index.php/fm/article/view/887/796> Accessed 25 September 2011.

Sears, F.W., M.W. Zemansky, and H.D. Young. 1987. *University Physics.* Reading: Addison-Wesley Publishing Company.

Shaviro, S. 2003. *Connected, or What It Means to Live in the Network Society.* Minneapolis: University of Minnesota Press.

Simkin, M. 2003. 'South Korea – Computer Games.' *Foreign Correspondent.* Canberra: ABC. Broadcast, 19 August 2003.

Sinclair, I.R. 1997. *Collins Dictionary of Personal Computing.* Glasgow: HarperCollins Publishers.

Smith, Adam. 1976. *An Inquiry into the Nature and Causes of the Wealth of Nations.* Oxford: Clarendon.

Smith, Anthony. 1986. 'Technology, Identity and the Information Machine.' *Daedalus* 115(3): 155–69.

Smith, D. 2011. 'Flow, Code and Stock: A Note on Deleuze's Political Philosophy.' *Deleuze Studies* 5 (Supplement): 36–55.

Soderberg, J. 2002. 'Copyleft Vs. Copyright: A Marxist Critique.' *First Monday* 7(3) <http://firstmonday.org/htbin/cgiwrap/bin/ojs/index.php/fm/article/view/938/860 > Accessed 25 September 2011.

Soja, E.W. 1989. *Postmodern Geographies: The Reassertion of Space in Critical Social Theory*. London: Verso.

Solove, D.J. 2007. *The Future of Reputation: Gossip, Rumor, and Privacy on the Internet*. New Haven: Yale University Press.

Stiegler, B. 1998. *Technics and Time, 1: The Fault of Epimetheus*, Trans. R. Beardsworth and G. Collins. Stanford: Stanford University Press.

Stiegler, B. 2009a. *Technics and Time, 2: Disorientation*, Trans. S Barker. Stanford: Stanford University Press.

Stiegler, B. 2009b. 'Teleologics of the Snail the Errant Self Wired to a WiMax Network.' *Theory, Culture & Society* 26(2–3): 33–45.

Stiegler, B. 2010a. *Taking Care of Youth and the Generations*, Trans. S. Barker. Stanford: Stanford University Press.

Stiegler, B. 2010b. *Technics and Time, 3: Cinematic Time and the Question of Malaise*, Trans. S. Barker. Stanford: Stanford University Press.

STG. 2001. 'In the Company of Strangers: Mobile Phones and the Conception of Space.' *Technospaces: Inside the New Media*, ed. S.R. Munt. London: Continuum. [Where STG refers to the Sussex Technology Group].

Stone, A.R. 1995. 'Split Subjects, Not Atoms; or, How I Fell in Love with My Prosthesis.' *The Cyborg Handbook*, ed. C.H. Gray. New York: Routledge.

Stone, A.R. 2001. 'Will the Real Body Please Stand Up? Boundary Stories about Virtual Cultures.' *Reading Digital Culture*, ed. D. Trend. Oxford: Blackwell Publishers.

Strandh, S. 1979. *Machines: An Illustrated History*. Melbourne: Rigby.

Stratton, J. 2000. 'Cyberspace and the Globalization of Culture.' *The Cybercultures Reader*, ed. D. Bell and B.M. Kennedy. London: Routledge.

Sturken, M., L. Cartwright. 2009. *Practices of Looking: An Introduction to Visual Culture*. Oxford: Oxford University Press.

Terranova, T. 2007. 'Futurepublic on Information Warfare, Bio-Racism and Hegemony as Noopolitics.' *Theory, Culture & Society* 24(3): 125–45.

Thacker, E. 2004. *Biomedia*. Minneapolis: University of Minnesota Press.

Thacker, E. 2005. *The Global Genome: Biotechnology, Politics, and Culture*. Cambridge: The MIT Press.

Thacker, E. 2008. 'Biophilosophy for the 21st Century.' *Critical Digital Studies: A Reader*, ed. A. Kroker and M. Kroker. Toronto: Toronto University Press.

Tonn, B.E. and D. Feldman. 1995. 'Non-Spatial Government.' *Futures* 27(1): 11–36.

Turkle, S. 1995. *Life on the Screen: Identity in the Age of the Internet*. New York: Simon & Schuster.

Ushahidi. 2011. *Ushahidi* <http://www.ushahidi.com/> Accessed 25 September 2011.

Valentine, J. 2000. 'Information Technology, Ideology and Governmentality.' *Theory, Culture & Society* 17(2): 21–43.

Vegh, S. 2002. 'Hacktivists or Cyberterrorists? the Changing Media Discourse on Hacking.' *First Monday* 7(10) <http://firstmonday.org/htbin/cgiwrap/bin/ojs/index.php/fm/article/view/998/919 > Accessed 25 September 2011.

Venn, C. 2007. 'Cultural Theory, Biopolitics, and the Question of Power.' *Theory, Culture & Society* 24(3): 111–24.

Virilio, P. 1986. *Speed and Politics: An Essay on Dromology*, Trans. M. Polizzoti. New York: Semiotext(e).

Virilio, P. 1991. *The Lost Dimension*, Trans. D. Moshenberg. New York: Semiotext(e).

Virilio, P. 1995. *The Art of the Motor*, Trans. J. Rose. Minneapolis: University of Minnesota Press.

Virilio, P. 2001. 'Speed and Information: Cyberspace Alarm!' *Reading Digital Culture*, ed. D. Trend. Oxford: Blackwell Publishers.

Wachowski, L. and A. Wachowski. 1999. *The Matrix* dir. L. Wachowski and A. Wachowski. USA: Warner Bros.

Wajcman, J. 1991. *Feminism Confronts Technology*. St. Leonards: Allen and Unwin.

Wark, M. 2007. *Gamer Theory*. Cambridge: Harvard University Press.

Weber, M. 1978. *Economy and Society: An Outline of Interpretive Sociology*, ed. G. Roth and C. Wittich, Trans. E. Fischoff et al. Berkely: University of California Press.

Webster, F. 1994. 'What Information Society?' *The Information Society* 10(1): 1–23.

White, L., Jr. 1962. *Medieval Technology and Social Change*. Oxford: Oxford University Press.

Winner, L. 1977. *Autonomous Technology: Technics-Out-of-Control as a Theme in Political Thought*. Cambridge: MIT Press.

Winner, L. 1986. *The Whale and the Reactor: A Search for Limits in an Age of High Technology*. Chicago: The University of Chicago Press.

Winner, L. 1999. 'Who Will We Be in Cyberspace?' *Computer Media and Communication*, ed. P.A. Mayer. Oxford: Oxford University Press.

Winner, L. and D. Brien. 2005. 'On Technologies as Forms of Life and Other Matters.' <http://www.cgjungpage.org/index.php?option= com_content&task= view&id= 682&Itemid= 40> Accessed 25 September 2011.

Winokur, M. 2008. 'The Ambiguous Panopticon: Foucault and the Codes of Cyberspace.' *Critical Digital Studies: A Reader*, ed. A. Kroker and M. Kroker. Toronto: Toronto University Press.

Wollstonecraft, M. [1792] 1992. *A Vindication of the Rights of Women*. London: Penguin.

Yergin, D. 2008. *The Prize: The Epic Quest for Oil, Money and Power*. New York: The Free Press.

Index

Note: The locators followed by the letter 'n' refer to note numbers cited in the text.

Printed and bound in the United States of America.